THE RISE OF OUR INDIAN EMPIRE

BEING THE HISTORY OF BRITISH INDIA FROM ITS ORIGINS TILL THE PEACE OF 1783

THE RISE OF OUR INDIAN EMPIRE

BY
LORD MAHON
PHILIP HENRY STANHOPE
(NOW EARL STANHOPE)

BEING THE HISTORY OF BRITISH INDIA FROM ITS ORIGINS TILL THE PEACE OF 1783

EXTRACTED FROM

LORD MOHON'S HISTORY OF ENGLAND

GYAN

Published by

GYAN

Gyan Publishing House
5, Ansari Road
Daryaganj, New Delhi-110002
Phone: 011-47034999, 9811692060
E-mail: books@gyanbooks.com

Distribution Network
gyanbooks.com
India, USA, Canada, UK, Australia

ISBN: 978-93-6433-145-6 (HB)
First Published, 1859

2nd Impression 2024

Printed at: Gyan Press, Delhi.

THE RISE OF OUR INDIAN EMPIRE: BEING THE HISTORY OF BRITISH INDIA FROM ITS ORIGINS TILL THE PEACE OF 1783 SERICULTURE IN THAT COUNTRY

AUTHOR: LORD MAHON,PHILIP HENRY STANHOPE

THE

RISE OF OUR INDIAN EMPIRE.

BY LORD MAHON

(NOW EARL STANHOPE).

BEING

THE HISTORY OF BRITISH INDIA

FROM ITS ORIGIN TILL THE PEACE OF 1783

EXTRACTED FROM

LORD MAHON'S HISTORY OF ENGLAND.

PREFACE.

In the year 1851 some extracts of the author's History of England which gave an account of the romantic enterprise of Prince Charles Stuart were published in a small volume, entitled "The Forty-Five." In like manner those chapters from the same work which treat of British India are now in a separate form submitted to the public. No alterations whatever have been made in them to suit passing events; the reprint being exactly from the last corrected editions of 1853 and 1854.

January, 1858.

CONTENTS.

CHAPTER I.

(CHAP. XXXIX. OF THE HISTORY.)

CHAPTER II.

(CHAP. XL. OF THE HISTORY.)

CHAPTER III.

(CHAP. LXVII. OF THE HISTORY.)

CHAPTER IV.

(CHAP. LXVIII. OF THE HISTORY.)

CHAPTER V.

(CHAP. LXIX. OF THE HISTORY.)

THE HISTORY OF BRITISH INDIA

FROM ITS ORIGIN TILL THE PEACE OF 1783.

CHAPTER I.

(CHAP. XXXIX. OF THE HISTORY.)

If in some fairy tale or supernatural legend we were to read of an island, seated far in the Northern seas, so ungenial in its climate and so barren in its soil that no richer fruits than sloes or blackberries were its aboriginal growth, —whose tribes of painted savages continued to dwell in huts of sedge, or, at best, pile together altars of rude stone, for ages after other nations widely spread over the globe had already achieved wondrous works of sculpture and design, the gorgeous rock-temples of Ellora, the storied obelisks of Thebes, or the lion-crested portals of Mycenæ;—If it were added, that this island had afterwards by skill and industry attained the highest degree of artificial fertility, and combined in its luxury the fruits of every clime,—that the sea, instead of remaining its barrier, had become almost a part of its empire,—that its inhabitants were now amongst the foremost of the earth in commerce and in freedom, in arts and in arms, —that their indomitable energy had subdued, across fifteen thousand miles of ocean, a land ten times more extensive than their own,—that in this territory they now peacefully reigned over one hundred and twenty millions of subjects or dependents,—the race of the builders of Ellora, and the heirs of the Great Mogul;—If, further still, we were told that in this conquest the rule of all other conquests had been reversed,—that the reign of the strangers, alien in blood, in language, and in faith, had been beyond any other in that region fraught with blessings,—that humanity and justice, the security of life and property, the progress of improvement and instruction, were far greater under the worst of the foreign governors than under the best of the native princes;—with what scorn might we not be tempted to fling down the lying scroll,—exclaiming that even in fiction there should be some decent bounds of probability observed,—that even in the Arabian Nights no such prodigies are wrought by spells or talismans,—by the lamp of Aladdin or the seal of Solomon!

To the marvels of this the most remarkable event in politics since the discovery of the New World,—the subjugation of India by the English,—might be added, how seldom and how imperfectly its particulars are known to the English themselves. Men of education and knowledge amongst us will generally be found far better versed in other modern achievements of much less magnitude, and in which our countrymen had no concern. The reason is, I conceive, that the historians of British India, some of them eminent in other respects, all require from their readers for their due comprehension a preliminary stock of Eastern lore. Perhaps a stronger popular impression might attend a less learned and less copious work. Meanwhile, to trace the origin of our Eastern greatness in a slight but clear and faithful outline,—however feebly performed, is at least no unworthy aim. I shall endeavour in this and the following chapter to shadow forth the first part of the career,—sometimes, it is true, marred by incapacity, and sometimes stained by injustice,—but on the whole the career of genius and of valour, by which in less than fifty years a factory was changed into an empire.

The earliest authentic accounts of India and its inhabitants are derived from the expedition of Alexander. Modern critics have remarked with surprise how well the descriptions given by his officers portray what we now behold in that country at the distance of two thousand years. The delicate and slender forms of the people; their dark complexion; their black uncurled hair; their cotton raiment; their vegetable food; their training of elephants to battle; their division into separate castes; the prohibition of intermarriage from one caste to another; the name of Brachmani or Bramins to their priests; the custom of widows burning themselves on the funeral piles of their husbands;—these, and several other particulars which Arrian has recorded, apply to the modern quite as perfectly as to the ancient Hindoos.*

* Robertson's Historical Disquisition, p. 21. and 187. ed. 1791.

The progress of Alexander in India itself did not extend beyond the district of the Punjaub, and the navigation of the Indus between that district and the sea. But on Affghanistan he made a more lasting impression; a dynasty which he founded in that country is proved by its coins to have subsisted during several generations; and a monument which he raised even now remains.—When, in May 1842, a melancholy train of captives, the survivors of the greatest military disaster that England had ever yet to mourn, — were slowly wending up the mountain-passes of Cabul, they beheld, towering high above them, the column of the Macedonian conqueror.*

Many ages after Alexander's expedition, the tide of Mahometan invasion, which had already overwhelmed the kingdom of Persia, approached the shores of the Indus and the Ganges. The gentle unwarlike Hindoos, with their antiquated forms of idolatry, were ill-fitted to withstand the enthusiasm of a new religion, and the energy of a fiercer race. But it is remarkable, that, widely as the disciples of the Koran spread in India, there was never, as in like cases, any amalgamation between the conquered and the conquerors, — between the old faith and the new. Although the Mahometans have succeeded in converting almost every man of almost every other nation that they conquered, and although in India they formed the sovereign and controlling power in so many states and for so many years, yet they do not now exceed, and never have exceeded, one seventh of the whole Indian population.

At the period of Alexander's invasion, as during most of the Mahometan conquests, the provinces of India do not appear combined in any general system, nor ruled by any single sovereign. Alexander found there separate and it would seem independent chiefs,— such as Porus,— whose appellation, according to modern commentators, was not a name, but a title; — merely the Greek ending

* Compare, on Alexander's Pillar, Lady Sale's Journal (p. 354.) with Lieut. Eyre's (p. 301.). For the Greek reigns in Affghanistan I would refer the reader to the learned and important work of Professor H. H. Wilson, *Ariana Antiqua*, London, 1841, and to a note in the excellent History of early India by my much respected friend, Mr. Mountstuart Elphinstone (vol. i. p. 468—476.).

added to the Indian POOR or prince.* Thus also neither Mahmoud of Ghuznee, nor Gengis-Khan, nor Tamerlane, had to encounter a sole monarch of India. But at the beginning of the sixteenth century of our era (I pass by the earlier dynasties) a great empire was founded at Agra by a race of Moguls. The first of these Emperors was Zehur-ood-Deen Mahomed, surnamed Baber, or the "Tiger," a descendant of the great Tamerlane. His own Memoirs, which are still preserved, relate in detail the exploits by which he overcame, and the arts by which he circumvented, his numerous opponents. He died in 1530, when on the point of carrying his arms beyond Bahar. But his schemes of conquest were fulfilled or exceeded by his successors, each of whom became known in Europe by the title of the Great Mogul. Above all, however, the name of Baber's grandson, Akbar, is yet famous through the East. During a reign of fifty years, concluding in 1605, he was ever waging fierce and successful wars, sometimes against rebellious provinces, sometimes against Hindoo tribes, and sometimes against Mahometan neighbours. Nevertheless, while thus extending his empire, he did not neglect its internal improvement; on the contrary, so numerous were his measures of legislation and finance that they rather seemed to betoken a period of uninterrupted peace.

Another reign, distinguished by conquest, and extending to half a century, was that of Aurungzebe. His armies spread far in the south of the Deccan, and overthrew the powerful RAJAHS or Princes of Beejapour and Golconda. But by far his most formidable enemy in this quarter was Sivajee, the founder of the Mahratta dominion. For many years did this intrepid and wily chieftain balance on the south of the Nerbudda the fortunes of the Great Mogul. The tidings of his death, in 1680, at the untimely age of fifty-two, were as joyful to Aurungzebe as those of any victory; nor did the Emperor then attempt to conceal either his own satisfaction or the merits of his foe. "He was," said Aurungzebe, "a great captain, and the only one who has had the mag-

* Vincent on Nearchus, p. 19. Mitford's History of Greece, vol. viii. p. 206. ed. 1829.

" nanimity to raise a new kingdom, whilst I have been
" endeavouring to destroy the ancient sovereignties of
" India. My armies have been applied against him for
" nineteen years, and nevertheless his state has been
" always increasing." *

The loss of Sivajee was, for the time at least, irreparable to the Mahrattas. Though never subdued, they were defeated and dispersed, and compelled to take shelter in their hill forts or impervious jungles. Among other tribes, the Rajahs readily acknowledged themselves the tributaries or dependents of the Mogul Empire. Other states, again, became governed by SOUBAHDARS or Viceroys, under the immediate appointment of the Emperor. On the whole, it is probable that there never yet had been a time in Hindostan when the whole peninsula was so nearly brought beneath the supreme dominion of one man.

The power of Aurungzebe, and the magnificence of the Court of Delhi (for to Delhi had the seat of empire been again transferred), are described by more than one intelligent European traveller. " In riches and resources," says Tavernier, " the Great Mogul is in Asia what the
" King of France is in Europe. . . . . When I took leave
" of His Majesty on the 1st of November 1665 he was
" pleased to desire that I should stay, and see the festivals
" in honour of his birth-day. . . . . On this occasion the
" Emperor is weighed in state, and if he is found to weigh
" more than on the preceding year there are great public
" rejoicings. The grandees of the empire, the Viceroys of
" the provinces, and the ladies of the Court, came to make
" their offerings, which, in precious stones, gold and
" silver, rich carpets and brocades, elephants, camels, and
" horses, amounted when I was present to upwards of
" thirty millions of our livres. . . . . The tents are of red
" velvet, embroidered with gold, so heavy that the poles
" which support them are as thick as the masts of ships,
" and some of them from thirty-five to forty feet in height.
" . . . . . The Great Mogul has seven splendid thrones;

* Orme's Historical Fragments of the Mogul Empire, p. 94. ed. 1805. From another passage (p. 263.) it appears that Aurungzebe used to call Sivajee " the Mountain Rat," which, like the ὄνος of Homer (Il. lib. xi. vers. 557.), was designed for praise.

"one covered with diamonds, another with rubies, with "emeralds, or with pearls. The value of the one most "precious (called the Peacock Throne) is estimated by "the Royal Treasurers at a number of lacs of rupees "equivalent to above one hundred and sixty millions of "livres. . . . . While the Emperor is on his throne fifteen "horses stand ready caparisoned on his right and as many "on his left, the bridles of each horse enriched with pre- "cious stones, and some great jewel dependent from his "neck. . . . . Elephants are trained to kneel down before "the throne, and do His Majesty reverence with their "trunks; and the Emperor's favourite elephant costs five "hundred rupees of monthly expense, being fed on good "meat with abundance of sugar, and having brandy to "drink. . . . . When the Emperor rides abroad on his "elephant he is followed by a great number of his "OMRAHS, or nobles, on horseback,—and the meanest "of these Omrahs, commands two thousand cavalry."* Another traveller, Gemelli Carreri, in the year 1695, visited the camp of the Great Mogul. According to his description, "the Imperial army consisted of 60,000 horse- "men and 100,000 infantry; there were for the baggage "5,000 camels and 3,000 elephants, but the number of "suttlers and camp-followers was immense; so that the "camp contained above half a million of people. It was "thirty miles in circuit. . . . . Aurungzebe himself was "of slender figure and of delicate features; a little bent "at this time, with the weight of fourscore years. His "beard, which was white and full, shone forth in strik- "ing contrast to his olive complexion."†

Aurungzebe expired in 1707; almost the only instance of either sovereign or statesman who has approached the age of one hundred years. The character of his successors,—as compared to his own, to Akbar's and to Baber's,—was feeble and unwarlike. Throughout the East the fortunes of the state ever follow in quick succession the disposition of the Monarch; and thus the decline of the Mogul dynasty was most rapid and most com-

* I have here abridged a chapter of Tavernier. (Voyages, vol. ii. p. 266—272. ed. 1679.)

† Anecdotes Orientales, vol. ii. p. 441. ed. 1773.

plete. In little more than thirty years from the death of Aurungzebe the Persians under Nadir Shah had sacked the city of Delhi.* The Mahrattas, emerging from their fastnesses, had resumed their expeditions, and begun to aim at empire. The conquered Rajahs, or the appointed Soubahdars, — though still professing themselves dependent,—had ceased to pay any real obedience and submission to the Mogul throne.

In this distinction between nominal and substantial authority, the state of India might be, not unaptly, compared to the state at the same period of Germany. According to ancient forms, the princes who had long since become independent of the Germanic Emperor,—nay, who were sometimes hostile to him,—still continued, in name, the humblest of his vassals. The Margrave of Brandenburg was still Great Chamberlain, and the Elector of Hanover Arch-Treasurer of the Empire.† Yet Frederick the Second of Prussia would not have been more surprised had he been summoned, in conformity with his patent, to carry a white wand and a golden key in the pageantries of the palace at Vienna, than would the contemporary Rajahs of the Deccan if required to pay tribute or do homage to the Court of Delhi.

At nearly the same period that the Moguls were founding their empire along the Ganges did the Portuguese discover the passage of the Cape of Good Hope. Vasco de Gama and his brave companions stepped on the Indian shore at Calicut in the month of May 1498. Seldom have truth and poetry been so closely combined; the achievement of that voyage by Vasco de Gama is the greatest feat of the Portuguese in arms; the celebration of that voyage by Luis de Camoens is their greatest feat in letters. The valour of their captains,—of their Albuquerque and their John de Castro,—overcame the resistance of the native chiefs, and made good their settlements from the coast of Malabar to the gulph of Persia,

* Histoire de Nader Chah traduite par Sir W. Jones, vol. ii. p. 74. The bombast of Eastern panegyric extends even to the Sovereign's horse. "Le coursier de Sa Majesté, dont les pas étaient semblables "à ceux du soleil, et dont les traces s'étendaient dans tout l'univers," &c. &c. (p. 21.)

† Butler's Revolutions of the Germanic Empire, p. 105., &c.

— at Goa and Ormuz. For some time it appears to have been thought by other European Powers, that the discovery of the passage round Africa by the Portuguese gave them some exclusive claim to its navigation. But after the year 1580 the conquest of Portugal by Spain, and the example of the Dutch who had already formed establishments not only in India but the Spice Islands, aroused the commercial enterprise of England. In 1599 an Association was formed for the Trade to the East Indies; a sum was raised by subscription, amounting to 68,000*l.*; and a petition was presented to the Crown for a Royal Charter. Queen Elizabeth wavered during some time, apprehending fresh entanglements with Spain. At length, in December 1600, the boon was granted; the "Adventurers" (for so were they termed at that time) were constituted a body corporate, under the title of "the Governor and Company of Merchants of London "trading into the East Indies." By their Charter they obtained the right of purchasing lands without limitation, and the monopoly of their trade during fifteen years, under the direction of a Governor, and twenty-four other persons in Committee, to be elected annually. In the exercise of those privileges they had to contend against numerous opponents, at home as well as abroad, but they did not want powerful friends and allies. "I confess," writes Lord Bacon to King James on another occasion, "I did "ever think that trading in Companies is most agreeable "to the English nature, which wanteth that same general "vein of a Republic which runneth in the Dutch, and "serveth to them instead of a Company, and therefore I "dare not advise to venture this great trade of the kingdom, which hath been so long under Government, in a "free or loose trade."* Thus, in 1609, the Charter of the new Company was not only renewed but rendered perpetual, — with a saving clause, however, that should any national detriment be at any time found to ensue, these exclusive privileges should, after three years' notice, cease and expire.

It does not seem, however, that the trade of the new

* Bacon was here referring to the Woollen Trade. Letter to the King, February 25. 1615. Bacon's Works, vol. iv. p. 614. ed. 1740.

Company was extensive. Their first voyage consisted of four ships and one pinnace, having on board 28,742*l.* in bullion, and 6,860*l.* in goods, such as cloth, lead, tin, cutlery, and glass. Many other of their voyages were of smaller amount; thus, in 1612, when they united into a Joint Stock Company, they sent out only one ship, with 1,250*l.* in bullion and 650*l.* in goods. But their clear profits on their capital were immense; scarcely ever, it is stated, below 100 per cent.*

During the Civil Wars the Company shared in the decline of every other branch of trade and industry. But soon after the accession of Charles the Second they obtained a new Charter, which not only confirmed their ancient privileges but vested in them authority, through their agents in India, to make peace and war with any prince or people, not being Christians, and to seize within their limits, and send home as prisoners, any Englishmen found without a licence. It may well be supposed that in the hands of any exclusive Company this last privilege was not likely to lie dormant. Thus, on one occasion, when one of their Governors had been urged to enforce the penalties against interlopers with the utmost rigour, and had replied, that unhappily the laws of England would not let him proceed so far as might be wished,— Sir Josiah Child, as Chairman of the Court of Directors, wrote back in anger, as follows: "We expect that our "orders are to be your rules, and not the laws of England, "which are a heap of nonsense, compiled by a few ig-"norant country gentlemen, who hardly know how to "make laws for the good of their own families, much less "for the regulating of Companies and foreign Com-"merce."†

The period of the Revolution was not so favourable to the Company as that of the Restoration. A rival Company arose, professing for its object greater freedom of trade with the East Indies, and supported by a majority in the House of Commons. It is said that the competition of these two Companies with the private traders

* Mill's History, vol. i. p. 25. ed. 1826.

† Hamilton's New Account of India, vol. i. p. 232., as cited by Bruce and Mill.

and with one another had well nigh ruined both.* Certain it is that appointments under the new Company were sought as eagerly as under the old. I have found, for example, in the diplomatic correspondence of that period, an account of an English gentleman at Madrid, "who is "resolved to return in hopes to be entertained to go as a "Writer to the East Indies in the service of the New "Company."†

An Union between these Companies, essential, as it seemed, to their expected profits, was delayed by their angry feelings till 1702. Even then, by the Indenture which passed the Great Seal, several points were left unsettled between them, and separate transactions were allowed to their agents in India for the stocks already sent out. Thus the ensuing years were fraught with continued jarrings and contentions. But in 1708 the Government having required from each Company a loan without interest towards the expenses of the war, both heartily combined to avert, if they could, or at least to mitigate, the common danger. Their remaining differences were referred to the arbitration of the Lord Treasurer, Godolphin; and his award, which an Act of Parliament confirmed, placed the affairs of the two Companies on a firm and enduring basis. It was enacted, that the sum of 1,200,000*l.*, without interest, should be advanced to the Government by the United Company, which, being added to a former loan of 2,000,000*l.* at eight per cent., made upon the whole 3,200,000*l.* with five per cent. interest,—that they should be empowered to borrow, through their Court of Directors and upon their common seal, to the amount of 1,500,000*l.*,—and that their privileges should be continued till three years' notice after 1726, and till repayment of their capital.—In 1712 they obtained a prolongation of their term till 1736; in 1730 till 1769; and in 1743 till 1783.‡

* Wealth of Nations, book v. ch. i.

† Hon. Alexander Stanhope to his son, Madrid, June 1. 1699.

‡ Anderson's History of Commerce, vol. ii. p. 257. 326. and 372. ed. 1764. In 1730 Sir Robert Walpole stipulated the abatement of the interest paid to them from five to four per cent., and their payment of 200,000*l.* towards the public service. In 1743 they agreed to advance another million at three per cent.

After the grant of the first Charter by Queen Elizabeth, and the growth of the Company's trade in India, their two main factories were fixed at Surat and Bantam. Surat was then the principal sea-port of the Mogul Empire, where the Mahometan pilgrims were wont to assemble for their voyages towards Mecca. Bantam, from its position in the island of Java, commanded the best part of the Spice trade. But at Surat the Company's servants were harassed by the hostility of the Portuguese, as at Bantam by the hostility of the Dutch. To such heights did these differences rise that in 1622 the English assisted the Persians in the recovery of Ormuz from the Portuguese, and that in 1623 the Dutch committed the outrage termed the "Massacre of Amboyna,"—putting to death, after a trial, and confession of guilt extorted by torture, Captain Towerson and nine other Englishmen, on a charge of conspiracy. In the final result, many years afterwards, the factories both at Bantam and Surat were relinquished by the Company. Other and newer settlements of theirs had, meanwhile, grown into importance.—In 1640 the English obtained permission from a Hindoo Prince in the Carnatic to purchase the ground adjoining the Portuguese settlement of St. Thomé, on which they proceeded to raise Fort St. George and the town of Madras. "At the Company's "first beginning to build a fort,"—thus writes the Agency,—"there were only the French PADRE's and "about six fishermen's houses!"* But in a very few years Madras had become a thriving town.—About twenty years afterwards, on the marriage of Charles the Second to Catherine of Braganza, the town and island of Bombay were ceded to the King of England as a part of the Infanta's dowry. For some time the Portuguese Governor continued to evade the grant, alleging that the patent of His Majesty was not in accordance with the customs of Portugal; he was compelled to yield; but the possession being found on trial to cost more than it produced, it was given up by King Charles to the East India Company, and became one of their principal stations.

* See a note to Orme's Historical Fragments on the Mogul Empire, p. 230.

Nor was Bengal neglected. Considering the beauty and richness of that province, a proverb was already current among the Europeans, that there are a hundred gates for entering and not one for leaving it.* The Dutch, the Portuguese, and the English had established their factories at or near the town of Hooghly on one of the branches — also called Hooghly — of the Ganges. But during the reign of James the Second the imprudence of some of the Company's servants, and the seizure of a Mogul junk, had highly incensed the native Powers. The English found it necessary to leave Hooghly, and drop twenty-five miles down the river, to the village of Chuttanuttee. Some petty hostilities ensued, not only in Bengal but along the coasts of India; several small factories of the Company were taken and plundered, nor did they speed well in their endeavours either for defence or reprisal. It was about this period that their settlement at Surat was finally transferred to Bombay. So much irritated was Aurungzebe at the reports of these hostilities, that he issued orders for the total expulsion of the Company's servants from his dominions, but he was appeased by the humble apologies of the English traders, and the earnest intercession of the Hindoo, to whom this commerce was a source of profit. The English might even have resumed their factory at Hooghly, but preferred their new station at Chuttanuttee, and in 1698 obtained from the Mogul, on payment of an annual rent, a grant of the land on which it stood. Then, without delay, they began to construct for its defence a citadel, named Fort William, under whose shelter there grew by degrees from a mean village the great town of Calcutta, — the capital of modern India. Perhaps no other city, excepting its contemporary, Petersburg, has ever in a century and a half from its origin attained so high a pitch of splendour and importance.† A letter is now before me which I once received from a Governor General of India, accus-

* Anecdotes Orientales, vol. ii. p. 342. ed. 1773.

† It is remarkable how much these two cities resemble each other. Bishop Heber writes from Calcutta: "The whole is so like some "parts of Petersburg that it is hardly possibly for me to fancy myself "any where else." Journal, October 11. 1824.

tomed to all the magnificence of European Courts, but describing with eloquent warmth his admiration and astonishment at the first view of Calcutta,—"the City of "Palaces," as he declares it most truly termed.

At nearly the same period another station,—Tegnapatam, a town on the coast of Coromandel, to the south of Madras,—was obtained by purchase. It was surnamed Fort St. David, was strengthened with walls and bulwarks, and was made subordinate to Madras for its government.

Thus then before the accession of the House of Hanover these three main stations,—Fort William, Fort St. George, and Bombay,—had been erected into Presidencies, or central posts of Government; not, however, as at present, subject to one supreme authority, but each independent of the rest. Each was governed by a President and a Council of nine or twelve members, appointed by the Court of Directors in England. Each was surrounded with fortifications, and guarded by a small force, partly European and partly native, in the service of the Company. The Europeans were either recruits enlisted in England or strollers and deserters from other services in India. Among these the descendants of the old settlers, especially the Portuguese, were called Topasses,—from the TOPE or hat which they wore instead of turban. The natives, as yet ill-armed and ill-trained, were known by the name of Sepoys,—a corruption from the Indian word SIPAHI, a soldier. But the territory of the English scarcely extended out of sight of their towns, nor had their military preparations any other object than the unmolested enjoyment of their trade. Far from aiming at conquest and aggrandisement, they had often to tremble for their homes. So lately as 1742 the "Mahratta Ditch" was dug round a part of Calcutta, to protect the city from an inroad of the fierce race of Sivajee.

Even before the commencement of the eighteenth century it might be said that all rivalry had ceased in India between the Company's servants and the Dutch or Portuguese. The latter, besides their treaties of close alliance with England, had utterly declined from their ancient greatness and renown. The Dutch directed by far their principal attention to their possessions in Java and the adjoining islands. But another still more formidable power had already struck root on the Indian soil.—The French under Louis the Fourteenth had established an East India Company, in emulation of our own; like us, they had obtained a settlement on the Hooghly river; — at Chandernagore, above Calcutta; like us, they had built a fort on the coast of the Carnatic, about eighty miles south of Madras, which they called Pondicherry. In Malabar and Candeish they had no settlement to vie with Bombay; but, on the other hand, they had colonised two fertile islands in the Indian Ocean;—the one formerly a Dutch possession, and called Mauritius, from Prince Maurice of Orange; the second, discovered by the Portuguese, with the appellation of Mascarenhas, from one of their Indian Viceroys.* The first now received the name of Isle de France, and the second of Isle de Bourbon, and both, under the assiduous care of their new masters, rapidly grew in wealth and population. On the whole, the settlements of the French on the Indian coasts and seas were governed by two Presidencies, — the one at Isle de France, the other at Pondicherry.

It so chanced, that at the breaking out of the war between France and England in 1744 both the French Presidencies were ruled by men of superior genius. Mahé de La Bourdonnais commanded at Isle de France; a man of Breton blood, full of the generous ardour, of the resolute firmness, which have ever marked that noble race. Since his tenth year he had served in the Navy on various voyages from the Baltic to the Indian seas, and he had acquired consummate skill, not only in the direction and pilotage but in the building and equipment of a fleet. Nor was he less skilled in the cares of civil administration. It is to him that the Mauritius owes the first dawn of its present prosperity. In the words of an eye-witness: "Whatever I have seen in that island most usefully "devised or most ably executed was the work of La

* This was, I conceive, Don Pedro de Mascarenhas, the eighth Viceroy. Camoens has addressed to him some spirited lines (Lusiad, canto x. stanzas 55—57.), which, however, I can only admire through a translation.

"Bourdonnais."* Ever zealous for his country's welfare, he was yet incapable of pursuing it by any other means than those of honour and good faith.

Dupleix was the son of a Farmer General, and the heir of a considerable fortune. From early youth he had been employed by the French East India Company, and had gradually risen to the government of Pondicherry and of all the subordinate factories on the continent of Hindostan. During his whole career he had zealously studied the interests of the Company, without neglecting his own, and the abilities which he had displayed were great and various. The calculations of commerce were not more habitual or more easy to him than the armaments of war or the wiles of diplomacy. With the idea of Indian sovereignty ever active in his mind, he had plunged headlong into all the tangled and obscure intrigues of the native Powers. Above all he caballed with the native NABOB or deputed Prince of Arcot, or, as sometimes called, of the Carnatic, (Arcot being the capital, and Carnatic the country,) and with his superior the Soubahdar or Viceroy of the Deccan, more frequently termed the NIZAM. Beguiled by a childish vanity, he was eager to assume for himself, as they did, the pompous titles of NABOB and BAHAUDER, which, as he pretended, had been conferred upon him by the Court of Delhi. It would almost seem, moreover, as if in this intercourse or this imitation he had derived from the neighbouring Princes something of their usual duplicity and falsehood, their jealousy and their revenge. His breach of faith on several occasions with his enemies is even less to be condemned than his perfidy to some of his own countrymen and colleagues. But fortunate was it perhaps for the supremacy of England in the East, that two such great commanders as Dupleix and La Bourdonnais should by the fault of the first have become estranged from any effective combination, and have turned their separate energies against each other.

On the declaration of war in 1744 an English squadron

* Bernardin de St. Pierre (Préâmbule à Paul et Virginie). He adds, bitterly: "Oh vous qui vous occupez du bonheur des hommes "n'en attendez point de recompense pendant votre vie!"

under Commodore Barnet had been sent to the Indian seas. M. de La Bourdonnais, on his part, exerting his scanty means with indefatigable perseverance, succeeded in fitting out nine ships, but nearly all leaky and unsound, and he embarked upwards of 3,000 men, but of these there were 400 invalids and 700 Caffres or Lascars. On the 6th of July, New Style, 1746, the two fleets engaged near Fort St. David, but the battle began and ended in a distant cannonade. Next morning the English stood out to sea, while the French directed their course to Pondicherry. The object of La Bourdonnais was the capture of Madras, and he made a requisition on Dupleix for some stores and sixty pieces of artillery. But the jealous mind of Dupleix could ill brook contributing to his rival's success. He refused the stores, allowed only thirty cannon of inferior calibre, and sent on board water so bad as to produce a dysentery in the fleet.*

Not disheartened, however, by these unexpected difficulties, La Bourdonnais appeared off Madras in September 1746, and proceeded to disembark his motley force. The city, though at this period rich and populous, was ill-defended; one division, called "the Black Town," only covered by a common wall; the other, "the White Town," or Fort St. George, begirt with a rampart and bastions, but these very slight and faulty in construction. There were but 300 Englishmen in the colony, and of them only 200 were soldiers. Under such circumstances no effective resistance could be expected; nevertheless the garrison sustained a bombardment during three days, and obtained at last an honourable capitulation. It was agreed that the English should be prisoners of war upon parole, and that the town should remain in possession of the French until it should be ransomed, La Bourdonnais giving his promise that the ransom required should be fair and

* From the commencement of hostilities in 1746 I find a sure and faithful guide in Mr. Orme. (History of Military Transactions, 2 volumes, ed. 1803.) Mr. Mill's narrative is much less minute, but drawn in some measure from other materials, and with a different point of view. The Life of Clive by Sir John Malcolm (3 vols. ed. 1836), though ill-digested, is fraught with many interesting facts and letters, and the article upon it by Mr. Macaulay, (Edinburgh Review, No. cxlii,) is equally accurate and brilliant.

moderate. The sum was fixed some time afterwards between the French Commander and the English Council at 440,000*l.* On these terms the invaders marched in; the keys were delivered by the Governor at the gate, and the French colours were displayed from Fort St. George. La Bourdonnais had been the more readily induced to grant this capitulation since his instructions were peremptory against his retaining any English factory which he might succeed in seizing.* — Not a single Frenchman had been killed during the siege, and only four or five English from the explosion of the bombs.

There were two persons, however, even among his own confederates, to whom the success of La Bourdonnais gave no pleasure; the Nabob of Arcot and the Governor of Pondicherry. At the first news of the siege, this Nabob, Anwar-ood-Deen by name, sent a letter to Dupleix, vehemently complaining of the presumption of the French in attacking Madras without his permission as prince of the surrounding district. Dupleix pacified his ally with a promise that the town, if taken, should be given up to him, — a promise which, there is little risk in affirming, Dupleix had never the slightest intention to fulfil. But Dupleix could not restrain his own resentment when he heard the terms of the capitulation. To his views of sovereignty in India it was essential that the English should be expelled the country, and Madras be either retained or razed to the ground. Accordingly, when La Bourdonnais again disembarked at Pondicherry, with the spoils of the conquered town, a long and fierce altercation arose between the rival chiefs. La Bourdonnais urged, "Madras is my conquest, and I am bound in "honour to keep the capitulation by which I entered it." — Dupleix answered, "Madras once taken becomes a "town within my sphere and under my jurisdiction, and "can only be disposed of as my judgment may determine." — "You know the instructions which I have received "from the King," pursued La Bourdonnais; "they prohibit me from retaining any conquest." — "You do not

* "Il est expressément defendu au Sieur de la Bourdonnais de "s'emparer d'aucun établissement ou comptoir des ennemis pour le "conserver." Signé ORRY, CONTROLEUR GENERAL. (Mill, vol. iii. p. 61 ed. 1826.)

"know the instructions which I have received from the "Company," retorted Dupleix; "they authorise me to "keep Madras." *

These differences with Dupleix prevented La Bourdonnais from pursuing, as he had designed, his expedition against the other British settlements in India. A part of his fleet had been scattered and disabled by the Monsoon; but, on the other hand, he had been joined by a squadron from France, and, on the whole, his force was far superior to any that the English could at this time and in this quarter bring against him. All his proposals, however, for an union of counsels and resources were scornfully rejected by Dupleix, who had now no other object than to rid himself of an aspiring colleague. For this object he stooped at length to deliberate falsehood. He gave a solemn promise to fulfil the capitulation of Madras, on the faith of which La Bourdonnais consented to re-embark, leaving a part of his fleet with Dupleix, and steering with the rest to Acheen, in quest of some English ships. Not succeeding in the search, he returned to the Mauritius, and from thence to France, to answer for his conduct. On his voyage home he was taken by the English, and conveyed to London, but was there received with respect, and dismissed on parole. At Paris, on the contrary, he found himself preceded by the perfidious insinuations of his rival. He was thrown into the Bastille, his fortune plundered, his papers seized, and his will torn open; himself secluded from his wife and children, and even debarred the use of pen and ink for his defence. When, at length, after many months' suspense, he was examined before a Royal Commission, he heard his services denied, his integrity questioned, and the decline of commerce resulting from the war urged as his reproach. "Will you explain," asked of him one of the East India Directors, "how it happened that under "your management your own private affairs have thriven "so well, and those of the Company so ill?"—"Because," answered La Bourdonnais, without hesitation, "I ma-

* I derive this summary of the discussion or correspondence from the article DUPLEIX in the Biographie Universelle — an article written by the son of Lally, in part from MS. documents.

"naged my own affairs according to my own judgment, "and I managed the Company's according to your in- "structions!"* After many harassing inquiries, and three years' detention, his innocence was publicly acknowledged; but his long imprisonment had broken his health, or rather, perhaps, his heart; he lingered for some time in a painful illness, and in 1754 expired. The Government, wise and just too late, granted a pension to his widow.

Only seven days after La Bourdonnais had sailed from Pondicherry, Dupleix, in utter defiance of his recent promise, obtained a warrant from his Council annulling the capitulation of Madras. Thus, so far from restoring the city within a few weeks, on payment of the stipulated sum, the principal inhabitants were brought under a guard to Pondicherry, and paraded in triumph through the streets. Such conduct had, at least, the advantage of absolving them from the obligation of their previous parole, and several of them, assuming Hindoo attire or other disguises, made their way from Pondicherry to Fort St. David, the two settlements being less than twenty miles asunder. Among those who thus escaped was young Robert Clive, then a merchant's clerk, afterwards a conqueror and statesman.

It was not long ere some troops were sent out by Dupleix (Dupleix himself was no warrior) for the reduction of Fort St. David; but the Nabob of Arcot, to whom the cession of Madras had been promised, being now disappointed in his hopes, and filled with resentment, joined his forces to the English, and the invaders were repulsed with loss. Not discouraged, Dupleix opened a new negotiation with the Nabob, who, on some fresh lures held out to him, consented to desert the English, and again embrace the French interest, with the usual fickleness of an Asiatic despot. Thus, in March 1747, Dupleix could under better auspices resume his expedition against Fort St. David, and his soldiers were advancing, as they thought, to a certain conquest, when a number of ships were descried in the offing as about to anchor in the roads. These were no sooner recognized as English than

* Bernardin de St. Pierre, Œuvres, vol. vi. p. 17. ed. 1820.

the French relinquished their design, and hastened back to Pondicherry.

The English fleet, thus opportune in its appearance, was commanded by Admiral Griffin, who had been sent from England with two men of war to strengthen the Bengal squadron. In the next ensuing months further reinforcements, both naval and military, were brought at different times by Admiral Boscawen and Major Lawrence; the former taking the chief command at sea, and the second on shore. So large was this accession of force as to turn at once, and heavily, the scale against the French. It became possible, nay, even, as it seemed, not difficult, to retaliate the loss of Madras by the capture of Pondicherry. With this view the English took the field in August 1748, having in readiness 2,700 European troops, 1,000 sailors, who had been taught the manual exercise during the voyage, and 2,000 Sepoys in the service of the Company. At the news of this armament, the greatest, perhaps, from modern Europe which India had yet seen, the Nabob of Arcot hastened to change sides once more, and declare himself an English ally; he even promised the succour of 2,000 horse, but only sent 300. Dupleix, on his part, could muster 1,800 Europeans and 3,000 Sepoys, but his dispositions were by far the more skilful and able. Though accused of too much considering his own safety, and always keeping beyond the reach of shot *, he, at all events, knew how to inspire his men with military ardour, while the English were dispirited by the want of practice in their commanders, wasted by sickness, and harassed by the rains, which had begun three weeks before the usual season. At length they found it necessary to raise the siege, after thirty-one days of open trenches, and the loss of 1,000 men. The French Governor, in his usual boastful strain, immediately proclaimed his triumph by letters to all the chief Soubahdars of India, and even to the Great Mogul.

* This was one of the accusations afterwards brought against Dupleix by the French East India Company. Dupleix does not seem to have denied the facts, but he pleaded *que le bruit des armes suspendait ses reflexions et que le calme seul convenait à son genie!* (Mill's Hist. vol. iii. p. 74.)

Such was the state of affairs in India when the tidings came that a peace had been signed at Aix La Chapelle, and that a restitution of conquests had been stipulated. It became necessary for Dupleix to yield Madras to the English, which he did with extreme reluctance, and after long delay. On this occasion of recovering Madras, the English also took possession of St. Thomé, which the natives had conquered from the Portuguese, but which of late "seemed," says Mr. Orme, "to belong to nobody, "for there were no officers, either civil or military, acting "with authority in the place." *

The rival settlements of Pondicherry and Madras, though now debarred from any further direct hostility, were not long in assailing each other indirectly, as auxiliaries in the contests of the native Princes. A new scene was rapidly opening to the ambition of Dupleix. The Nizam, or Viceroy of the Deccan under the Mogul, had lately died, and been succeeded by his son, Nazir Jung, but one of his grandsons, Mirzapha Jung, had claimed the vacant throne. At the same time, in the dependent province of the Carnatic, Chunda Sahib, son-in-law of a former Nabob, appeared as a competitor to the reigning Prince, Anwar-ood-Deen. There seems the less necessity to weigh the justice of these various claims, since it scarcely formed an element in the consideration of those who espoused them. Neither the French nor the English at this period had any object in such struggles beyond their own aggrandizement, and the humiliation of their rivals; and, moreover, so loose and unsettled were then the politics of India,—with the authority of the Great Mogul supreme in theory and null in fact,—that plausible arguments might have been found in favour of the worst pretensions. Dupleix eagerly seized the opportunity to enhance his own importance, by establishing through his aid a Viceroy of the Deccan and a Nabob of the Carnatic. He promised his support to the two pretenders, who had combined their interests and their armies, and who were now reinforced with 2,000 Sepoys and several hundred Europeans. Nor did they want skilful officers from Pondicherry; one, above all, the

* Orme's Hist., vol. i. p. 131.

Marquis de Bussy, showed himself no less able in the field than Dupleix was in council. In August 1749 a battle ensued beneath the fort of Amboor, when the discipline of the French auxiliaries turned the tide of victory, and when the veteran and subtle Nabob, Anwar-ood-Deen, was slain. His capital, Arcot, and the greater part of his dominions, fell into the hands of the conquerors. His son, Mahomed Ali, with the wreck of his army, fled to Trichinopoly, and endeavoured to maintain himself, assuming the title of Nabob of Arcot, and acknowledged as such by the English; but their zeal in his behalf was faint and languid, and, moreover, they were at this juncture entangled with some insignificant operations in Tanjore. Dupleix, on the contrary, was all activity and ardour. Even on learning that his confederate, Mirzapha Jung, had suffered a reverse of fortune, and was a prisoner in the camp of Nazir Jung, he did not slacken either in warfare or negotiation. When, at length, in December 1750, the army which he had set in motion came in sight of Nazir Jung's, the Indian prince viewed its scanty numbers with scorn, calling out that it was only "the mad attempt of a parcel of drunken "Europeans!" But even before the trumpets sounded to battle Nazir Jung found cause to rue the power of Dupleix. A conspiracy had been formed by the French among his own followers; one of them aimed a carabine as Nazir Jung rode up on his elephant, and the Indian prince fell dead on the plain. His head was then severed from his body, and carried on a pole before the tent of Mirzapha Jung, who, freed from his fetters, was by the whole united army—thus sudden are the turns of Oriental politics!—hailed as the Nizam.

The exultation of Dupleix knew no bounds. On the spot where Nazir Jung had fallen he began to build a town, with the pompous title of Dupleix Fatihabad,—"the City of the Victory of Dupleix,"—and in the midst of that town he laid the foundation of a stately pillar, whose four sides were to bear inscriptions, proclaiming in four different languages the triumph of his arms. With the same vain-glorious spirit he resolved to celebrate, at the seat of his own government, the installation of the new Nizam. On the day of that ceremony he might have passed for an Asiatic potentate, as he entered the town in the same palanquin with his ally, and in the garb of a Mahometan Omrah, with which the Prince himself had clothed him. He accepted, or assumed, the government, under the Mogul, of all the country along the eastern coast between the river Kistna and Cape Comorin; a country little less in extent than France itself. A still higher honour, and still more important privilege, in the opinion of the natives, was the leave he obtained to carry, among his other trappings, the emblem of a fish.* No petition was granted by the Nizam unless signed by the hand of Dupleix; no money was henceforth to be current in the Carnatic except from the mint of Pondicherry. "Send me reinforcements," wrote Bussy to his chief, "and in one year more the Emperor shall "tremble at the name of Dupleix!"† But the French Governor soon discovered that his own vanity had been a fatal bar in the way of his ambition. His rivals at Fort St. George and Fort St. David took an alarm at his lofty titles which they might not have felt so soon at his extended power. How superior was their own conduct in prudence! how superior in success! The English in India have continued to call themselves traders long after they had become princes; Dupleix, on the contrary, had assumed the title of Prince while still, in truth, a trader.

It appeared on this occasion, to the heads of the English factory, that, although the contest for the Deccan had been decided by the fall of Nazir Jung, they might still advantageously take part in the contest for the Carnatic. Accordingly they sent several hundred men under Captain Gingen to reinforce their confederate, Mahomed Ali; but these troops were put to flight at Volcondah, and compelled to take shelter with Mahomed Ali in his last stronghold of Trichinopoly. There he was soon besieged and closely pressed by the army of Chunda Sahib and the auxiliaries of Dupleix. If the place should fall it was clear that the French would gain the mastery over

* Orme's Hist., vol. i. p. 161. "This distinction," he adds, "was "never granted but to persons of the first note in the Empire."—Bishop Heber says that it is considered even a badge of Royalty. Journal, October 28. 1824.

† Article Dupleix in the Biographie Universelle by Count de Lally Tollendal.

all the provinces adjoining Fort St. George and Fort St. David, and would at the first opportunity renew their attack upon those settlements. On the other hand, the English were at this time ill prepared for any further active hostilities; their only officer of experience, Major Lawrence, had gone home, and the garrisons remaining for their own defence were extremely small. There seemed almost equal danger in remaining passive or in boldly advancing. These doubts were solved, these perils overcome, by the energy of one man, — Robert Clive.

The father of Clive was a gentleman of old family, but small estate, residing near Market-Drayton in Shropshire. There Robert, his eldest son, was born in 1725. From early childhood the boy showed a most daring and turbulent spirit. His uncle thus writes of him, even in his seventh year: "I hope I have made a little further con-"quest over Bob. . . . . But his fighting, to which he is "out of measure addicted, gives his temper so much "fierceness and imperiousness that he flies out upon "every trifling occasion; for this reason I do what I can "to suppress the hero." * — The people at Drayton long remembered how they saw young Clive climb their lofty steeple, and seated astride a spout near the top, — how, on another occasion, he flung himself into the gutter to form a dam, and assist his playmates in flooding the cellar of a shopkeeper with whom he had quarrelled. At various schools to which he was afterwards sent he appears to have been idle and intractable. Even in after life he was never remarkable for scholarship; and his friendly biographer admits, that, wide as was his influence over the native tribes of India, he was little, if at all, acquainted with their languages.† His father was soon offended at his waywardness and neglect of his studies, and, instead of a profession at home, obtained for him a writership in the East India Company's service, and in the Presidency of Madras. Some years later, when the old gentleman was informed of his son's successes and distinctions, he used to exclaim, half in anger and half in pride, "After all the booby has sense!"

* Letter, June 9. 1732. Malcolm's Life of Clive, vol. i. p. 32.
† Malcolm's Life, vol. ii. p. 173.

The feelings of Clive during his first years at Madras are described in his own letters. Thus he writes to his cousin: "I may safely say I have not enjoyed one happy "day since I left my native country. I am not acquainted "with any one family in the place, and have not assurance "enough to introduce myself without being asked. . . . "Letters to friends were surely first invented for the "comfort of such solitary wretches as myself." * There is no doubt that the climate at Madras was unfavourable to his health, and his duty at the desk ill-suited to his temper. But worse than any other discomfort was his own constitutional and morbid melancholy, — a melancholy which may yet be traced in the expression of his portraits, and which, afterwards heightened as it was by bodily disease and mental irritation, closed the career of this great chief, by the act of his own hand, before he had attained the age of fifty years. As a writer at Madras he twice one day snapped a pistol at his own head. Finding it miss fire, he calmly waited until his room was entered by an acquaintance, whom he requested to fire the pistol out of the window. The gentleman did so, and the pistol went off. At this proof, that it had been rightly loaded Clive sprang up, with the exclamation, "Surely "then I am reserved for something!" and relinquished his design.

I have already found occasion to relate how Clive was led a prisoner from Fort St. George to Pondicherry, and how he effected his escape from Pondicherry to Fort St. David. At this latter station his daring temper involved him in several disputes. Once he fought a duel with an officer whom he had accused of cheating at cards. They met without seconds; Clive fired, and missed his antagonist, who immediately came close up to him, and held the pistol to his head, desiring him to recant the accusation, and threatening instant death as the alternative. "Fire!" answered Clive, with an oath, "I said you "cheated; I say so still, and I will never pay you!" —Awestruck at so much boldness, the officer flung away his pistol, exclaiming that Clive was mad.†

* Letter, February 16. 1745.

† This story is related in the biographichal sketch by Henry Beaufoy, Esq., M.P., drawn up from family papers and information, and (like the former) is admitted by Sir John Malcolm.

From this time forward, however, the undaunted spirit of Clive found a nobler scope against the public enemy. During the petty hostilities which ensued, — when the merchants' clerks were almost compelled in self-defence to turn soldiers, — the name of Ensign or Lieutenant Clive is often, and always honourably, mentioned; and during the intervals of these hostilities he returned to his ledgers and accounts. But on the emergency produced by the successes of Dupleix, the siege of Trichinopoly, and the departure of Major Lawrence, he accepted a Captain's commission, and bade adieu to trade. With no military education, with so little military experience, this young man of twenty-five shone forth, not only, as might have been foreseen,—a most courageous, but a most skilful and accomplished commander;—a commander, as Lord Chatham once exclaimed, "whose resolution would "charm the King of Prussia, and whose presence of "mind has astonished the Indies." *—At this crisis he discerned, that, although it was not possible to afford relief to Trichinopoly, a diversion might still be effected by a well-timed surprise of Arcot, thus compelling Chunda Sahib to send a large detachment from his army. The heads of the Presidency, on whom he strenuously urged his views, not only approved the design, but accepted the offer of his own services for its execution. Accordingly, in August 1751, Captain Clive marched from Madras at the head of only 300 Sepoys and 200 Europeans. Scanty as seems this force, it could only be formed by reducing the garrison at Fort St. David to 100 and the garrison of Madras to 50 men; and of the eight officers under Clive, six had never before been in action, and four were merchants' clerks, who, incited by his example, took up the sword to follow him. A few days' march brought the little band within ten miles of Arcot, and within sight of the outposts of the garrison. There a violent storm of thunder, lightning, and rain arose, through which, how-

* Lord Orford's Memoirs, vol. ii. p. 276. In a speech in the House of Commons (March 30. 1772) we find Clive disclaim all knowledge of trade. "My line has been military and political. I owe all I have "in the world to my having been at the head of an army, — and as to "cotton, — I know no more about it than the Pope of Rome!" (Parl. Hist. vol. xvii. p. 332.)

ever, Clive undauntedly pushed forward. Slight as seems this incident, it became attended with important results, for the garrison, apprised by their outposts of the behaviour of the English, were seized with a superstitious panic, as though their opponents were in league with the Heavens, and they fled precipitately, not only from the city, but from the citadel. Thus Clive, without having struck a blow, marched through the streets amidst a concourse of an hundred thousand spectators, and took quiet possession of the citadel or fort. In that stronghold the Arcot merchants had, for security, deposited effects to the value of 50,000*l.*, which Clive punctually restored to the owners; and this politic act of honesty conciliated many of the principal inhabitants to the English interest.

Clive, learning that the fugitive garrison had been reinforced, and had taken post in the neighbourhood, made several sallies against them; in the last he surprised them at night, and scattered or put them to the sword. But his principal business was to prepare against the siege which he expected, by collecting provisions and strengthening the works of the fort. As he had foretold, his appearance at Arcot effected a diversion at Trichinopoly. Chunda Sahib immediately detached 4,000 men from his army, who were joined by 2,000 natives from Vellore, by 150 Europeans from Pondicherry, and by the remains of the fugitive garrison. Altogether, the force thus directed against Arcot exceeded 10,000 men, and was commanded by Rajah Sahib, a son of Chunda Sahib. The fort in which the English were now besieged was, notwithstanding some hasty repairs, in great measure ruinous; with the parapet low and slightly built, with several of the towers decayed, with the ditch in some parts fordable, in others dry, and in some choked up with fallen rubbish. But Clive undauntedly maintained, day after day, such feeble bulwarks against such overwhelming numbers. Nor did he neglect, amidst other more substantial means of defence, to play upon the fears and fancies of his superstitious enemy. Thus he raised on the top of his highest tower an enormous piece of ordnance, which he had found in the fort, and which, according to popular tradition, had been sent from Delhi in the reign of Aurungzebe, dragged along by a thousand yoke of oxen.

This cannon was useless for any real practical effect, but being discharged once a day with great form and ceremony, it struck, as we are told, no small alarm into Rajah Sahib and his principal officers.*

The exertions and the example of Clive had inspired his little band with a spirit scarce inferior to his own. "I have it in my power," writes Sir John Malcolm, "from "authority I cannot doubt, to add an anecdote to the ac-"count of this celebrated siege. When provisions be-"came so scarce that there was a fear that famine might "compel them to surrender, the Sepoys proposed to Clive "to limit them to the water (or gruel) in which the rice "was boiled. 'It is,' they said, 'sufficient for our sup-"'port; the Europeans require the grain.'—This fact "is as honourable to Clive as to those under his command, "for the conduct of the native troops in India" (Sir John might, perhaps, have said the same of any troops in any country,) "will always be found to depend upon the cha-"racter of the officers under whom they are employed." †

After several weeks' siege, however, the besiegers, scanty and ill-served as was their artillery, had succeeded in making more than one practicable breach in the walls. Some succour to the garrison was attempted from Madras, but in vain. Another resource, however, remained to Clive. He found means to despatch a messenger through the enemy's lines to Morari Row, a Mahratta chieftain, who had received a subsidy to assist Mahomed Ali, and who lay encamped with 6,000 men on the hills of Mysore. Hitherto, notwithstanding his subsidy, he had kept aloof from the contest. But the news how bravely Arcot was defended fixed his wavering mind. "I never thought "till now," said he, "that the English could fight. Since "they can I will help them." And accordingly he sent down a detachment of his troops from the hills.

Rajah Sahib, when he learnt that the Mahrattas were approaching, perceived that he had no time to lose. He sent a flag of truce to the garrison, promising a large sum

* Orme's Hist., vol. i. p. 191. See, in the Memoires du Baron de Tott, the consternation produced among the Turks by the discharge of another such enormous and useless piece of artillery at the Dardanelles in 1770 (vol. ii. p. 75. ed. 1785).

† Life of Lord Clive, vol. i. p. 96.

of money if Clive would surrender, and denouncing instant death if Clive awaited a storm; but he found his offers and his threats received with equal disdain. Exasperated at the scornful answer, he made every preparation for a desperate attack on the morrow. It was the 14th of November, the fiftieth day of the siege, and the anniversary of the festival in commemoration of that martyr of early Islam, Hosein *, when, according to the creed of the Mahometans of India, any one who falls in battle against unbelievers is wafted at once into the highest region of Paradise. But, not solely trusting to the enthusiasm of the day, Rajah Sahib had recourse, moreover, to the excitement of BANG, an intoxicating drug, with which he plentifully supplied his soldiers. Before daybreak they came on every side rushing furiously up to the assault. Besides the breaches which they expected to storm, they had hopes to break open the gates by urging forwards several elephants with plates of iron fixed to their foreheads; but the huge animals, galled by the English musketry, as of yore by the Roman javelins †, soon turned, and trampled down the multitudes around them. Opposite one of the breaches where the water of the ditch was deepest another party of the enemy had launched a raft, with seventy men upon it, and began to cross. In this emergency Clive, observing that his gunners fired with bad aim, took himself the management of one of the field-pieces with so much effect that in three or four discharges he had upset the raft and drowned the men. Throughout the day his valour and his skill were equally conspicuous, and every assault of his opponents was repulsed with heavy loss. In the first part of the night their fire was renewed, but at two in the morning it ceased, and at the return of daylight it appeared that they had raised the siege, and were already out of sight,

* The fate of Hosein is eloquently and pathetically told by Gibbon. (Hist., vol. ix. p. 343—346. ed. 1820.) He adds in a note, the key to the excellence of his description: "The pathetic almost always "consists in the details of little circumstances."

† "Elephanti, in quorum tergis infixa stetere pila, ut est genus "anceps, in fugam versi etiam integros avertere . . . . Eo magis "ruere in suos belluae . . . . . Elephanti quoque duo in ipsâ portâ "conruerant." (Liv. Hist., lib. xxvii. c. 14.)

leaving 400 men dead upon the ground, with all their ammunition and artillery.

Elated at this result of his exertions, Clive was not slow in sallying forth, and combining his little garrison with the detachment from Morari Row, and with some reinforcements from Europe which had lately landed at Madras. Thus strengthened, he sought out Rajah Sahib, and gave him battle near the town of Arnee. On this occasion he beheld for the first time in action,—happily for him, ranged on his own side,—the activity and bravery of the Mahrattas. "They fight," says an excellent historian, "in a manner peculiar to themselves; their cavalry "are armed with sabres, and every horseman is closely "accompanied by a man on foot armed with a sword and "a large club; and some instead of a club carry a short "strong spear; if a horse be killed, and the rider remains "unhurt, he immediately begins to act on foot; and if "the rider falls, and the horse escapes, he is immediately "mounted, and pressed on to the charge by the first foot-"man who can seize him." * On the other hand, Rajah Sahib, though the greater part of his own troops were dispersed, had been reinforced from Pondicherry with 300 Europeans and nearly 3,000 Sepoys. The issue of the battle, however, was a complete victory to Clive; the enemy's military chest, containing a hundred thousand rupees, fell into the hands of his Mahrattas; and not less than 600 of the French Sepoys, dispirited by their failure, came over with their arms, and consented to serve in the English ranks.

Clive next proceeded against the great PAGODA, or Hindoo temple, of Conjeveram, into which the French had thrown a garrison. Their governor, who had lately surprised and taken two wounded English officers, sent Clive warning, that if the pagoda were attacked the prisoners should be exposed on the walls to the first fire of their countrymen. But a private note was added by the brave officers themselves,—their names deserve to be recorded; Lieutenants Revel and Glass,—entreating Clive to take no heed of their safety, and to do his duty at all risks. The barbarous threat was not, however,

* Orme's Hist. vol. i. p. 198

put in execution, and Clive, entering the place, after three days' cannonade, found the French garrison escaped by night, and the English officers unhurt.

Notwithstanding these events, Rajah Sahib was not disheartened. In January 1752, finding that Clive had marched to Fort St. David, he suddenly collected a body of his own troops and of his French auxiliaries, and pushed forwards to Madras. There was little or no force to withstand him in the open field, and he laid waste, without resistance, the gardens and the countryhouses of the British merchants. Clive was recalled in haste from the south; and at the village of Coverpauk he again encountered Rajah Sahib; again with complete success. From the scene of action he marched back in triumph to Fort St. David, passing on his way near the newly raised "City of the Victory of Dupleix," and the foundation of the pompous Pillar. By a just requital, Clive directed that these monuments of premature exultation should be razed to the ground.

At Trichinopoly the effect of Clive's earliest successes had been to turn the siege into a languid blockade, and with a little more energy on the part of the English garrison it might no doubt have been wholly raised; but all our leaders were not Clives. The indecision and want of enterprise of Captain Gingen excited the murmurs even of his own soldiers, and yet more of his auxiliaries. "Surely," cried one of the Mahrattas, "these are not "the same race of men as those we saw fighting at "Arcot!"

Such being the state of affairs, the heads of the English Presidency resolved to send a new expedition to Trichinopoly under Clive's command. At this period, however, Major Lawrence returned from Europe. Many a junior officer, flushed with successes, such as Clive's, might have disdained to serve under a senior. Many a senior officer, on the other hand, might have been jealous of such a junior. To the credit both of Clive and of Lawrence no such feelings appear to have sprung up between them. Clive continued his strenuous exertions in the public cause; and Lawrence, a good, though not a brilliant soldier, always readily employed and warmly acknowledged the talents of his second in command.

The expedition to Trichinopoly, led by Lawrence and Clive, was crowned with triumphant success. Lawrence adopted the daring proposal of Clive to divide,—at the risk of receiving a separate attack,—the army into two divisions, so as to surround the French. There arose some difficulty from the strict rules of seniority in our service to give, as Lawrence desired, the command of one division to Clive, who was the youngest Captain of his force. But his doubts were speedily solved by his auxiliaries, the Mahrattas and Mysoreans, who declared that they would take no part in this enterprise unless it were directed by the defender of Arcot.* In the result the French besiegers of Mahomed Ali were themselves besieged in the island of Seringham in the river Cavery, and were compelled to lay down their arms. Chunda Sahib himself surrendered to a native chief named Monackjee, who took an oath for his safety on his own sabre and poniard,—the most sacred of all oaths to an Indian soldier,—but who, nevertheless, shortly afterwards put his prisoner to death. "The Mahrattas," says Mr. Orme, "scarcely rate the life of a man at the value of his "turban."

The severed head of Chunda Sahib, a man whose benevolence and humanity are acknowledged even by his enemies,—was borne into the city of Trichinopoly, and into the presence of the Nabob, Mahomed Ali, who now for the first time beheld the face of his rival. After exhibiting the gory trophy in triumph to his courtiers, it was by his directions tied to the neck of a camel, and carried five times round the walls of the city, attended by an hundred thousand spectators, and insulted by every form of outrage.—Such were the customs and the feelings from which India has been freed by the British dominion!

It might have been expected that such successes,—and, above all, the murder of one of the competitors,—would finally decide the conquest for the government of the Carnatic. But immediately after his victory Mahomed Ali had become involved in dissensions with his allies, the Mahrattas and Mysoreans, to whom he had promised, without ever really intending, the cession of

* Orme's Hist., vol. i. p. 220. Malcolm's Life of Clive, vol. i. p. 110.

Trichinopoly. These bickerings gave fresh life and spirit to Dupleix. Although he found his recent policy disapproved by his employers in Europe,—although he received from them only reproofs instead of supplies,—although the recruits sent out to him were, according to his own description, no other than "boys, shoe-blacks, "and robbers," * — he yet clung to his own schemes with unconquerable perseverance. He laboured to train and discipline his recruits; and, in the want of other funds, he advanced for the public service not less than 140,000*l.* of his own money. He hastened to acknowledge Rajah Sahib as Nabob of Arcot; and on the incapacity of that competitor becoming apparent, still not discouraged, he proclaimed another chieftain in his place. Nor did he intermit the most active negotiations with the Nizam. This was no longer Mirzapha Jung, who had survived his elevation only a few months, but his successor, Salabat Jung, who had been elected mainly by the French influence, and generally leaned to the French interest. At the Court of this prince Dupleix had for some time past stationed his best officer, Bussy, whose abilities had gained him great weight, and enabled the Nizam to prevail over his numerous opponents. "Had I only a second Bussy," writes Dupleix, "I should long ago have put an end to "the war in the Carnatic." † It was with other and far inferior officers that Dupleix now resumed hostilities,—again attempted Arcot, and again besieged Trichinopoly. Notwithstanding all his exertions, the warfare proved weak and languid, and was far from enabling the French to recover their lost ground.

Clive had for some time continued to distinguish himself in the desultory operations which followed the surrender of Seringham. He had reduced in succession the two important forts of Covelong and Chingleput. But his health was beginning to fail beneath the burning sun of India; his return to England had become essential to his recovery, and he embarked at Madras early in the year 1753, immediately after his marriage to Miss Mar-

* "Enfans, decrotteurs, et bandits!" Lettre à M. de Machault, le 16 Octobre 1753. The English recruits in India were little better.

† Lettre à M. de Machault, le 16 Octobre 1753.

garet Maskelyne. He found himself received at home with well-earned approbation and rewards. The Court of Directors at one of their public dinners drank the health of the young Captain by the name of "General Clive," * and, not satisfied with this convivial compliment, voted him the gift of a sword set with diamonds. It is greatly to the honour of Clive that he refused to accept this token of esteem, unless the same were bestowed on his old and worthy commander, Major Lawrence, which was done accordingly.

Far different were the feelings which the Directors of the French East India Company entertained towards Dupleix. They looked with slight interest on the struggles for the Carnatic, and thought the failure of their Dividends an unanswerable argument against the policy of their Governor. A negotiation for the adjustment of all differences was carried on for some time in London between them and their English rivals. At length they determined to send over M. Godeheu, as their Commissioner, to India, with full powers to conclude a peace, and to supersede Dupleix. Godeheu landed at Pondicherry in August 1754, and hastened to sign with the chiefs of the English Presidency a provisional treaty, to be confirmed or annulled in Europe, according to which the French party yielded nearly all the points at issue, and virtually acknowledged Mahomed Ali as Nabob of the Carnatic.

Dupleix, who looked on this pacification with unavailing grief and anger, had, even before its final conclusion, embarked for France. There he found neither reward for the services he had rendered nor even repayment for the sums he had advanced.—Where was now that proud and wily Satrap, so lately bedecked with pompous titles, and glittering with the gold of Trichinopoly or the diamonds of Golconda?—Had any curious travellers at the time sought an answer to that question they might have found the fallen statesman reduced, as is told us by himself, to the most deplorable indigence,—compiling in some garret another fruitless Memorial, or waiting for many a weary hour in some Under-Secre-

* Letter to Clive from his father, December 15. 1752.

tary's antechamber. For several years he pursued most unavailingly his claims and his complaints, until in 1763 he expired, sick at heart and broken in fortunes, like his rival and his victim, La Bourdonnais.

CHAPTER II.

(CHAP. XL. OF THE HISTORY.)

WITHIN two years the health of Clive grew strong in his native air, and his spirit began to pine for active service. On the other hand, experience of his merits, and apprehension of a war with France, rendered both the King's Ministers and the East India Company eager to employ him. From the former he received the rank of Lieutenant Colonel in the army, from the latter the office of Governor of Fort St. David. Landing at Bombay with some troops in November 1755, he found there Admiral Watson and a British squadron. There was little at that time on the coast of Coromandel to demand the exertions of these two commanders, and they thought the opportunity tempting to reduce in conjunction a formidable nest of pirates, about two degrees south of Bombay. These pirates had for above half a century formed a predatory state like Tunis or Algiers, holding 120 miles of coast, and commanded by chiefs who always bore the name of Angria. Although their vessels were but small and slightly armed, the richest merchants in those seas had either to purchase their passes or to fear their depredations. One of their fortresses, Severndroog, had been taken by Commodore James several months before; it was against the other, Gheriah, that Clive and Watson now proceeded. The place was of great strength, built on a rocky headland almost surrounded by the sea; but the pirates were struck with terror, and surrendered with little resistance. Their spoils, valued at 120,000*l.*, were shared as prize-money between the naval and military captors.

Having performed this service in February 1756, Clive pursued his voyage to Fort St. David, and took the charge of his government on the 20th of June, — the very day, by a remarkable coincidence, when the Nabob of Bengal was storming Fort William.—In fact a crisis had now occurred on the shores of the Hooghly, threatening the utmost danger, and calling for the utmost exertion.

The Viceroys of Bengal, like the Viceroys of the Deccan, retained only a nominal dependence on the Mogul Empire. From their capital, Moorshedabad,—"a city," says Clive, "as extensive, populous, and rich as the city "of London,"—they sent forth absolute and uncontrolled decrees over the wide provinces of Bengal, Orissa, and Bahar, ill disguised by the mockery of homage to that empty phantom "the King of Kings" at Delhi.* The old Nabob, Aliverdi Khan, had died in April 1756, and been succeeded by his grandson, Surajah Dowlah, a youth only nineteen years of age. Surajah Dowlah combined in no small degree a ferocious temper with a feeble understanding. The torture of birds and beasts had been the pastime of his childhood, and the sufferings of his fellow-creatures became the sport of his riper years. His favourite companions were buffoons and flatterers, with whom he indulged in every kind of debauchery, amongst others, the immoderate use of ardent spirits. Towards the Europeans, and the English especially, he looked with ignorant aversion, and still more ignorant contempt. He was often heard to say that he did not believe there were 10,000 men in all Europe.†

Differences were not slow to arise between such a prince as Surajah Dowlah and his neighbours, the British in Bengal. One of his revenue officers had escaped from his custody with a large treasure, as was suspected, and had found a safe refuge at Calcutta. Moreover, the Presidency of that place had begun to improve their fortifications, from the prospect of another war with France. This greatly displeased the Nabob, and he was only the more incensed at the explanation, which implied that these audacious strangers might presume to bring their hostilities into his dominions. Without further parley he

* Even at a later period, and a much lower pitch of degradation, the Mogul Court still retained the most pompous forms and titles. See in Bishop Heber's Journal (December 31. 1824) the account of his own presentation at Delhi.

† Orme's Hist., vol. ii. p. 120.

seized the British factory at Cossim-Bazar, the port of Moorshedabad upon the river, and he retained the chiefs of that settlement as his prisoners. The Presidency of Fort William were now thoroughly alarmed, and hastened to make the most abject apologies, offering to accept any terms which Surajah Dowlah might be pleased to dictate. But Surajah Dowlah had heard much of the wealth at Calcutta; that wealth he was determined to secure; and he soon appeared before the gates at the head of a numerous army.

The defences of Calcutta, notwithstanding the wrath which they had stirred in the Nabob, were at this time slight and inconsiderable. For a garrison there were less than 200 Europeans, and scarcely more than 1,000 natives, hastily trained as militia, and armed with matchlocks. No example of spirit was set them by their chiefs. On the contrary, the Governor, Mr. Drake, and the commanding officer, Captain Minchin, being struck with a disgraceful panic, embarked in a boat, and escaped down the Hooghly. Under these circumstances, a civilian, Mr. Holwell, though not the senior servant of the Company, was by the general voice called to the direction of affairs. At this time the Nabob's artillery was already thundering at the walls, yet under every disadvantage Mr. Holwell protracted for two days longer the defence of the fort. When, at length, on the evening of the 20th of June, all resistance had ceased, the Nabob seated himself in the great hall of the factory, and received the congratulations of his courtiers on his prowess. Soon after he sent for Mr. Holwell, to whom he expressed much resentment at the presumption of the English in daring to defend their fort, and much dissatisfaction at his having found so small a sum,—only 50,000 rupees,—in their treasury. On the whole, however, he seemed more gracious than his character gave reason to expect, and he promised, "on the word of a soldier," as he said, that the lives of his prisoners should be spared.

Thus dismissed by the tyrant, and led back to the other captives, Mr. Holwell cheered them with the promise of their safety. We are told how, relieved from their terrors, and unconscious of their doom, they laughed and jested amongst themselves. But their joy and their jesting were of short duration. They had been left at the disposal of the officers of the guard, who determined to secure them for the night in the common dungeon of the fort, — a dungeon known to the English by the name of "the Black Hole," — its size only eighteen feet by fourteen; its airholes only two small windows, and these overhung by a low veranda. Into this cell, — hitherto designed and employed for the confinement of some half dozen malefactors at a time, — was it now resolved to thrust an hundred and forty-five European men and one Englishwoman, some of them suffering from recent wounds, and this in the night of the Indian summer-solstice, when the fiercest heat was raging! Into this cell accordingly the unhappy prisoners, in spite of their expostulations, were driven at the point of the sabre, the last, from the throng and narrow space, being pressed in with considerable difficulty, and the doors being then by main force closed and locked behind them.

Of the doleful night that succeeded narratives have been given by two of the survivors, Mr. Holwell and Mr. Cooke.—The former, who even in this extremity was still in some degree obeyed as chief, placed himself at a window, called for silence, and appealed to one of the Nabob's officers, an old man, who had shown more humanity than the rest, promising him a thousand rupees in the morning if he would find means to separate the prisoners into two chambers. The old man went to try, but returned in a few minutes with the fatal sentence that no change could be made without orders from the Nabob, — that the Nabob was asleep, — and that no one dared to disturb him.

Meanwhile within the dungeon the heat and stench had become intolerable. It was clear to the sufferers themselves that, without a change, few, if any, amongst them would see the light of another day. Some attempted to burst open the door; others, as unavailingly, again besought the soldiers to unclose it. As their dire thirst increased, amidst their struggles and their screams, "Water! Water!" became the general cry. The officer, to whose compassion Mr. Holwell had lately appealed, desired some skins of water to be brought to the window; but they proved too large to pass through the iron bars, and the sight of this relief, so near and yet withheld, served only to infuriate and well-nigh madden the miserable captives; they began to fight and trample one another down, striving for a nearer place to the windows, and for a few drops of the water. These dreadful conflicts, far from exciting the pity of the guards, rather moved their mirth; and they held up lights to the bars, with fiendish glee, to discern the amusing sight more clearly. On the other hand, several of the English, frantic with pain, were now endeavouring by every term of insult and invective to provoke these soldiers to put an end to their agony by firing into the dungeon. "Some of our "company," says Mr. Cooke, "expired very soon after "being put in; others grew mad, and having lost their "senses, died in a high delirium." At length, and by degrees, these various outcries sunk into silence,—but it was the silence of death. When the morning broke, and the Nabob's order came to unlock the door, it became necessary first to clear a lane, by drawing out the corpses, and piling them in heaps on each side, when,—walking one by one through the narrow outlet,—of the 146 persons who had entered the cell the evening before, only twenty-three came forth; the ghastliest forms, says Mr. Orme, that were ever seen alive!

It does not appear that Surajah Dowlah had in any degree directed or intended the horrors of that night. But he made himself what might be termed in legal phrase an accessary after the fact. He expressed neither sympathy with those who had suffered nor resentment at those who had wrought the inhuman outrage. When in the morning Mr. Holwell was by his orders again brought before him,—unable to stand, and propped up between two guards,—the Nabob talked only of the great treasure which he was sure the English had buried, and threatened further injuries, unless it were revealed. But after sufferings like those of Mr. Holwell threats can no longer cause dismay. In Mr. Holwell's own words: "Such "intimations gave me no manner of concern, for at that "juncture I should have esteemed death the greatest "favour the tyrant could have bestowed upon me."—In his treatment of the dead, as of the living, the brutal temper of the tyrant was shown. The corpses drawn from the Black Hole were rudely and promiscuously cast into a large trench dug without the castle-wall. An Englishwoman, the only one of her sex among the sufferers, and who, strange to add, had been found among the few survivors, was consigned to the Haram of the Nabob's general, Meer Jaffier. The English of inferior rank were suffered to escape, but their property was plundered, and Mr. Holwell, with two other chief men, were sent as prisoners to Moorshedabad; there loaded with irons, lodged in a cow-house, and allowed only rice and water for their food, until, some time afterwards, their release was granted to the humane intercession of a native lady, the widow of Aliverdi Khan.

At Calcutta meanwhile Surajah Dowlah was lending a ready ear to the praises of his courtiers, who assured him that his reduction of the British settlement was the most heroic and glorious achievement performed in India since the days of Tamerlane. In memory of the Divine blessing (for so he deemed it) on his arms, he ordered that Calcutta should thenceforward bear the name of ALINAGORE,—"the Port of God." Another edict declared that no Englishman should ever again presume to set foot within the territory. Then, leaving a garrison of 3,000 men in Calcutta, and levying large sums, by way of contribution, from the Dutch at Chinsura and the French at Chandernagore, Surajah Dowlah returned in triumph to his capital.

It was not till the 16th of August that tidings of the events of Calcutta reached Madras. Measures were then in progress for sending a detachment into the Deccan, to counteract the influence of Bussy. But all other considerations were overborne by the cry for vengeance against Surajah Dowlah, and the necessity of an expedition to Bengal. It happened fortunately that Admiral Watson and his squadron had returned from the western coast, and were now at anchor in the roads. It happened also, from the projected march to the Deccan, that the land-forces were at this period combined, and ready for action. Difficulties, however, immediately arose as to the chief command. Colonel Adlercron and Colonel (lately Major) Lawrence might urge the claims of seniority, but the former had no experience of Indian warfare, and the health of the latter was declining. Under these circumstances Mr. Orme, the historian, who was then a member of the Council at Madras, had the honour of suggesting the name of Clive; and Colonel Lawrence, no less to his credit, warmly supported the proposal. Adopting these views, the Presidency summoned Clive from Fort St. David, and appointed him chief of the intended expedition. Colonel Adlercron, much incensed, declared, in his zeal for the public service, that unless the command were vested in himself he would not allow the Royal Artillery or the King's guns and stores to proceed; and, though they were already on board, they were again disembarked by his orders. The young hero of Arcot, however, could still reckon on some of the best troops in the King's service, — great part of the Thirty-ninth Foot. That gallant regiment, so conspicuous for many other services, — which for its brave deeds at Gibraltar bears on its colours the Castle and the Key, MONTIS INSIGNIA CALPE, — has no less nobly earned the lofty title, as founder of our Eastern empire: PRIMUS IN INDIS.*

On the whole, the force entrusted to Clive amounted to 900 Europeans, and 1,500 Sepoys. The powers granted him were to be in all military matters independent of the Members of the Council of Calcutta; but his instructions were positive and peremptory, to return at all events and under any circumstances by the month of April next, about which time a French expedition was expected on the coast of Coromandel.

The armament of Clive and Watson, having been delayed two months by quarrels at Madras, and two more

* This regiment also distinguished itself in the campaigns of the Peninsula and South of France. At Hellette, writes the Duke of Wellington, "two attacks of the enemy were most gallantly received "and repulsed by the 39th." (To Earl Bathurst. February 20. 1814.) Even while these pages are passing through the press, this regiment has gained new and brilliant laurels on the field of Maharaj-poor. Lord Ellenborough speaks of it as follows, in his General Orders of January 4. 1844. "Her Majesty's 39th Regiment had the peculiar for- "tune of adding to the honour of having won at Plassey the first "great battle which laid the foundation of the British empire in "India, the further honour of thus nobly contributing to this, as it "may be hoped, the last and crowning victory by which that empire "has been secured."

by contrary winds at sea, did not enter the Hooghly until the middle of December. At the village of Fulta, near the mouth of the river, they found the fugitives from the British settlement, including the principal Members of the Council, who formed a Select Committee of direction. Having combined measures with them, Clive and Watson pushed forward against Calcutta. The scanty garrison left by Surajah Dowlah ventured to sally forth, under its commander, Monichund, but was easily routed with the loss of 150 men, Monichund himself receiving a shot through his turban. Calcutta, after one or two random discharges from the wall, was quietly abandoned to the English, who thus on the 2d of January 1757 again became masters of the place. Nay, more, after this first success, Clive and Watson advanced against the town of Hooghly, which they stormed and sacked with little loss. This was the first opportunity of distinction to Captain Coote, afterwards Sir Eyre.

At these tidings, Surajah Dowlah, much irritated, but also in some degree alarmed, marched back from Moorshedabad at the head of 40,000 men. By this time intelligence had reached India of the Declaration of War between France and England, and the Nabob proposed to the French at Chandernagore that they should join him with their whole force, amounting to several hundred Europeans. But the memory of their reverses on the coast of Coromandel was still present in their minds, and they not only rejected the Nabob's overture, but made an overture of their own to the English for a treaty of neutrality. Formerly, they said, war had been waged in India between France and England while the two countries were in peace at home. Why not now reverse the rule, and maintain quiet in Bengal, though hostilities might prevail elsewhere? As, however, the French at Chandernagore did not, like the English at Calcutta, form a separate Presidency, but were dependent on the government of Pondicherry, they had not in truth the powers to conclude the treaty they proposed, and for this and other reasons it was finally rejected by the British chiefs.*

* There is some contradiction between the several statements of this overture, but they are judiciously reconciled in a note to Mr. Thornton's History of India, vol. i. p. 214.

During this time Surajah Dowlah had advanced close upon Fort William, at the head of his large but ill-disciplined and irregular army. Clive, considering the disparity of numbers, resolved to surprise the enemy in a night attack. According to his own account, "about "three o'clock in the morning I marched out with nearly "my whole force; about six we entered the enemy's "camp in a thick fog, and crossed it in about two hours, "with considerable execution. Had the fog cleared up, "as it usually does about eight o'clock, when we were "entire masters of the camp without the ditch, the action "must have been decisive; instead of which it thickened, "and occasioned our mistaking the way." * It may be added from other reports, that the loss of the English in the action which ensued was no less than 100 Sepoys and 120 Europeans, — a great proportion of their little army. Yet if the object of Clive had been mainly to show the superiority of the Europeans in warfare, and to strike terror into the mind of the Nabob, that object was fully attained. Surajah Dowlah passed from an ignorant contempt of the English to a kind of timid awe; and though the latter feeling in his mind proved as evanescent as the former, it strongly inclined him at the time to peace on terms most favourable to his opponents. He agreed to grant them the confirmation of their previous privileges, — the right to fortify Calcutta in any manner they pleased, — the exemption of all merchandise under their passes from fees and tolls, — and the restoration of or compensation for all such of their plundered effects as had been carried to the Nabob's account. Three days after a peace had been signed on these conditions the new-born friendship of the Nabob for the English, joined to some fear of a northward invasion from the Affghans, led him so far as to propose another article, for an intimate alliance, offensive and defensive. It seemed ignominious, and a stain on our national honour, to conclude such a treaty, or indeed any treaty, with the author of the atrocities of the Black Hole, while those atrocities remained without the slightest satisfaction, requital, or apology. But, as Clive had previously complained, the

* Letter to the Secret Committee, February 22. 1757.

gentlemen at Calcutta were then callous to every feeling but that of their own losses. "Believe me," says Clive, "they are bad subjects, and rotten at heart. . . . . The "riches of Peru and Mexico should not induce me to live "among them."* — Nevertheless it must be observed, that, whatever may have been Clive's feelings on this occasion, he showed himself to the full as eager and forward as any of the merchants in pressing the conclusion of the treaty of alliance. Among the chiefs none but Admiral Watson opposed it, and it was signed and ratified on the 12th of February, the same day that it was offered.

This new and strange alliance seemed to the English at Calcutta to afford them a most favourable opportunity for assailing their rivals at Chandernagore. Clive wrote to the Nabob applying for permission, and received an evasive answer, which he thought fit to construe as assent. Operations were immediately commenced; Clive directing them by land, and Watson by water. To the latter especially high praise is due. "Even at the pre-"sent day," says Sir John Malcolm, "when the naviga-"tion of the river is so much better known, the success "with which the largest vessels of this fleet were navi-"gated to Chandernagore, and laid alongside the batteries "of that settlement, is a subject of wonder."† The French made a gallant resistance, but were soon overpowered, and compelled to surrender the settlement, on which occasion above 400 European soldiers became prisoners of war.

The Nabob, who by this time had gone back to his capital, was most highly exasperated on learning the attack upon Chandernagore, which he had never really intended to allow. It produced another complete revolution in his sentiments. His former hatred against the English returned, but not his former contempt. On the contrary, he now felt the necessity of strengthening himself by foreign alliances against them, and with that view he entered into correspondence with M. de Bussy in the Deccan. His letters pressed that officer to march

* Letter to the Governor of Madras, January 8. 1757.

† Life of Clive, vol. i. p. 192.

to his assistance against the Englishman, SABUT JUNG, "The daring in war," — a well-earned title, by which Clive is to this day known among the natives of India. "These disturbers of my country," writes his Highness, "the Admiral and Sabut Jung, — whom may ill fortune "attend! — without any reason whatever are warring "against the Governor of Chandernagore. I, who in all "things seek the good of mankind, assist him in every "respect. . . . . I hope in God these English will be "punished. . . . . Be confident; look on my forces as your "own." — Copies of these letters fell into the hands of the English, and left them no doubt as to the hostile designs of the Nabob. In the same spirit, Surajah Dowlah conferred secretly and more than once with M. Law, the chief of the French factory at Cossim-Bazar. This Law, a nephew of the Mississippi projector, had under his command a force, partly his own and partly of fugitives from Chandernagore, amounting to nearly 200 Europeans and Sepoys. It was now demanded by the English, in conformity with the treaty of alliance, that Surajah Dowlah should dismiss this small force from his dominions. On the other hand, Law warned the Nabob of the plots and conspiracies already rife at his own Court, and urged him to declare boldly and at once against the English. The Nabob, as usual with weak minds, adopted a middle course. He pretended to banish Law from the province as far as Patna, but continued to supply him secretly with money, and said, on his taking leave, that if there should happen any thing new, he would send for him again. — "Send for me again!" replied the resolute Frenchman. "Be assured, my Lord "Nabob, that this is the last time we shall ever see "each other; remember my words; we shall never meet "again."

At this time the English Resident at the Court of Moorshedabad was Mr. Watts, lately chief of the factory at Cossim-Bazar, and selected for his new office at the Nabob's own request. From the information he supplied, Clive reports as follows: "One day the Nabob tears my "letters, and turns out our VAKEEL (envoy), and orders "his army to march; the next countermands it; sends "for the Vakeel, and begs his pardon for what he has "done. Twice a week he threatens to impale Mr. Watts! "In short he is a compound of every thing that is bad. ".... It is a most disagreeable circumstance to find that "the troubles are likely to commence again, but the "opinion here (at Calcutta) is universal, that there can "be neither peace nor trade without a change of government."*

With this conviction strongly rooted in his mind, and the danger to Bengal full before his eyes, the bold spirit of Clive determined to set aside of his own authority the instructions commanding his immediate return to Madras. He entered eagerly into the conspiracy forming at Moorshedabad to depose Surajah Dowlah, and to place on the throne the General of the forces, Meer Jaffier. It may readily be supposed that in these negotiations Meer Jaffier was liberal, nay lavish, in his promises of compensation to the Company, and rewards to their soldiers. Still more essential was the engagement into which he entered, that, on the approach of an English force, he would join their standard with a large body of his troops. It was the energy of Clive which formed the soul of the whole design—which upheld the faltering courage of the conspirators at Moorshedabad, and fixed the doubtful judgment of the Committee (or Council) at Calcutta. Thus he writes to Mr. Watts: "Tell Meer Jaffier to fear "nothing, and that I will join him with 5,000 men who "never turned their backs."† Yet it seems difficult to believe that Clive could really expect, at that juncture, to muster much more than half the numbers that he named.

In these negotiations between the native conspirators and the English chiefs, the principal agent next to Mr. Watts was a wealthy Hindoo merchant of the name of Omichund. A long previous residence at Calcutta had made him well acquainted with English forms and manners, while it had lost him none of the craft and subtlety that seemed almost the birthright of a Bengalee. As the time for action drew near, he began to feel,—not scruples at the treachery,—not even apprehensions as to

* Letter to the Governor of Madras, April 30. 1757.

† Letter to Mr. Watts, May 2. 1757.

the success, — but doubts whether his own interests had been sufficiently secured. He went to Mr. Watts, and threatened to disclose the whole conspiracy to Surajah Dowlah unless it were stipulated that he should receive thirty lacs of rupees, or 300,000*l.*, as a reward for his services, — which stipulation he insisted on seeing added as an article in the treaty pending between Meer Jaffier and the English. Mr. Watts, in great alarm for his own life, soothed Omichund with general assurances, while he referred the question as speedily as possible to the Members of the Select Committee at Calcutta. There was little disposition on the part of these gentlemen to concede the grasping demands of the Hindoo. Meer Jaffier, it is true, had promised a donative of forty or fifty lacs in case of his success; but these the Committee designed partly for the army and navy, and partly for themselves. Though often at variance with each other, they were never found to disagree when their own profit was at stake. Thus, one of the Members, Mr. Becher, having moved, "That as they, the Committee, had set the machine in motion, it was reasonable and proper that they should be considered," — or, in other words, share in the spoils, the Resolution was carried with enthusiastic unanimity.*

Under these circumstances the Committee were equally unwilling to grant and afraid to refuse the exorbitant claim of Omichund. But an expedient was suggested by Clive. Two treaties were drawn up; the one on white paper, intended to be real and valid, and containing no reference to Omichund, the other on red paper, with a stipulation in his favour, but designed as fictitious, and merely with the object to deceive him. The Members of the Committee, like Clive, put their names without hesitation to both treaties; but Admiral Watson, with higher spirit, would only sign the real one. It was foreseen that the omission of such a name would rouse the suspicion of Omichund, and in this emergency Clive directed another person to counterfeit the Admiral's signature.

For his share in these transactions Clive was many years afterwards taunted to his face in the House of

* Malcolm's Life of Clive, vol. i. p. 253.

Commons. Unable to deny he endeavoured to defend his conduct. "It was," he said, "a matter of true policy "and of justice to deceive so great a villain as Omi- "chund." * The villany of Omichund, however, appears mainly this,—that for the treachery which the English encouraged and abetted he claimed a larger reward than the English were willing to pay. But even admitting to the fullest extent the guilt of the Hindoo intriguer, this does not suffice to vindicate the British chief; this does not prove that it was justifiable, as he alleges, to deceive the deceiver, and to foil an Asiatic by his own Asiatic arts. Such expedients as fictitious treaties and counterfeited signatures are not, as I conceive, to be cleared by any refinements of ingenuity, or any considerations of state advantage †, and they must for ever remain a blot on the brilliant laurels of Clive.

Omichund having thus been successfully imposed upon, and the conspiracy being now sufficiently matured, Mr. Watts made his escape from Moorshedabad, and Clive set his army in motion from Calcutta. He had under his command 3,000 men, all excellent troops, and one third Europeans. The terror of Surajah Dowlah was increased by a haughty letter from Clive, alleging the Nabob's infraction of the recent alliance, and his new designs against the English. Much perturbed, the Nabob, however, proceeded to assemble near the village of Plassey

* Speech, May 19. 1773. Parl. Hist., vol. xvii. p. 876.

† See the elaborate defence of Sir John Malcolm in the sixth chapter of his Life of Clive. He argues, that Admiral Watson knew and permitted the signature of his name by another hand. But in the first place, and *primâ facie*, it appears utterly incredible that any man refusing on conscientious grounds his signature to a delusive treaty would give his consent to the counterfeiting of that signature. Secondly, I observe, that no such apology is ventured upon by the contemporary historian, Mr. Orme, notwithstanding his personal friendship for Clive (Hist. vol. ii. p. 155.). Thirdly, I find that the expressions ascribed to Watson by Mr. Cooke, the Secretary to Government, are merely as follows: "The Admiral said he had not "signed it, but left them to do as they pleased,"—expressions which, I think, can imply no more than that the other parties might proceed or not, as they could or would, in their own course of policy, without him. Watson died of jungle-fever only a few weeks after these events.

his whole force amounting to 15,000 cavalry, and 35,000 foot. Nor was it merely in numbers of men that he surpassed the English; while Clive brought only eight field pieces and two howitzers, Surajah Dowlah had above forty pieces of cannon of the largest size, each drawn by forty or fifty yoke of white oxen, and each with an elephant behind, trained to assist in pushing it over difficult ground. Forty Frenchmen in the Nabob's pay directed some smaller guns. The greater part of the foot were armed with matchlocks, the rest with various weapons, —pikes, swords, arrows, and even rockets. The cavalry, both men and horses, were drawn from the northern districts of India, and, to the eye at least, appeared more formidable than those encountered by Clive in the wars of the Carnatic. But in truth these numbers were an army only in name and outward show; not cheered by military spirit, nor jealous of military reputation; with no confidence in themselves, and no attachment to their leader.

The Nabob, distrustful of Meer Jaffier, had before he left the capital exacted from him an oath of fidelity upon the Koran. Either a respect for this oath, or, what is far more probable, a doubt as to the issue of the war, seemed to weigh with Meer Jaffier; he did not perform his engagement to the English, of joining them with his division at the appointed place of meeting, but kept aloof, sending them only evasive answers or general assurances. When, therefore, the English army came within one march of the Nabob's at Plassey,—with the wide stream of the Hooghly flowing between them,—can we wonder if doubts assailed even the resolute spirit of Clive, how far relying on the slippery faith of the Hindoo conspirator, or on his own brave but scanty force, he might venture to pass the river, and bring the enemy to battle? He well knew, as he said himself, that "if a defeat ensued not one man would have returned to tell it." Under these circumstances he assembled a Council of War. Sixteen years afterwards he observed that this was the only Council of War which he had ever held, and that if he had abided by its decision it would have been the ruin of the East India Company. But these words, if taken alone, would not convey an accurate impression of what passed. Having called together his officers, to the number of twenty, he proposed to them the question, whether it would be prudent, without assistance, to attack the Nabob, or whether they should wait until joined by some native force. Contrary to the usual form in Councils of War, beginning with the youngest Member, Clive gave his own opinion first, and that opinion was, not to venture. Twelve officers concurred with their chief; seven others, among whom was Major Eyre Coote, voted for immediate action. Thus a large majority approved the judgment of Clive; but his own doubts returned more forcibly than ever, and he began to feel that not only honour but safety pointed forwards. It was said at the time that his purpose had been changed by one hour of tranquil meditation under the shade of some trees; but Clive himself declared in his Evidence in England, that after the Council he had taken "about "twenty-four hours' mature consideration." Be this as it may, he came forth fully resolved to put every thing to the hazard. The troops were led across the river; they accomplished in eight hours a toilsome march of fifteen miles, and at one o'clock in the morning of the memorable 23d of June, 1757, they reached the mangoe-grove of Plassey. The mingling sounds of drums, clarions, and cymbals, — the usual tokens of a night-watch in an Indian army, — convinced them that they were now within a mile of the Nabob's camp. For the remainder of that night Clive took up his quarters in a small hunting-house belonging to the Nabob, but could not sleep; while his soldiers, less concerned than their General, stretched themselves to rest beneath the adjoining trees.*

At sunrise Clive ascended the roof of the hunting-house, and surveyed with a steadfast eye the rich array and the spreading numbers of his enemy. He saw them advance from several sides, as if to enclose him, but they halted at some distance, and began a cannonade, which

* The proceedings of the Council of War, and the march of Clive, are in some points of less importance, differently told by different writers. These points are clearly drawn out and well discussed by Mr. Thornton in two notes. (Hist. of India, vol. i. p. 235. and 237.) Sir John Malcolm adopts two conflicting statements without explanation or remark. (Life of Clive, vol. i. p. 161. and 164.)

was returned by the English, and which continued during several hours. It was found that the cumbrous ordnance of the Indians did far less execution than the light field-pieces of Clive. So careless, besides, were the former troops in carrying or handling ammunition, that several explosions were observed in their own ranks, and that about noon a passing shower damaged a great part of their powder, and compelled them to slacken their fire. At nearly the same time one of their most trusted leaders fell, and one of their divisions consequently showed some symptoms of disorder. This news came to the Nabob, who had remained in his tent beyond the reach of danger, surrounded by officers, one half of whom were parties to the conspiracy against him. He now received the perfidious or timid counsel, — to which his own fears readily responded, — of commanding a retreat towards his capital; the order was issued, and the army began to fall back. At such favourable indications, a charge upon the enemy was begun, without orders, by two companies under Major Kilpatrick *, and soon afterwards was renewed by Clive, at the head of his whole line. They met with faint resistance, except from the gallant little band of Frenchmen; drove the enemy from the advanced position; and became possessed of some rising ground near an angle of the Indian camp. Meer Jaffier, on his part, seeing to which side the fortune of the day was tending, drew off his body of troops. Before five o'clock the victory of Clive was not only certain but complete. It had cost him no more than twenty-two soldiers slain and fifty wounded, while the loss of the vanquished also did not exceed 500 men; but they were pursued for six miles, scattering in every direction, and leaving behind all their artillery and baggage.

The field of Plassey, — on which with such slender loss the fate, not only of Bengal, but of India, was in truth decided, — continued for many years an object of interest

* "Colonel Clive chanced at this time to be lying down in the "hunting-house. Some say he was asleep, which is not improbable, "considering how little rest he had had for so many hours before; "but this is no imputation either against his courage or conduct." (Orme's Hist. vol. ii. p. 176.)

and curiosity to the passing stranger. It was visited, amongst several other British officers, by the Duke of Wellington, whom I have heard describe it; but more recently it has become difficult, nay, almost impossible, to trace the scene of this great achievement. The river has here entirely changed its course, and encroached upon the plain; the Nabob's hunting-house, once the abode of Clive, has crumbled away, and even the celebrated mangoe-grove is no longer to be found.*

Of this battle it may be said, that it was gained against a disparity of force nearly such as the Spaniards encountered in Mexico and Peru. But there is a difference highly honourable to the English. The natives of Mexico and Peru were wholly ignorant of gunpowder, and viewed the Spaniards with their fire-arms as demi-gods, wielding the lightning and thunder of the Heavens. The natives of India, on the contrary, were well acquainted with the natives of Europe; they looked on them with no superstitious awe; and, however unskilful in the use of artillery, they were at least not surprised at its effects.— From the day of Plassey dates our supremacy above them. From that day they began to feel that none of the things on which they had heretofore relied,—not their tenfold or twentyfold numbers,—their blaze of rockets,—the long array of their elephants,—the massy weight of their ordnance,—their subterfuges and their wiles,—would enable them to stand firm against the energy and discipline of the island-strangers. They began to feel that even their own strength would become an instrument to their subjugation; that even their own countrymen, when, under the name of Sepoys, trained in European discipline, and animated by European spirit, had been at Plassey, and would be again, the mainstay and right arm of the British power. From that day the British flag in Hindostan has never (and the Hindoos know it) been unfurled in vain; its very sight has more than once awed, without a blow, aggressors to submission, and ever inspired with undoubting confidence those who are ranged beneath it, and can claim it for their own. That feeling, now prevalent through the East, has in our day been forcibly

* Hamilton's East India Gazetteer, article PLASSEY, ed. 1828.

described by one of our naval officers, when beset with his boat's crew in a great city of China. — "I found," he writes, in words whose truth and earnestness are nearly akin, and perhaps superior, to eloquence, "that the top-" mast of the flag-staff had been struck since the exe-" cution; but I immediately desired that the boat's ensign " should be taken up, and made fast to the lower mast-" head, for I well knew, my Lord, that there is a sense " of support in the sight of that honoured flag, fly where " it will, that none can feel but men who look upon it in " some such dismal strait as our's." *

On the morning after the battle Meer Jaffier appeared at the English camp, far from confident of a good reception since his recent conduct. As he alighted from his elephant the guard drew out, and rested their arms to do him honour; but Meer Jaffier, not knowing the drift of this compliment, started back in great alarm. Clive, however, speedily came forward, embraced his trembling friend, and hailed him Nabob of Bengal, Orissa, and Bahar. It was agreed between them that Meer Jaffier should immediately push forward with his division to Moorshedabad, and that Clive and his English should follow more at leisure. But they neither expected nor found the slightest further resistance.

Even before the day of Plassey was decided Surajah Dowlah had mounted a camel, and ignominiously fled from the field. He scarcely rested until he reached Moorshedabad. There he heard his councillors advise, — some, surrender to the English,—others, perseverance in the war, — others, again, a prolongation of his flight. To his own cowardly temper this last advice was by far the most congenial. In the evening he assumed a mean dress for a disguise, let himself down from a by-window of his palace, and embarked in a small boat, with the most precious of his jewels, and the favourite of his women. His design was to ascend the Ganges as far as Patna, and throw himself upon the protection of Law's detachment. Already had he reached the point where the blue hills of Rajmahal, — the first outposts of the

* Captain Elliot to Lord Palmerston, March 30. 1839. Parliamentary Papers, — CHINA.

Himalaya, — rise above the wide level of Bengal. At this place he landed to pass the night on shore, but was recognised by a peasant who had incurred his displeasure some months before, and whose ears he had caused to be cut off. The injured man now revealed the secret to some soldiers; and thus the Nabob was discovered and seized, and brought back in chains to the palace of Moorshedabad, — to the very presence chamber, once his own, now that of Meer Jaffier. The fallen prince, still more abject in spirit than in fortunes, flung himself down before his triumphant subject, and with an agony of tears implored his life. It is said that Meer Jaffier was touched with some compassion, and merely directed that his prisoner should be led away; but his son Meeran, a youth no less ferocious and cruel than Surajah Dowlah himself *, gave the guards orders that he should be despatched in his cell. Barely sufficient respite was granted him, at his own urgent entreaty, to make his ablutions, and to say his prayers. Next morning the mangled remains were exposed to the city on an elephant, and then carried to the tomb of Aliverdi, while Meer Jaffier excused himself to the English for the deed of blood committed without their knowledge and consent.

The installation of Meer Jaffier, as Nabob of Bengal, was performed with great solemnity. Clive himself led his friend to the MUSNUD, or seat of honour, and, according to the Indian custom, presented him with a plate full of gold rupees; he then, through an interpreter, addressed the native chiefs, exhorting them to be joyful that Fortune had given them so good a Prince. Nor did the new Nabob fail to bestow on his allies marks as splendid and more substantial of his favour. It was agreed, according to the previous stipulation, that the English should have the entire property of the land within the Mahratta ditch, and for 600 yards beyond it, and also the ZEMINDARY, or feudal tenure on payment of rent, of all the country between

* Of Meeran Clive writes, two years afterwards: "Sooner or later "I am persuaded that worthless young dog will attempt his father's "overthrow. How often have I advised the old fool against putting "too much power into the hands of his nearest relations!" To Warren Hastings, Resident at Moorshedabad, September 21, 1759.

Calcutta and the sea. The money granted them in compensation for their losses, and in donatives to the fleet, the army, and the Committee, amounted to no less than 2,750,000*l.**, although, as the wealth of Surajah Dowlah proved far less than was expected, it was not found possible to pay the whole of this sum at once. Clive accepted for his own share a gift of above 200,000*l.* When, some years afterwards, before a Committee of the House of Commons, he was accused for taking so much, he defended himself by saying, that he might, if he had pleased, have taken much more. "When I recollect," he said, "entering the Nabob's treasury at Moorshedabad, "with heaps of gold and silver to the right and left, and "these crowned with jewels," — here he added an oath, and violently struck his hand to his head, — "at this moment do I stand astonished at my own moderation!" †

A painful office remained, — to tell Omichund, that, notwithstanding the promise in his favour, he should have no share in all this wealth. As interpreter and spokesman for that purpose the British chief employed Mr. Scrafton, a civil servant of the Company. A meeting having been held at the house of one of the principal SOUCARS or bankers of Moorshedabad, Clive, at its conclusion, said to Mr. Scrafton: "It is now time to undeceive "Omichund." Mr. Scrafton, as if ashamed of the task, performed it in the fewest and shortest words. "Omichund, the red paper is a trick; you are to have "nothing." — At this announcement the unhappy dupe staggered back, as from a blow; he fainted away, and was borne by an attendant to his house, where, on recovering from his swoon, he remained for many hours silent and abstracted, and then began to show symptoms of imbecility. Some days afterwards he visited Clive, who received him kindly, advised him, for change of scene, to undertake a pilgrimage to some one of the Indian shrines, and was willing, on his return, to employ him again in public business. But the intellect of Omichund had been wholly unhinged, and he expired

* Orme's Hist., vol. ii. p. 180.

† Malcolm's Life, vol. i. p. 313.

not many months from this period in a state of second childhood.

The return of Clive to Calcutta was attended with general rejoicing and applause, and from this time forward, during several years, he was, in truth, master of Bengal. The East India Directors had, indeed, formed a most unwise scheme for conducting the government of Calcutta, by a system of rotation, but at the news of the victory of Plassey they gladly conferred the office of Governor on Clive. As a statesman he displayed scarcely less ability than as a soldier. It was his energy as both which upheld the feeble character and the tottering throne of Meer Jaffier. Thus, when, in 1759, Shah Alum, the eldest son of the Emperor of Delhi, succeeded in collecting a large army of adventurers, and marched down upon Bahar, the terrified Nabob was eager to purchase peace by the cession of a province or the payment of a tribute. Far different were the views of the British chief. "I would not," he wrote to Meer Jaffier, "have "you think of coming to any terms. . . . . . Rest assured "that the English are staunch and firm friends, and that "they never desert a cause in which they have once "taken a part." * Yet at this time the British force of Clive was much diminished by an expedition which he had sent out to the southern coast. With a little army, comprising less than 500 Europeans, he undauntedly marched to the aid of his ally; and such were now the terrors of his name, that at his approach the mighty host of Shah Alum melted away; the siege of Patna was raised, and the war ended without a blow. In gratitude for this great service Meer Jaffier bestowed upon Clive a splended JAGHIRE or domain, producing, according to Clive's own computation, an income of 27,000*l.* a year.

At nearly the same period Clive was directing from afar hostilities in the districts known in the Carnatic by the name of the "Northern Circars"; a tract of coast extending from the mouth of the Kistna to the pagoda of Juggernaut. These districts had been invaded by Bussy from the Deccan, and on his departure a French force, commanded by the Marquis de Conflans, had been left

* Letter, February 10. 1759.

for their defence. On the other hand, Clive sent thither a large detachment, under Colonel Forde, an officer trained under his own eye. The result was complete success; the French were worsted in a pitched engagement, and the English reduced Masulipatam against a garrison superior in numbers to themselves.

Towards the close of the same year, 1759, the English in Bengal were threatened with danger, equally great and unforeseen, from the Dutch in Java. Although peace prevailed between the two nations the Dutch could not view without jealousy the success and renown of their commercial rivals; they entered into secret negotiations with Meer Jaffier, who, with the usual fickleness of Asiatics, had become desirous of deserting the English alliance; and they sent into the Hooghly an armament of seven large ships and 1,400 soldiers. The pretext was to reinforce their own settlement at Chinsura, and to obtain redress for the grievances which they alleged against the Presidency of Calcutta, especially the compelling Dutch ships to take English pilots on the river. It was a moment of anxious consideration for Clive. In the first place, although Colonel Forde had returned from the Circars, other detachments had gone out to assist their countrymen at Madras; and the squadron, commanded since the decease of Admiral Watson by Admiral Pocock, had long since sailed in the same direction. If Clive suffered the Dutch ships to pass up the river, and the Dutch troops to join the Nabob's, the English might be overpowered and driven from Bengal. If he attempted to stop them, there was the risk of kindling a war between the two nations, or, on the other hand, of being disavowed by the authorities in England, and consigned to disgrace and ruin. Nor were other personal motives wanting to dissuade Clive from action. At this very period he had entrusted a large share of his fortune to the Dutch East India Company, for speedy remittance to Europe. Nevertheless, in this emergency, Clive showed himself, as ever, firm, resolute, unwavering. He was informed that the Dutch had landed their troops, and committed various acts of violence, and a letter was addressed to him by Colonel Forde, stating, that if he had an Order of Council he could now attack the invaders with a fair prospect of destroying them. Clive was playing at cards in the evening when he received this letter, and without leaving the table he wrote an answer in pencil: "Dear Forde, "fight them immediately. I will send you the Order of "Council to-morrow."* Accordingly the Dutch were attacked both by land and water, and, notwithstanding their superiority of force in both, in both were they defeated. Of their seven ships every one fell into the hands of the English. At these tidings the chiefs of the settlement at Chinsura hastened to sue for peace, disavowing the acts of their naval commander, owning themselves the aggressors, and agreeing to reimburse the English Company for the charges of the war,—on which terms they obtained the restitution of their ships. Thus it happened that the news of their apology reached Europe nearly as soon as the news of the attack upon them, so as effectually to prevent any complaint or remonstrance on the part of the Government of Holland.†

Only a few weeks after these events, in February, 1760, Clive, who was suffering from ill-health, embarked for England. "With him it appeared" (to use the strong language of a contemporary) "that the soul was depart-"ing from the body of the government of Bengal." At home he was rewarded with an Irish peerage, as Lord Clive, Baron of Plassey, and speedily obtained a seat in the English House of Commons. During his second residence in India, a period of less than five years, he had acquired a fortune amounting at the very lowest computation to 40,000*l.* a year.‡ Several of the transactions in which he had engaged for the public advantage or his own seem to me, as I have elsewhere stated, repugnant to justice and good faith. Those who explore his character with minute attention may, perhaps, moreover detect, not merely some great faults, but some little foibles. Thus, although he was plain and free from all ostentation in the field, he might be thought in society

* Malcolm's Life of Clive, vol. ii. p. 97.

† See on this point a note to Favre's Memoir on Holland, in the *Politique de tous les Cabinets de l'Europe* (vol. ii. p. 154. ed. 1802). By a shortly subsequent treaty the Dutch at Chinsura further engaged to raise no fortification and maintain no troops in Bengal.

‡ Malcolm's Life, vol. ii. p. 187.

fonder of fine clothes than becomes a hero. At one of the busiest periods of his public career,—the year of Plassey,—he could find leisure to weigh the comparative merits for a Court suit of "a scarlet coat with handsome "gold lace," or "the common wear of velvet," *—and to instruct his friend Mr. Orme, the historian, to send him "two hundred shirts, the best and finest you can get "for love or money; some of the ruffles worked with a "border either in squares or points, and the rest plain." † But with every drawback or deduction which can fairly be made from his character, there will still remain very much to call forth praise and inspire admiration. He was indeed, as Chatham once called him, "a Heaven-"born General," ‡—who, with no military training, had shown consummate military genius. With nearly as little study of politics he displayed nearly as great abilities for government. Energy,—which, perhaps, of all human qualities, is the one most conducive to success,—energy and fearlessness, were peculiarly his own. Whatever gratitude Spain owes to her Cortes, or Portugal to her Albuquerque, this—and in its results more than this—is due from England to Clive. Had he never been born I do not believe that we should—at least in that generation—have conquered Hindostan; had he lived longer I doubt if we should—at least in that generation—have lost North America.

The narrative of the events that followed in Bengal,—the misrule of Clive's successors,—the dethronement and the reinstatement of Meer Jaffier,—though occurring in part before the peace of 1763, belongs more properly to a later period, when producing Clive's third and final visit to India. I therefore pass at once to the important transactions of which the Carnatic had meanwhile been the scene.—The Declaration of War between France and England found the chiefs both at Pondicherry and Madras ill-prepared for any expedition of importance, and engaging in none but desultory and feeble hostilities. The English set fire to Wandewash; the French, in re-

* Letter from Captain Latham, August 5. 1757.

† Letter, August 1. 1757.

‡ This was in 1758. Lord Orford's Memoirs, vol. ii. p. 276.

taliation, to Conjeveram. The latter, under M. d'Auteuil, besieged Trichinopoly; the former, under Captain Calliaud, relieved the place. But the attention of both parties was intently fixed on a great armament which France had announced the intention of despatching to the Indian seas; comprising nearly 1,200 regular troops, and commanded by Lieutenant General Comte de Lally. This officer was sprung from an Irish family which had followed James the Second into exile; his true name being Lally of Tully-dale, since Gallicised to Tollendal. — A soldier from his earliest years, he had highly distinguished himself both at Dettingen and Fontenoy; in December 1745 he had warmly pressed the expedition against England from Dunkirk, and had been appointed one of its chiefs. Brave, active, and zealous, he was well qualified for military service; but a hasty temper and a caustic wit too frequently offended his inferiors, and marred his exertions.

The armament of Lally was delayed by various causes, both in its departure and on its voyage, and it was not till near the close of April 1758 that it cast anchor before Pondicherry. Almost immediately on its arrival the French squadron, which was commanded by the Comte d'Aché, was engaged by the British under Admiral Pocock, but the battle proved indecisive, with little result to either party, beyond the loss of a few men and some damage to the ships. In August another naval engagement, equally indecisive, ensued. The Comte d'Aché, satisfied with this result, and with having landed the troops, then sailed back to the Mauritius.

Lally, who had brought out a commission as Governor General of the French in India, displayed from the first hour of his landing the impetuosity of his temper. His instructions prescribed the siege of Fort St. David, and he sent forth a body of troops for that object on the very same night that he arrived. So much haste bodes little real speed; the troops thus in hurry despatched, without provisions or guides, arrived before Fort St. David way-worn and hungry, and ill-disposed for action. In a few days, however, they were quickened by large reinforcements, and by the presence of Lally. The works of the siege were now vigorously pushed forward; a part in them all being urged by compulsion on the reluctant and scrupulous natives. "In India," says Mr. Orme, "even "the lower Castes have their distinctions, insomuch that "the COOLIE, who carries a burden on his head, will "not carry it on his shoulder. Distinctions likewise pre-"vail amongst the soldiery, for the man who rides will "not cut the grass that is to feed his horse; nor at this "time would the Sepoy dig the trench which was to "protect him from a cannon-ball." * — Such prejudices, which a wise ruler will ever consult, until he is able to correct, were now derided and set at nought by Lally. Thus he carried his immediate object, but thus also he forfeited for ever all claim to the attachment and regard of the native population. According to another historian, "the consternation created by such an act was greater "than if he had set fire to the town, and butchered every "man whom it contained." †

At this juncture Fort St. David was the strongest that the East India Company possessed, and it held a sufficient garrison; but the commanding officer was far from able, and part of the men are represented as drunken and disorderly. So early as the 2d of June terms of surrender, by no means honourable to themselves, were proposed by the besieged, and on the evening of the same day were accepted by the besiegers. Lally, in pursuance of the instructions which he had brought from France, immediately razed the fortifications to the ground, nor have they ever since been rebuilt. Thus the name of Fort St. David, — up to that time so conspicuous in the annals of the Company, — henceforth no longer appears.

Elated with this conquest, Lally pursued his warfare; he failed in an expedition against Tanjore, but succeeded in an expedition against Arcot. His aspiring views extended to the siege of Madras, and to the extinction of the British name in the Carnatic. For this great object he mustered every man at his disposal, even recalling Bussy from the Deccan, which had so long been the scene

* Orme's Hist. vol. ii. p. 305. "Hence," he adds, "the numerous "train of followers and assistants which always accompanies a camp "in India."

† Mill's Hist. vol. iii. p. 193. ed. 1826.

of that officer's active and able exertions. His want of money was no small obstacle in the way of his designs; to supply it he again offended the natives by plundering a pagoda of its wealth; and in a more praiseworthy spirit subscribed largely from his own private funds, exhorting his subordinates to follow his example. But he had already made nearly all of them his personal enemies by his haughty reproaches and his bitter jests. Thus, for example, when he found his Council less alert than they might have been in providing the beasts of burthen he required, he exclaimed that he could not do better than harness to his waggons the Members of Council themselves! * All his letters at this period were filled with invectives of no common asperity.†

In December 1758 Lally appeared before Madras, at the head of 2,700 European and 4,000 native troops. The English had already, in expectation of a siege, called in nearly all their garrisons and outposts, and could muster within their walls 4,000 soldiers, of whom 1,800 were of European race. Besides these there was a small body under Captain Calliaud, which had marched from Trichinopoly, and which hung upon the rear of the French, most effectually intercepting their supplies and harassing their detachments. "They are like flies," said Lally himself, "no sooner beaten off one place than they settle in "another!"—The French had no difficulty in making themselves masters of the Black Town; but this, from the large stores of arrack it contained, proved rather an obstacle to their further progress, as augmenting the insubordination of the men. On the other hand, the English steadily continued the defence of Fort St. George; they made on one occasion a most vigorous sally, under Colonel Draper; and their Governor, Mr. Pigot, displayed throughout the siege both spirit and judgment. Lally had, no doubt, many obstacles to encounter, but perhaps the greatest of all was his own unpopularity. He

* Voltaire, Siécle de Louis XV. ch. 34.

† "L'Enfer m'a vomi dans ce pays d'iniquités, et j'attends comme "Jonas la baleine qui me recevra dans son ventre." (Lettre du Comte de Lally, le 27 Decembre 1758.) In another letter he says he would rather have to govern the Caffres in Madagascar than the Europeans in India.

found that, though he might enforce obedience, it was not so easy to stifle discontent or to inspire alacrity. When, after nearly two months' investment, a breach had been effected by his batteries, his principal officers declared that it was not accessible, adding their opinion that a prolongation of the siege would be merely a wanton waste of human lives. At this time the supply of provision was scanty and uncertain, and the pay of the troops several weeks in arrear. The Sepoys had deserted in great numbers, and some of the Europeans threatened to follow their example. Under such discouraging circumstances, Lally, with bitter mortification, resolved to burn the Black Town and to raise the siege of the White. Happily, of these two designs, the first was prevented, and the second quickened by the opportune appearance, on the 16th of February 1759, of Admiral Pocock and his squadron, which had sailed to Bombay several months before, and now returned with some fresh troops on board. The French, apprehensive of a combined attack upon them, commenced that very night their march to Arcot, leaving behind their sick and wounded, fifty-two pieces of artillery, and a hundred and fifty barrels of gunpowder.

After this great reverse to the French arms, and the return of their chief to Pondicherry, hostilities languished for some time between the rival nations. But in the autumn there ensued another naval engagement, from another voyage of the Admiral Comte d'Aché to this coast. On the 2d of September his squadron was encountered by Pocock's; the English having nine ships of the line and the French eleven, with a great superiority both in guns and men. Nevertheless, after a cannonade of two hours, the French sailed away in great confusion, leaving to the English the honours of victory. The result, however, as on the two last occasions, was by no means decisive; the loss of men was nearly equal on both sides, and the English, though the victors, suffered the most damage in their ships. D'Aché immediately proceeded to disembark a few men and a little money at Pondicherry, and then, notwithstanding the vehement remonstrances of the Governor and Council, returned with his squadron to the islands.

At nearly the same period the English at Madras were cheered with the tidings that Eyre Coote had been promoted in England to the rank of Lieutenant Colonel, and was coming over at the head of the King's 84th Regiment and other reinforcements. Major Brereton, who meanwhile commanded in the field, appears to have been desirous of distinguishing himself before the arrival of his chief. Thus he attempted to reduce the fort of Wandewash by three divisions in a night-attack, but signally failed, with the loss of 200 men. So indignant was Brereton himself at his repulse, that, on seeing the crowd of English fugitives, he drew his sword, and ran the first man he met through the body! *

Colonel Eyre Coote, with the last division of his force, landed at Madras on the 27th of October 1759. Born in 1726, Coote was now in the prime of life, with none of those infirmities of body or mind which clouded over his later years, and obscured the lustre of his fame. His influence over the native soldiers was great, and not forgotten by them to this day; and he showed himself on all occasions not less active and resolute than prudent and wary. — One of his earliest measures on reaching the Carnatic was to retrieve the recent check to the British arms, by a more regular and skilful attack on Wandewash. In this enterprise Major Brereton did good service at the head of a division, and the fort was carried with little loss on the last day of November.

At this news Lally took the field. His dissensions with the civil service still continued, and his want of money to pay the troops had already produced more than one mutiny among them. He had, however, obtained as auxiliaries a body of Mahrattas, and he had under his command the sagacious and experienced Bussy, but, unhappily for himself, was jealous of his influence and distrustful of his counsels. Bussy strongly urged the imprudence of attempting to recover Wandewash, in the face of the English army. Lally, however, thought the honour of his arms at stake, and persevered in the design. He accord-

* Orme's Hist. vol. ii. p. 521. He adds: "Unfortunately the man "was one of the bravest in the army, so that this example carried "little influence."

ingly proceeded to the attack of the fort so lately lost, when Coote, who had been in expectation of this movement, at once marched upon him with his whole force. Lally had no other choice than to raise the siege, or to give battle on the ground selected by his enemy. He preferred the latter alternative. On the morning of the 22d of January 1760 he perceived the English, after some skilful manœuvres, advancing along the base of the mountain of Wandewash, protected on their left by the rugged height, and on their right by the fire of the fort. Immediately, while yet maintaining his batteries of siege, he drew up the remainder of his army on the open plain. This was, for the most part, stony ground, but here and there intersected with rice fields, so as to render nearly useless the superiority of the French in cavalry. According to the English computation, the French numbers in line of battle were 2,250 Europeans, 300 of them horse, and 1,300 Sepoys. There were also 3,000 Mahrattas; but these kept carefully aloof at the hour of action. The English had 1,900 Europeans, of whom only eighty were cavalry, 2,100 Sepoys, and 1,250 native horsemen. At nearly the commencement of the battle, the French horse, led on by Lally in person, was thrown into disorder by two English pieces of artillery, and was driven back to the encampment. Lally hastened to put himself at the head of the foot soldiers, and cheered them on to the charge. In pursuance of his brave example, the French regiment of Lorraine especially displayed the utmost gallantry; it formed in a column twelve in front, and came rushing full upon the King's 84th. In a moment the two regiments were mingled at the point of the bayonet. The battle now became general, and fiercely contested among the Europeans, but ere long began to declare in favour of Coote, — a result hastened by the accidental explosion of a tumbril in the French ranks. Among other brave soldiers, Major Brereton fell mortally wounded, and when fallen refused the assistance of the men next to him, bidding them not mind him, but follow up their victory. On the other side, M. de Bussy, attempting to rally the fugitives, and fighting with undaunted spirit at the head of a handful of men that still adhered to him, was surrounded and made prisoner sword in hand. The day was now decided. The French, notwithstanding the efforts of Lally, gave way in all directions from the field. In the battle or pursuit their loss was estimated at nearly 600 men; the English had 190 killed and wounded. It deserves notice that the brunt of the conflict had fallen entirely on the Europeans of both armies, the native troops taking no part in it since the first cannonade. In the evening the officers of the English Sepoys came to congratulate Colonel Coote on his victory, and with great coolness thanked him for the sight of such a battle as they never yet had seen.*

The English at Madras, who felt their own fate dependent on the issue of this battle, were watching with feverish anxiety for its earliest tidings. At sunrise the next morning one of the black spies of the English camp brought them some vague rumours of success, but it was not till noon that they received a note of two lines in pencil, written by Coote from the field of battle. Then, indeed, relieved from all their fears, they burst forth into exclamations of delight; acknowledging also, with well-deserved applause, the skill and intrepidity of the British commander. The joy this day at Madras, says a contemporary, could only be compared to that at Calcutta on the news of Plassey. In truth, as the one victory gained us Bengal, so did the other the Carnatic. It is remarkable, however, in all these operations by or against Lally, how little weight the native Powers threw into either scale. Scarcely does it appear worthy of commemoration that Mahomed Ali was present with the English at Madras during the first part of the siege, and afterwards passed to Trichinopoly; or that Salabat Jung, after the departure of Bussy, consented to renounce the French alliance.

I may also observe on this occasion of the three most eminent chiefs who ever fought in British India,—Lord Clive, Sir Eyre Coote, and Sir Arthur Wellesley,—that they gained the battles of Plassey, of Wandewash, and of Assaye, at the ages respectively of thirty-two, thirty-three, and thirty-four. It may hence, perhaps, be doubted (notwithstanding some recent and most brilliant examples

* Orme's Hist. vol. ii. p. 589.

to the contrary) whether the more modern practice of sending forth to military command in that unwholesome climate veterans already bending beneath the weight of years be in all cases entirely consistent with the means by which our Eastern greatness was achieved.

Had Coote been aware how ill Pondicherry was then provided, and how discordantly governed, he might probably have pushed forward to that city immediately after his triumph at Wandewash; but knowing how large was still the force of the enemy, he first applied himself to besiege and reduce the outposts of their dominion. Arcot, Trincomalee, Devi-Cottah, Cuddalore, and several other places fell successively into his hands. During this time the French were making strenuous efforts to obtain some native reinforcements. With that view they opened a secret negotiation with Hyder Ali, afterwards the founder of the great kingdom of Mysore, and at this period the General in chief of the Mysorean army. It was stipulated that Hyder Ali should send, as auxiliaries, a body of 3,000 horse and 5,000 foot, and receive in return from the French the fort of Thiagur, one of their last remaining strong-holds in the Carnatic. The first division of the Mysoreans marched accordingly, and a detachment, chiefly of Sepoys, having been sent out by Coote to repel them, was itself totally routed. Nevertheless, the result of this treaty proved of little advantage to the French. Only a few weeks after the auxiliaries had arrived intelligence reached them of a revolution in Mysore, threatening danger to their chief, upon which, without any notice to Lally, they set off by night, and hastened home.

The net was now closing round Pondicherry itself. Through the boundary-hedge of thorns and prickly plants, which, as in many other Indian towns, encompassed its outer defences, the inhabitants could discern the hostile army encamped, and ready for the siege. The departure of D'Aché's squadron had left the English undisputed masters of the sea, and scarce any further supplies, either by land or water, could reach the beleaguered city. The French valour, — the rainy season, — and a most violent storm in the roads, — interposed, however, considerable obstacles in the way of Coote. Nor was Discord, which raged so fiercely within the walls of Pondicherry, altogether absent from the English camp. In consequence of orders from home, given in ignorance of the late events, a dispute as to the chief command arose between Colonel Coote and Colonel Monson. At one period Coote had already relinquished his post, and was preparing to embark for Bengal; but Monson receiving a severe wound, and becoming for a time disabled, the leadership happily reverted to the victor of Wandewash.

In the night between the 8th and 9th of December four English batteries opened against the walls of Pondicherry. The besieged were firm and resolute in their defence, fighting every foot of ground, and making more than one successful sally. They had also, to spare their provisions, put themselves upon half rations, and sent forth from the town the remaining native inhabitants; a wretched multitude, which remained famishing and helpless between the gates and the batteries, and was debarred access at either, until, after some days, the humanity of the English allowed them to pass. Notwithstanding such strong measures, it was found, before the middle of January, that there only remained sufficient provisions for two days. In this extremity Lally and his Council sent deputies to capitulate, and failing to obtain more favourable terms, were compelled to surrender at discretion. Accordingly, on the 16th of January 1761, the English marched into the place. Great civilities passed between the chiefs; Coote dining that day at Lally's table; but Lally and his French, still amounting to above 2,000, remained prisoners of war. "All," says a contemporary, "wore the face of famine, fatigue, or disease. The grenadiers of Lorraine and Lally, once the ablest-bodied men in the army, appeared the most impaired, having constantly put themselves forward to every service; and it was recollected that from their first landing, throughout all the services of the field, and all the distresses of the blockade, not a man of them had ever deserted to the English colours." *

Almost immediately after the surrender a dispute arose among the victors for the possession of the place. Coote and his officers claimed it for the King; Mr. Pigot and

* Orme's Hist. vol. ii. p. 722.

the other civilians from Madras claimed it for the Company. The quarrel grew high, until at length Mr. Pigot declared, that unless his pretensions were admitted he should refuse to supply funds for the subsistence of the troops. This threat barred all further argument.—In return for the destruction of Fort St. David, and in pursuance of orders from home, Mr. Pigot took measures for razing to the ground the fortifications of Pondicherry, nay, even all the buildings that stood within them.

Thus ended the French power in India. For although Pondicherry was restored to them by the peace of 1763, and although the stipulation in that peace against their raising fortresses or maintaining troops applied only to Bengal, yet even in the Carnatic they could never again attain their former influence nor recover their lost ground; and the extinction of their East India Company speedily ensued.

This result, however mortifying to French ambition, has been acknowledged by French writers as a just retribution on that Company, and on the Government of Louis the Fifteenth, for their cruel oppression of almost every great commander who had served them faithfully in India.* The closing scenes of La Bourdonnais and of Dupleix have been already described; there remains to tell the still more tragic fate of Lally. On arriving a prisoner in England, and hearing of the charges brought against him in France, he wrote to Pitt, soliciting that he might return on his parole, and confront his accusers †, and with this request the British Minister complied. But no sooner was Lally at Paris than he was thrown into the Bastille, where he remained fifteen months without even a preliminary examination. When at length his trial did come on before the Parliament of Paris, it was pressed with the utmost acrimony, both by the Crown and East India Company; and a legal quibble on the term "High Treason" enabled his judges to sentence him to death. When informed of their decision, "Is this,"

* "Oh combien cette Compagnie des Indes Française avait merité "sa chute !"—Biograph. Univ. art. Dupleix. See also Sismondi, Hist. des Français, vol. xxix. p. 303.

† See his letter in the Chatham Correspondence, vol. ii. p. 144.

he passionately cried, "the reward of forty-five years ser-"vice!" — and snatching up a compass with which he had been drawing maps during his imprisonment, he struck it at his breast. His hand, however, was held back by some person near him; and that same afternoon, the 9th of May 1766, he was dragged along to public execution in a dung-cart, with a gag between his lips, and beheaded on the Place de Grève. Such was the end of a veteran, who had fought and bled for his adopted country, seldom, indeed, with prudence and discretion, but always with courage and honour.

By the downfal of the Portuguese, the Dutch, and, above all, the French power in India, a wide and still-extending scope was left to that of England. The best chance of supremacy to the native states had lain in resisting Europeans by Europeans, — in setting the skill and energy of one northern race against another. Single-handed they fell one by one, — some dropping from their own rottenness, like fruit from a tree, — others striving fiercely, but without avail, against us. From the precarious tenure of some two or three petty forts, — from the mere Mahratta-ditch of Calcutta, or the "bound-"hedge" of Madras, — our empire has spread far and wide; from Ceylon to Gujerât, — from the snows of the Himalaya to the sea-line of the Sunderbunds,—along the loftiest mountains and the widest plains in the known world. In India at this moment the number of our subjects and dependents is in all probability greater than Alexander, than Augustus, than Charlemagne, than Napoleon, ever knew. And if that vast people be as yet low in the scale of nations, — long enslaved, and still debased by a succession of tyrannies, — and led astray by foul superstitions and revolting rites, — their depression gives them only the stronger claim on our sympathy and care. Never did a Government stand more nearly in the parental relation to its subjects than the English Government of India. The English are as much superior to the Hindoos, — not in natural gifts, but in training, in knowledge, and in principles,— as a parent is superior to a child. God grant, that as we hold a parent's place we may fulfil a parent's duty, — not merely to command and direct, but to enlighten and reform! For many years, however, we did not act fully on these maxims, and our course in India, though far above any Asiatic, was yet below the European rules of right. Surely it behoves our chief statesmen, of whatever party, to take to heart the awful responsibility which this state of things devolves upon them, — to weigh well, and with scrupulous attention, every new appointment made, not only in India itself, but in the Indian department at home. Let them be assured that even the humblest of these appointments, if unwisely made, may become directly or indirectly the cause of suffering to unprotected millions, which are often too timid for complaint, or too distant for redress. To these millions let us prove that we have higher objects than additions of territory or accumulations of wealth. Let us aim at the overthrow of the idol-temples, not rashly, not through violence and persecution, but by affording means to know the truth, — their overthrow by the hands of their own worshippers, converted and reclaimed. Let us cast aside for ever the base, the miserable fear, lest the Hindoos, as they approach our level of civilisation, may become less patient of our sway. It is, I trust, reserved for British counsels in the coming age to extend even much further the work auspiciously begun of good government in India, and to give even to the meanest peasant of that land fresh reason to bless God, in the fulness of his heart, that his lot is cast beneath the Great Company, instead of the Rajahs and Sultauns of former days!

CHAPTER III.

(CHAP. LXVII. OF THE HISTORY.)

WHENEVER, in any modern History of England, an attempt has been made to combine, year by year, the transactions in Europe and in India, the result, it may be said without presumption, is seldom satisfactory. Such frequent breaks in the narrative, and changes in the scene,—with so thorough a difference in race and language, in religion, and in laws,—may fulfil the duty of an annalist, but not, as I conceive, the higher aim of an historian. Avoiding that error, as on full reflection I believe it to be, I design in this and the following Chapter, and in a connected series, to pursue the sketch of British India, which in two former Chapters I commenced; and to bring down its tale to that period decisive of its welfare, when, in the autumn of 1783, the Ministry of Fox and North not only judged it right, but found it necessary, to propose, in some or other form, a new measure for the government of our Eastern empire.

The victories of the English in India, during Chatham's first administration, left to them a power great indeed, and nobly won, but as yet ill-administered and insecure. They had struck down their European rivals at Pondicherry, at Chandernagore, and at Chinsura. They had shot high above their titular liege-lords in the Deccan and Bengal. Of Bengal, indeed, they were in truth the masters, since Meer Jaffier, as their tool and instrument, sat enthroned on the Musnud of that province. On the other hand, they had no longer a chief of genius and of energy to guide them. The principal authority, since the departure of Clive, had devolved on Mr. Henry Vansittart, the father of the late Lord Bexley, a man of good intentions, but of moderate capacity. Thus the discipline of the victors was relaxed by their own successes. Thus their rapine ceased to be checked by a strong hand. Almost every Englishman in Bengal began to look upon speedy enrichment as his right, and upon the subservient natives as his prey.

Nor was it long ere a growing difference sprung up between them and their new Nabob. So early as the autumn of 1760, Meer Jaffier was found to engage in cabals against the Company. Mr. Vansittart and Colonel Caillaud deemed it necessary to advance with a few hundred of their troops to Cossim-Bazar, a suburb of Moorshedabad, beyond the river. They gave in their terms to Meer Jaffier. Meer Jaffier wavered and wrangled. Without further delay, he was surrounded in his palace at the dead of night, compelled to resign the Government, and then, at his own request, permitted to retire to Fort William, under the protection of the British flag; while his son-in-law, Meer Cossim, was in his stead proclaimed the Viceroy of Bengal.*

According to a compact made beforehand with the English, Meer Cossim forthwith yielded to them, as the price of their assistance, both an amount of treasure and an increase of territory. But his temper, which was bold and active, and by no means scrupulous, chafed at these sacrifices. Still less could he brook the oft-repeated acts of insolence and rapine of the GOMASTAHS,—the native factors or agents in the British pay. Ere long, therefore, he took some measures to shake off his subjection. He removed his Court from Moorshedabad to Monghir, two hundred miles further from Calcutta. He increased and disciplined his troops. He imprisoned or disgraced every man of note in his dominions who had ever shown attachment to the English. He began to enforce against the private traders the revenue laws, from which they claimed exemption. Angry disputes arose above all with the numerous English factory at Patna. Mr. Vansittart repaired to Monghir in the hope to avert hostilities. He concluded a treaty, agreeing that

* "The removal of Jaffier was an ill-advised measure . . . . . had "Clive remained in Bengal, there would probably have been no revo- "lution." (Note by Professor H. H. Wilson, to Mr. Mill's History. vol. iii. p. 310. ed. 1840.)

his countrymen should pay the inland duties to the amount of nine per cent.; and not refusing on that occasion a present to himself of seven Lacs of Rupees from Meer Cossim. But the Council of Calcutta voted the terms dishonourable. As a last effort to avert hostilities, another deputation was sent from Calcutta to Monghir. At its head was Mr. Amyatt, one of the principal members of the Council. Not only, however, did these gentlemen wholly fail in their mission, but while passing the city of Moorshedabad on their way back, they were inhumanly murdered by a body of Cossim's own troops. After such an outrage, peace was no longer possible. Thus, in the summer of 1763, war again commenced, the Council of Calcutta resolving to depose Meer Cossim, and proclaiming the restoration of Meer Jaffier.

The British forces that took the field in this campaign amounted at first to scarcely more than 600 Europeans, and 1,200 Sepoys. With these, however, their commander, Major Adams, obtained rapid and great successes. He drove the enemy from their strong-holds, entered Moorshedabad, gained a battle on the plains of Geriah, and, after a nine days' siege, reduced Monghir. Nothing was left to Meer Cossim but Patna, and even Patna he perceived that he should not be able to maintain. Accordingly, he prepared for flight to the dominions of his powerful neighbour, Sujah Dowlah, the Nabob of Oude. But first he wreaked his vengeance on the English by an act of savage barbarity, second in its horrors only to those of the Black Hole. His prisoners of the factory at Patna exceeded one hundred and fifty persons. They comprised many peaceful traders, they comprised one infant child. All these the tyrant indiscriminately doomed to death—the Massacre of Patna, as it has ever since been termed. For his purpose Meer Cossim found a congenial instrument in one Sombre, otherwise Sumroo, a Frenchman by birth, and a deserter from the European service. This wretch gave his victims a significant though trivial token of their coming doom by sending, in the first place, to seize and carry off all their knives and forks, which might have been weapons in their hands. Next day, the 5th of October, in the evening, was the time of slaughter. Then the prison-house was surrounded by Sumroo and his band. Then the butchery of the prisoners was begun. It is said that they made all the resistance in their power, by throwing bottles and stones at their murderers.* But, of course, in vain. Some were cut to pieces with sabres, others shot down with musketry, and then barbarously mutilated. In both cases, the mangled limbs were flung into two wells, which were afterwards filled up with stones. Of the whole number of intended victims, only one was spared; a surgeon known to the Nabob, and William Fullarton by name.†

The reduction of Patna by the English, which speedily followed the atrocious act within its walls, completed their conquest of Bengal. Under their auspices, Meer Jaffier was once more proclaimed as Nabob throughout the province. But, meanwhile, the thrusting forth of Meer Cossim — the dispossession by an European force of one of the native Princes — seemed to the latter an act far more atrocious than the Massacre of Patna. It gained favour for the exile at the Court of Oude; and the Court of Oude was then among the most powerful in India. Sujah Dowlah, besides the resources of his own vast province, could wield at his pleasure the authority, slender though it might be, that yet adhered to the Imperial name. The titular Emperor of Delhi, Shah Alum, had taken refuge with him, and had named him his Visier. Shah Alum, in real truth, was an exile and a wanderer, his very capital, Delhi, being held against him by Mahratta invaders, and half laid in ruins by their fury; but amidst every privation, in the eyes of the people he was still the "Great Mogul."

* Scott's Bengal, p. 427., and Thornton's History of India, vol. i. p. 448. But Mr. Thornton appears in error of two days as to the date of this transaction.

† The narrative of Mr. Fullarton, as the sole survivor of the Massacre, and as addressed to the Board at Calcutta, is (for whatever reason) extremely meagre. It is printed in the Third Report of the East India Committee, 1773, No. 62. Of his earlier letter, dated Nov. 3. 1763, in which he seems disposed to avoid any narrative at all, I obtained a MS. copy from the India House, through the kindness of my friend Sir James Weir Hogg.

Thus combining, the three princes advanced at the head of an army well provided with artillery, and which numbered 50,000 men. On the other side, the English with their utmost exertions could bring into the field no more than 8,000 Sepoys and 1,200 Europeans. Their commander, Major Adams, having died, his place was filled by Major, afterwards Sir Hector, Munro. But such in their ranks was the state of insubordination, nay, even mutiny, that the new chief found it necessary to make a most severe example of the ringleaders. He began by directing four and twenty native soldiers to be blown from the mouth of cannon. On this occasion, a touching incident occurred. When the orders were first given to tie four of these men to the guns from which they were to be blown, four others of the soldiers stepped forward and demanded the priority of suffering as a right, they said, which belonged to men who had always been first in the post of danger; and the claim thus preferred was allowed. An officer who was an eye-witness of the scene observes: "I belonged on this occasion to a detachment of marines. "They were hardened fellows, and some of them had "been of the execution-party that shot Admiral Byng; "yet they could not refrain from tears at the fate and "conduct of these gallant grenadier Sepoys." *

Having thus in some measure, as he hoped, awed the disaffected, Munro led his troops to Buxar, a position above Patna, more than one hundred miles higher up the Ganges. There, in October 1764, he was attacked by the army of Oude. The battle was fierce, but ended in a brilliant victory to the English; the enemy leaving 130 pieces of cannon and 4,000 dead upon the field.

On the day after the battle, Shah Alum, having with some followers made his escape from the army of his own Visier, drew near to the English camp. So long as he had been dependent on the Durbar of Oude, the English had shown little willingness to acknowledge his authority, but no sooner did he join their ranks and appear a ready instrument in their hands, than he became to them at once the rightful Sovereign of Hindostan. They con-

* Memoir by Captain Williams, as cited in Malcolm's Life of Clive, vol. ii. p. 300.

cluded a treaty with him, he undertaking to yield them certain districts, and they to put him in possession of Allahabad and the other states of the Nabob of Oude.

The battle of Buxar, though so great a victory, did not decide the war. Major Munro failed in two attempts to storm the hill-fort of Chunar on the Ganges, — a fort in which all the treasures of Cossim were thought to be contained; and Sujah Dowlah obtained the aid of Holkar, a powerful Mahratta chief. Nevertheless he sent to sue for peace. But Munro refused all terms, unless both Cossim and Sombre were first given up to punishment. Nor was his purpose changed by the offer of a large sum of money for himself. With a higher spirit than Vansittart's, he cried: "If the Nabob would give " me all the Lacs in his treasury, I would make no peace " with him until he had delivered up those murdering " rascals; for I never could think that my receiving " eleven or twelve Lacs of Rupees was a sufficient atone- " ment for the blood of those unfortunate gentlemen at " Patna."

Sujah Dowlah thought his honour concerned upon the other side. He refused to surrender the two exiles, but proposed an expedient altogether worthy an Asiatic Prince, that he would give secret orders for the assassination of Sombre, in the presence of any person whom the English General might send to witness the deed. That expedient being, of course, rejected, the war was resumed. A new tide of successes poured in upon the English. Early in 1765, they reduced the fortress of Chunar, scattered far and wide the force of the enemy, and entered in triumph his great city of Allahabad.

Through all these last years of strife it is gratifying to observe, not merely the valour, but also the mercy and forbearance, of the English owned, at least in private, by their enemies. The skill of Oriental scholars has laid open to us the records of a Mussulman historian of that period — the eye-witness, in some part, of the scenes which he describes: "It must be acknowledged," says he, " to the honour of those strangers, that as their " conduct in war and in battle is worthy of admiration, " so, on the other hand, nothing is more modest and " more becoming than their behaviour to an enemy.

"Whether in the heat of action, or in the pride of success "and victory, these people seem to act entirely according to the rules observed by our ancient chiefs and "heroes." But at the same time, and, no doubt, with equal truth, this historian cannot forbear lamenting the grievous suffering and misrule endured by the helpless Bengalees after the departure of Lord Clive. "Oh God!" thus in another passage citing the Koran, he concludes: "Oh God! come to the assistance of thy afflicted "servants, and deliver them from the oppressions they "bear!" *

Meanwhile, the transactions in India which followed the departure of Clive had produced no slight amount of discord and cabals in England. These were heightened by the want of any strong and well-framed authority in either country for Eastern affairs. In India, whether at Calcutta, at Madras, or at Bombay, the Governor was entitled to no more than one voice in the Council, with the advantage, should the numbers be found equal, of a second, or the casting vote. Moreover, the three Presidencies being as yet upon an equal footing, and with no central seat of power, were constant rivals, each envious of the other's successes, each believing that undue favour was accorded to the rest. In England, the whole body of twenty-four Directors was renewed by annual election. On such occasions, and indeed on many others, the India House became the scene of the most violent debates, and the keenest party-struggles. There were parties formed on every sub-division of selfish interests; the party of Bombay, the party of Madras, the party of Bengal, the party of Mr. Sulivan, the party of Lord Clive. Greater than all these, perhaps, in point of numbers, was the party anxious only for the high rate and the punctual payment of their Dividends. Nor were these cabals

* Seir Mutakhareen, vol. ii. pp. 102. and 166. These curious contemporary annals were written in Persian by Gholam Hossein, a nobleman of India, and first translated into English by a renegade Frenchman, who took the name of Haji Mustapha. His translation, which is now before me, was published at Calcutta in 1789, and comprises three quarto volumes. Another version has been undertaken by Colonel Briggs, in two volumes; of which, however, only the first (London, 1832,) has appeared.

altogether unconnected with the greater parties in the State. Mr. Sulivan, the paramount Director until the appearance of Clive, was supported by Lord Bute. Clive at that time was a follower of Pitt. Thus no one incentive to violence and rancour was wanting from these contests at the India House. At that time every share of *500l.* conferred a vote, and the manufactory of fictitious votes was carried on to a gigantic scale. Clive, according to his own account, spent in this manner no less a sum than 100,000*l.** It was not till 1765, that this evil practice was arrested by an Act of Parliament, which required that each Proprietor, before he voted, should take an oath that the Stock entered in his name was really and in truth his own, and had been so for the last twelve months.

Sulivan and Clive had not at first been enemies. But, as Clive complains, in a private letter:—"Sulivan has "never reposed that confidence in me which my services "to the East India Company entitle me to. The conse-"quence has been that we have all along behaved to one "another like shy cocks; at times, outwardly expressing "great regard and friendship for each other."† Besides, there was a great divergence in their views of Indian affairs. Sulivan was disposed to favour the gentlemen of Bombay, and Clive the gentlemen of Bengal. Sulivan looked mainly to commerce, and Clive mainly to empire. At last, an open breach ensued between them. In 1763, Clive made a desperately fought attempt to oust Sulivan, and Sulivan's friends, from the Direction. He failed; and the new Directors revenged themselves by confiscating, contrary to law, the Jaghire, or domain, which had been bestowed upon him by Meer Jaffier. It became necessary for Clive to seek relief by a Bill in the Court of Chancery.

Such was the petty warfare raging at the India House, when ship after ship from Bengal brought news of the growing disorganization of the British power, of misrule and plunder by its servants, of renewed hostilities with the native princes. It began to be felt on all sides that

* Life by Malcolm, vol. ii. p. 211.

† To Mr. Vansittart, November 22. 1762.

the crisis called for Clive,—that he alone could order the confusion and allay the storm. So strong was this feeling in his favour as to carry every thing before it. At a meeting of the Proprietors, held early in the spring of 1764, they proposed to the Directors the immediate restitution of the disputed Jaghire, and the appointment of Lord Clive as both Governor and Commander-in-Chief of Bengal. Clive, who was present, rose to speak. "It "would be vain for me," he said, "to exert myself as "I ought in India, if my measures are to be thwarted "and condemned at home, under the influence of a "Chairman who is known to be my personal and invete-"rate enemy. It is a matter of indifference to me who "fills the Chair, if Mr. Sulivan does not; but if he does, "I must decline to go." Some reply was attempted by Mr. Sulivan, even amidst the uproar which ensued. He endeavoured to point out the jealousies and heart-burnings which the nomination of Lord Clive might raise among the chiefs already in command. But the tumult around him, if it did not drown his voice, at least overruled his argument. The Directors found themselves, though most unwillingly, compelled to appoint Lord Clive to both the offices desired. It was now within a month of the annual elections; and Clive, in conformity with what he had declared at the last meeting, resolved to abide their issue before he made his decision. The 25th of April was the day of contest, Mr. Sulivan had prepared a list of twenty-three Directors, which he supported by the strenuous exertion of his followers, but at the close, he had not carried more than half his number, and was himself saved from exclusion by only a single vote.

Under these circumstances, not only the Chairman, but also the Deputy-Chairman, was chosen from among Clive's friends. The new Board of Directors, moreover, conferred upon him extraordinary powers. Aided by a Committee of persons of his own naming, he was made, unlike the other Governors, independent of his Council. Clive embarked with the full purpose to use his powers most firmly—to curb and to crush at once the abuses which prevailed. One of his letters, written on ship-board, speaks as follows: "Give me leave now to lead you for "a few moments into the civil department. See what "an Augean stable is to be cleaned! The confusion we "behold, what does it arise from? Rapacity and luxury; "the unwarrantable desire of many to acquire in an "instant what only a few can or ought to possess. Every "man would be rich without the merit of long services; "and from this incessant competition, undoubtedly springs "that disorder, to which we must apply a remedy, or "be undone; for it is not only malignant, but con- "tagious."*

In May 1765, after a long protracted passage, Clive landed at Calcutta. There he found another, a recent and a glaring, instance of the abuses which he came to quell. Meer Jaffier had lately died, and a question had arisen respecting his inheritance. One party at his Court declared for his base-born son, and another for his legitimate but infant grandson—the child of Meeran, who had been struck dead by lightning some years before. Both parties appealed to the Council at Calcutta, but the Council viewed it only as a matter of bargain and sale. They found it easiest to make terms with the illegitimate pretender. He was proclaimed as Nabob of the province, while they received from him, and divided among themselves, the sum of 140,000*l.* Such a course was directly in the teeth of recent orders from home, binding the servants of the Company for the future to accept no presents from the native princes. And Clive might justly complain, not only of the transaction itself, but also of the headlong haste with which, in order to avert his interference, it had been determined. As he writes to one of the gentlemen concerned in the ignominious bargain: "There could have been no danger in "declining an absolute conclusion of the treaty until our "arrival, which you know was expected every day."†

No time was lost by Lord Clive in assembling the Council, showing them the full powers of his Committee, and announcing his peremptory will. One member, Mr. Johnstone, who had been foremost among the new Nabob-makers, attempted a faint demur. "Do you dare to

* Letter dated April 17. 1765.

† To Mr. Spencer, May 13. 1765.

"dispute our authority?" asked Clive haughtily. "I "never had the least intention of doing such a thing!" answered the affrighted Johnstone. "Upon this"—as Clive in one of his private letters tells the story—"there "was an appearance of very long and pale countenances, "and not one of the Council uttered another syllable." Elsewhere he adds: "We arrived on Tuesday, and ef-"fected this on Thursday"—and in the interval Clive had to read over and make himself master of all the recent Minutes of proceedings.*

On the landing of Clive, the war with the native princes was by no means over. Sujah Dowlah lay encamped on the borders of Bahar. He was reinforced by bands both of Mahrattas and of Afghans, and wished to try the issue of another battle. But the name of Clive sounded terrible in his ears. No sooner did he learn that the victor of Plassey had again set foot in India, than he determined on unconditional submission. He informed Meer Cossim and Sombre that he could no longer protect them, and connived at their escape—the one seeking shelter among the Rohillas, the other among the Jauts. Then, dismissing his followers, he repaired to the camp of the English, and declared himself ready to accept whatever terms of peace they might impose.

To adjust these terms, Lord Clive himself repaired to Benares. The design of the Council of Calcutta while they pursued the war, had been to wrest from Sujah Dowlah the whole or greater part of Oude. But such were not the views of the new Governor. Instead of aiming at new conquests, it was wiser, he thought, in the first place to secure those already gained by a firmer and sounder tenure. "Let us guard," he said, "against "future evils, by doing for ourselves what no Nabob "will ever do for us."† On this principle he acted. To Sujah Dowlah, who continued to bear the rank and title of Visier, he gave back the greater part of Oude. He reserved only the two districts of Corah and Allahabad as an Imperial domain for Shah Alum, to whom it was also agreed that the Company should make from their re-

* Life by Malcolm, vol. ii. pp. 321. and 324.
† To General Carnac, May 3. 1765.

venues an annual payment of twenty-six Lacs of Rupees. On the other hand, he obtained from the fallen Emperor a DEWANNEE or public Deed, conferring on the English Company the sole right of administration throughout the provinces of Bengal, Orissa, and Bahar.

In this transaction, as in almost every other in India during the same period, it is striking how wide was the interval between nominal authority and effective power. Here we find the heir of Aurungzebe treated with as though still supreme, as though able at his pleasure to bestow upon the Europeans, or to withhold from them, the exercise of sovereignty in three great provinces. Yet at this very time, so low had his fortunes fallen, as to leave him destitute of even the common trappings or appurtenances of high state. During the solemn ceremony of the investiture, it was an English dining-table, covered over, that formed the Imperial Throne!* Such was the prince, of whom the English in India continued to call themselves the vassals, whose coin they struck at their mint, whose titles they bore upon their public Seal.

In this transaction, though it manifestly set aside the authority of the Musnud at Moorshedabad, there was no objection raised by the young Nabob. With him, as with most Asiatic despots, the contingent future was but an empty name; and his desire to obtain a fixed and regular income, no longer to be embezzled or diverted by his Ministers, overbalanced every other consideration in his feeble mind. As Lord Clive writes to Mr. Verelst: "He received the proposal of having a sum of money for "himself and his household at his will with infinite "pleasure, and the only reflection he made upon leaving "me was: 'Thank God! I shall now have as many "'dancing girls as I please!'"†

The sagacious views of Clive, on the contrary, went far beyond his treaty or his time. As he writes to the Directors, we find him urge proposals, all of which have since been carried into effect, but several not until a long course (which his foresight would have spared them) of

* Malcolm's Life of Clive, vol. ii. p. 338.
† To Mr. Verelst, July 11. 1765.

discord and confusion. We find him recommend that the Governor of Bengal should have a larger salary, but be restrained from trade — that Calcutta should be made the chief seat of the government of India — that a Governor-General should be nominated with the power, in cases of emergency, to take his decision independent of the Council. In a private letter to the Deputy-Chairman, he combats the anxiety resulting from such vast provinces to govern beyond so many thousand miles of sea: "With regard to the magnitude of our possessions "be not staggered. Assure yourself that the Company "must either be what they are or be annihilated." But even without any view as to the future, and looking solely at the present, Lord Clive might boast, that by his treaty he had secured to his countrymen a net revenue annually of 2,000,000*l.* He might boast, that he had freed them from any further dependence on the character or the conduct, the intrigues or the cabals, of the successive heirs of Meer Jaffier, whom he reduced, in fact, to little more than high pensioners of state.

Nevertheless, it formed a part of the policy of Clive, that the whole detail of the revenue department should still, for some time at least, be directed by a native Prime Minister, resident at Moorshedabad but responsible only to Calcutta. Two competitors appeared for this great office — Nuncomar at the head of the Brahmins — Mahomed Reza Khan at the head of the Mussulmans. There seemed a manifest advantage in preferring the former, as representing by far the greater numbers in race and in religion. Such was also the desire of Clive. But on full examination it appeared that the character of Nuncomar was stained by more than one act of fraud and even forgery. Moreover, at this very time, as Clive complains, he was seeking to establish a most pernicious influence on the mind of the young Nabob. "It is really "shocking," writes the hero of Plassey, "what a set of "miserable and mean wretches Nuncomar has placed "about him; men who the other day were horse-keepers." On the whole, therefore, after great deliberation, the choice of Clive fell upon Mahomed Reza Khan.

Having thus dealt with the Hindoos, Clive applied himself to the Europeans. He exacted from the civil servants of the Company a written covenant, pledging them to accept no future presents from the native princes. Many murmured, some resigned, but no one dared to disobey. Another measure which Clive considered most essential, and found most difficult, but which he succeeded in enforcing, was, to debar the men in high places from private trade, granting them, as some compensation, a share in the salt monopoly. With respect to the military officers, Clive announced his intention to deprive them of the large dole or additional allowance, which, under the name of DOUBLE BATTA, had been granted them by Meer Jaffier after the battle of Plassey, but which, as Clive had always explained to them, could not, in all probability, be continued by the Company. In fact, the Court of Directors had issued the most positive orders that the Double Batta should be discontinued. These orders had been several times repeated, but the remonstrances of the army had hitherto prevented the Governor and Council from giving them effect. For, according to the bitter sarcasm hurled against them at a later period, the military could not behold without a "virtuous emulation" the "moderate gains" of the civil service.* In abolishing their Double Batta, Clive had to encounter, not remonstrances merely, nor dissatisfaction, but even mutiny. Nearly two hundred officers, combining together, bound themselves by an oath of secrecy, and undertook to fling up their Commissions on one and the same day. It added not a little to the dangers of the league that it was, though in private, instigated by no less a man than Sir Robert Fletcher, the second in command to Clive, who had headed the troops, and with success, in the last campaign. Each officer separately pledged himself under a bond of 500*l.* not to resume his Commission, unless the Double Batta was first restored. In support of those who might be cashiered, a subscription was begun in camp, to which subscription, it is said, that no less than 16,000*l.* were added from the angry civilians at Calcutta.

The idea of the conspirators (for surely they deserve no milder name) was that in a country like India,—held

* Speech of Burke on Mr. Fox's East India Bill, December 1. 1783.

solely by the sword,—Clive could not dispense with their services even for a single day, and must succumb to their demands. Far from daunted, however, Clive set off in person for the camp at Monghir. The heavy rains and the stifling heat delayed his progress;. and he was further weighed down by an illness, resulting from fatigue of body and anxiety of mind. But his spirit never for one instant quailed. On his arrival, he assembled and addressed the officers and men, pointing out to them the guilt of their course on public grounds. The points that merely touched himself he passed by with generous disdain. There were two officers accused of declaring that they would attempt to stab or shoot him dead; and words to that effect were certainly used, though as certainly proceeding only from the heat and folly of the moment. Clive declared most justly that he gave no belief whatever to any such design. He was well assured, he said, that he was speaking to Englishmen and not assassins. Several of the officers were touched and reclaimed by his manly firmness. Several others, though but few, had stood by him from the first. The Sepoys, who had ever looked up to him with especial reverence, and comprising some perhaps of the same men who had offered to give up for him their rice at Arcot, cried out that nothing should make them swerve from their English hero,— Sabut Jung.* Clive, on his part, declared that nothing should make him swerve from his fixed purpose. If necessary, he would send for other officers from Madras. If necessary, he would summon clerks at their desks (such as in his outset he had been) to serve as soldiers. He would do all or any thing rather than yield to mutiny. Thus, while indulgent to the younger and less experienced officers, and willing to receive their tokens of contrition, he ordered the ringleaders into arrest, and sent them down the Ganges for trial at Calcutta. He did not shrink even from the bold measure of cashiering his second in command.

His letters to the members of his Council at Calcutta breathe a no less determined tone. "I tell you again; "remember to act with the greatest spirit. If the ci-

* See page 47.

" vilians entertain the officers, dismiss them the service; " and if the latter behave with insolence or are refractory, make them all prisoners and confine them in the " new fort. If you have any thing to apprehend, write " me word, and I will come down instantly and bring " with me the Third Brigade, whose officers and men can " be depended upon."*

By such firmness was averted the shame of a successful mutiny, — a shame which, in Clive's own strong language, all the waters of the Ganges could never wash away. The privates showed no disposition to support their officers, and scarce any of the latter but displayed symptoms of repentance. Of the chiefs of the mutiny at Monghir, who were sent away in boats for trial, many were seen to embark with tears in their eyes. The younger or less guilty officers, who at the outset had been threatened with death if they drew back, now pleaded with the greatest earnestness to be allowed to recall their resignations. In most cases, but always as an act of grace and favour, their humble supplications were allowed, while the remaining vacancies were filled by a judicious choice of subalterns.

All this time the conduct of Clive was giving a lofty example of disregard to lucre. He did not spare his own personal resources, and was able some years afterwards to boast in the House of Commons, that this his second Indian command had left him poorer than it found him. His enemies might indeed observe, that the virtue of disinterestedness is not so hard to practise when a fortune of forty thousand pounds a year has been already gained. Yet still the fact remains, that when presents from one of the native Princes laid the foundations of his wealth the practice of receiving them was both usual and allowed, and that when it ceased to be at least the latter he stood firm against all temptation. In vain did the Rajah of Benares press upon him two diamonds of large size. In vain did the Nabob Visier produce a rich casket of jewels and offer a large sum of money. Lord Clive, thus wrote an officer by no means his friend from India, might then have added at least half a million to his fortune; and we

* Letter to Mr. Verelst, May 28. 1766.

may further note, that the receipt of such gifts might have probably remained a secret, since even their refusal was not known until after his decease.

In the corrections which Lord Clive applied to both the civil and military services, and in his general course of policy, he had, on some points, no more than fulfilled the positive instructions of the Court of Directors. On other points he obtained their entire approbation. But there were one or two besides on which he did not shrink from the painful duty of daring their displeasure, and standing firm against their peremptory orders. On the whole it may be said, that his second command was not less important for reform than his first had been for conquest. By this, the foundations, at least, of good government were securely laid. And the results might have been far greater still, could Clive have remained longer at his post. But the burning climate, combined with ceaseless anxiety and toil, had grievously impaired his health. In December, 1766, we find him during several weeks disabled from all writing, and at the close of the ensuing month he found it necessary to embark for England. He left the government to a man of no more than average ability—Mr. Verelst; yet under him there still continued the impulse given by a stronger hand.

At this period, the main point of interest changes from the Presidency of Bengal to the Presidency of Madras. There, the English were becoming involved in another war. There, they had now, for the first time, to encounter the most skilful and daring of all the enemies against whom they ever fought in India—Hyder Ali. He was of humble origin, the grandchild of a wandering FAKIR or Mahomedan monk. Most versatile in his talents, Hyder was no less adventurous in his career; by turns a private man devoted to sports of the chase, a captain of freebooters, a partisan-chief, a rebel against the Rajah of Mysore, and commander-in-chief of the Mysorean army. Of this last position he availed himself to dethrone and supplant his master. Indeed, during his whole course, we seldom find him either restrained by scruples or bound by promises. One single instance of the kind will suffice to paint his character. A Brahmin, Khonde Row by name, at one time his close confederate, but afterwards his enemy, having taken the field against him, was reduced to the point of surrender. The Rajah and the ladies of the palace sent a joint message to Hyder, pleading for their friend the Brahmin, and inquiring what terms he might expect. "I will not only spare his life," said Hyder, "but I will cherish him like a parroquet." Nevertheless, no sooner was the Brahmin in his hands than he was treated with the utmost rigour, and imprisoned for the remainder of his life in an iron cage. When Hyder was thereupon gently reminded of his promise, he answered, that he had literally kept his word, referring in proof to the cage in which the captive was confined, and to the rice and milk allotted for his daily food! *

Pursuing his ambitious schemes, Hyder Ali became, not merely the successor of the Rajah, but the founder of the kingdom of Mysore. From his palace at Seringapatam, as from a centre, a new energy was infused through the whole of Southern India. By various wars and by the dispossession of several smaller princes, he extended his frontiers to the northward, nearly to the river Kistna. His posts on the coast of Malabar, Mangalore especially, gave him the means of founding a marine; and he applied himself with assiduous skill to train and discipline his troops according to the European models. The English at Madras were roused by his ambition, without as yet fully appreciating his genius. We find them at the beginning of 1767 engaged, with little care or forethought, in a confederacy against him with the Nizam and the Mahrattas. Formidable as that confederacy might seem, it was speedily dissipated by the arts of Hyder. At the very outset, a well-timed subsidy bought off the Mahrattas. The Nizam showed no better faith; he was only more tardy in his treason. He took the field in concert with a body of English commanded by Colonel Joseph Smith, but soon began to show symptoms of defection, and at

* Colonel Wilks's Historical Sketches of the South of India, vol. i. p. 434. Sir John Malcolm, in his first mission to Teheran, gives an account of *Tootee*, a young dancing-girl from Shiraz, and a favourite of the Shah. "*Tootee*," adds Sir John, "is the Persian "word for a parrot, a bird which is proverbial in Persian tales for "its knowledge and habits of attachment." (Sketches of Persia, p. 221., ed. 1845.)

last drew off his troops to join the army of Hyder. A battle ensued near Trincomalee, in September, 1767. Colonel Smith had under him no more than 1,500 Europeans and 9,000 Sepoys; while the forces combined on the other side were estimated, probably with much exaggeration, at 70,000 men. Nevertheless, Victory, as usual, declared for the English cause. The Nizam in this action showed himself destitute alike of conduct and of courage. At the outset, he had valiantly cried: "Sooner than "yield, I would share the fate of Nazir Jung."* Yet within an hour afterwards, the Indian prince was in full gallop to the westward; and his troops proved perfectly worthy of such a chief. Almost the only instance of spirit in his army was displayed by one of the ladies of his palace. These he had brought with him on a train of elephants, as spectators of his expected triumph. In his own panic he ordered that these elephants also should be turned for flight. Then, from one of the covered canopies a woman's voice was heard: "This elephant has not "been taught so to turn; he follows the standard of the "empire." Accordingly, though the English shot was falling thick around her, the female assertor of the honour of the empire would not allow her elephant to be drawn aside until first the standard had passed.†

On the other hand, the troops of Hyder Ali, both then and afterwards, displayed not merely the effects of a braver chief and of a better discipline, but also the energies of a robuster race. The people within the Ghauts or hill-passes of Southern India, though far below the mountain races of Afghan, are yet far superior to the Hindoos of the plains. In these, the delicacy of limbs and the softness of muscles must be reckoned among the foremost causes of their failure on a battle-field. In these, the utter want of strength in their bodily organisation is only, on some occasions and for some purposes, redeemed by its suppleness. It has been computed, that two English sawyers can perform in one day the work

* See page 23.

† Wilks's South of India, vol. ii. p. 38. I am sorry to spoil the story, but it appears that "the loss of several elephants was the "consequence of this damsel's demur."

of thirty-two Indians. Yet, as the same authority assures us, see the same men as tumblers, and there are none so extraordinary in the world. Or employ them as messengers, and they will go fifty miles a day for twenty or thirty days without intermission.*

Our victory at Trincomalee produced as its speedy consequence a treaty of peace with the Nizam. Hyder was left alone; but even thus proved fully a match for the English both of Madras and of Bombay. The latter had fitted out a naval armament which, in the course of the winter, reduced his sea-port of Mangalore and destroyed his rising fleet. Against these new enemies Hyder, like some wild beast at bay, made a sudden bound. Leaving to the eastward a force sufficient to employ and delude Colonel Joseph Smith, he silently descended the western Ghauts, and in May 1768, at the very time when least expected, appeared before the gates of Mangalore. The English garrison taken by surprise, hastily re-embarked in boats, relinquishing all their artillery and stores, and leaving also more than two hundred sick and wounded to the mercy, or rather the politic forbearance, of their crafty foe.

Returning to the eastward, Hyder Ali continued to wage the war against Colonel Smith; inferior on any field of battle, but prevailing in wiles and stratagems, in early intelligence, and in rapid marches. He could not be prevented from laying waste the southern plains of the Carnatic, as the territory of one of the staunchest allies of England, Mahomed Ali, the Nabob of Arcot. Through such ravages, the British troops often underwent severe privations. Moreover, Colonel Smith was trammelled by the same system so often and so justly complained of in the wars of Marlborough — the appointment of field-deputies. Two members of the Council of Madras had been sent into his camp with full powers to control — that is, to clog and thwart — his operations.

At length, in the spring of 1769, Hyder Ali became desirous of peace, and resolved to extort it on favourable terms. First, by a dexterous feint he drew off the

* See an essay by Mr. Orme, in his Historical Fragments of the Mogul Empire, p. 463.

British forces a hundred and forty miles to the southward of Madras. Then suddenly, at the head of five thousand horsemen, Hyder himself appeared at St. Thomas's Mount, within ten miles of that city. The terrified Members of the Council already, in their mind's eye, saw their country-houses given up to plunder and to flame, and were little inclined to dispute whatever might be asked by an enemy so near at hand. Happily his terms were not high. A treaty was signed, providing that a mutual restoration of conquests should take place, and that the contracting parties should agree to assist each other in all defensive wars.

In the career of Hyder Ali, this was by no means the first, nor yet the last occasion, on which he showed himself sincerely desirous of alliance with the English. He did not conceal the fact, that, in order to maintain his power and secure himself, he must lean either on them or on the Mahrattas. He would have preferred the first; it was the vacillation and weakness of the council at Madras that drove him to the latter. Finding his overtures of friendship slighted, he took his part, as always, decidedly and boldly. He became, even in the midst of peace, a known and ardent enemy of the English race and name; ever watchful for any opening to assail them; ever ready to league himself against them with the Mahratta chiefs at Poona, or the French Governors at Pondicherry.

It was no common enemy whom the Madras traders (who could, at that period call them statesmen?) thus neglected or defied. The vigorous administration of Hyder at his Court of Seringapatam, has been closely viewed and well described by more than one European in his service. Like the other Indian Princes, he was addicted to licentious pleasure. Unlike them, he was never enslaved by it. Many of his leisure hours were passed in the company of dancing girls. To intoxication likewise he was often prone; and one instance is recorded, how, in that state, he was seen by his whole Court to seize and most severely cane his grown-up son, Tippoo. It may be added, that, on common occasions, his toilet took up a considerable portion of his time. But no sooner did any peril threaten, or any object of ambition rise in view, than all such habits of indulgence were promptly cast aside; and Hyder passed whole days and nights untired in his council-chambers, or on horseback with his cavalry. At all times he was most easy of access; freely receiving all those who desired to see him, except only the Fakirs; a significant token of the degree of esteem in which he held his grandfather's profession. From all others he quickly drew whatever information he desired; and in dealing with them, manifested the keenest insight of their various characters. So far had his education been neglected, that he could neither read nor write. He made no later attempt at scholarship, but relied upon the powers of a most retentive memory, and upon a shrewdness hard to be deceived. He might be careless of his people's welfare for their sake, but he anxiously sought it for his own; he knew that to make them prosperous would, beyond all other causes, make him powerful; and thus through the wide extent of the kingdom that he founded, he never failed to guard them from all vague depredation or inferior tyranny.

By such means did he who had first set forth as a freebooter, with one or two score of followers, leave behind him at his peaceful end a well-appointed army ot a hundred thousand soldiers, and a treasure of three millions sterling. Yet, prosperous as he seemed, Hyder was not happy. It is recorded of one of his attendants, that after watching for some time his short and uneasy slumbers, he ventured at his waking to inquire of his dreams. "Believe me, my friend," said Hyder, "my "dominion, envied though it may be, is in truth far less "desirable than the state of the YOGEES (the religious "mendicants); awake, they see no conspirators; asleep, "they dream of no assassins!"*

In this war with Hyder, the English had lost no great amount of reputation, and of territory they had lost none at all. But as regards their wealth and their resources,

* The character and habits of Hyder Ali are described in his History by M. Le Maitre de La Tour, a Frenchman, who had commanded his artillery. Some considerable extracts from that work will be found in the Annual Register for 1784 (part ii. pp. 18—27.), and may be compared with various passages in Colonel Wilks's work (especially vol. i. pp. 247. and 351., and vol. ii. p. 142.)

they had suffered severely. Supplies, both of men and of money, had been required from Bengal, to assist the government at Madras; and both had been freely given. In consequence of such a drain, there could not be made the usual investments in goods, nor yet the usual remittances to England. Thus at the very time when the proprietors of the East India Company had begun to wish each other joy on the great reforms effected by Lord Clive, and looked forward to a further increase of their half-yearly Dividend, they were told to prepare for its reduction. A panic ensued. Within a few days, in the spring of 1769, India Stock fell above sixty per cent.*

At that period, indeed, as for some years before it, nothing could be more unsteady than the wishes, or more precarious than the prospects, of the great Company. Party-spirit continued to rage at their elections; the contests between the followers of Sulivan and the followers of Clive being renewed every year with varying success. Each party, when defeated, heaped the grossest imputations on the other, as on the lowest and basest of mankind; and in that respect the public were inclined to give an equal belief to both. In such a state of things the very existence of the Company seemed to hang upon the breath of any great man in Parliament. Thus was Lord Clive, while still in India, addressed by one of his principal agents in England, Mr. Walsh:— "I am very sorry you did not write a few lines to Mr. "Pitt, to conciliate him to your negotiations. I spoke a "few words to him just as he left the House of Commons, "and whilst he was getting on his great coat. . . . . He "answered me that he had heard of the great things "you had done; that you had gained much honour, but "that they were too vast. . . . . One word from him "would go far in making or unmaking the Company."† This was in May 1766, while Pitt was still a private Member of Parliament; but when, in the July following, he became Prime Minister, with the title of Chatham, still far greater importance, of course, attached to his opinions. In a former chapter I have fully shown how he entered office with the fixed determination to take

* Ann. Reg. 1769, p. 53

† Life by Malcolm, vol. iii. p. 189

into our own hands the government of our Eastern empire; how his purpose was baffled, not through any efforts of the East India Company, but through his own mysterious illness; and how the men succeeding him in power, though unable to pursue his policy, were reduced merely to stave off the main question, or to patch up temporary terms. But they, for their own part, were well satisfied, since the Company undertook, meanwhile, to pay to the revenue 400,000*l.* each year. As a further concession, arising from the financial embarrassments of 1769, it was agreed by the Directors that Commissioners of Inquiry, under the name of Supervisors, should be sent to India with full powers over the other servants of the Company. Three gentlemen of old standing and long service — Mr. Vansittart, Mr. Scrafton, and Colonel Ford — were selected for this important trust. Accordingly they embarked on their mission towards the close of the same year. But after leaving the Cape of Good Hope, the ship in which they sailed, the Aurora frigate, was never heard of again: it is supposed to have foundered at sea.

It is not improbable that this system of makeshifts might have still continued, and the necessity of any more decisive measures been longer postponed. But in the ensuing year, 1770, a new and more grievous calamity overspread Bengal. The usual rains having failed, there was no water in the tanks, and the rivers shrank into shallows. The rice-fields continued parched and dry, and could not yield their expected produce, while the conflagration of several large granaries completed the work of misery. A terrible famine ensued; a famine such as Europe, during the last few ages, has never known even in its rudest districts, or behind beleaguered walls. Throughout the wide valley of the Ganges, the country places were deserted, and the cities, where alone there might be hope of food, became thronged with starving multitudes, from whom piteous cries were heard. The common misery united, for the first and only time, the men of the most opposite castes — from the Brahmin of lofty lineage down to the humblest of the Niaidees.*

* The Niaidees were described a few years since in a Report from Mr. Conolly, Collector of Revenue in Malabar. "They are supposed

Even the Zenana now gave forth its guarded inmates, who, no longer veiled with jealous care, but prostrate and wailing on the ground, implored from the passers by, if not for themselves, at least for their little children, a handful — only a handful — of rice. Thousands and tens of thousands of human beings died daily in the streets, where the vultures swooped down and the dogs and jackals flocked in quest of their ghastly prey. In Calcutta alone there were daily employed one hundred men, on the Company's account, to pile the dead bodies upon sledges and cars, and throw them into the Ganges. The broad river was itself so far tainted that its fish ceased to be wholesome food. Hogs, ducks, and geese, which had likewise taken part in devouring the carcases, could no longer themselves be safely eaten; and thus, as the famine grew greater, the means of subsistence, even to the Europeans, grew less. It was computed, not in any rhetorical flight, not amidst the horror of the sufferings described, but in a grave despatch written two years afterwards, though even then perhaps with some exaggeration, that through Bengal this dreadful famine had destroyed in many places one half, and, on the whole, above one third, of the inhabitants.* These evil tidings from India did not come alone. Conjoined with them were rumours and charges that the distress had been greatly aggravated by the conduct of the Company's servants; that at the very outset of the famine they had engrossed all the rice of the country, and that afterwards they slowly doled it out at tenfold the price they had paid. If in truth there were any such cases, they can have been but few. They were in direct contravention

"to be the descendants of a Brahmin excommunicated many cen-"turies ago; and they are regarded as outcasts even by the slaves, "whom they are not allowed to approach within forty paces." (Despatch to the Government of Madras, May 7. 1845. MS.)

* Letter of the Governor and Council, Nov. 3. 1772, and Mr. Burke's Articles of Charge, xv. part i. It is remarkable that Mr. Mill, while devoting several large tomes to the History of British India, dismisses two of the most striking and important events of their time, — the Massacre of Patna, and the famine of Bengal, — in one sentence each! (Vol. iii. pp. 346. and 486., ed. 1840.) Thanks to Professor H. H. Wilson, these volumes are now enriched by many excellent notes and useful emendations.

of the Directors' orders, and of Lord Clive's rules. For my part, indeed, I strongly incline to the belief that, looking to the whole of this dismal period, and waiving, perhaps, some rare exceptions, the Hindoos were benefited, and so far as relief was possible, relieved, by the presence among them of their civilised and Christian rulers. Charges like these made against the latter, are common among every rude people at every dispensation of Providence. If there be a pestilence, they complain that the springs were poisoned by the malice of their enemies. If there be a famine, they feel sure that the grain has been fraudulently hoarded and usuriously dispensed.

Such charges, however, could not fail to make some impression on both the Ministry and Parliament of England. Even allowing them to be unfounded, there was yet an ample growth of abuses, rank and stubborn, to hew down in the Company's affairs. It was felt on all sides that there was more need than ever of investigation — more need and now more leisure also. The government of Lord North had by this time attained some degree of stability, and the nation some degree of repose. In the first place some legislation (perhaps to prevent any other more effective) was attempted by Mr. Sulivan, who had once more become the Deputy-Chairman of the Company. It was answered that as yet there was not sufficient information. Accordingly, in April 1772, and on the motion of General Burgoyne, there was appointed, by means of ballot, a Committee of Inquiry, bearing the title of "Select," though consisting of no less than thirty-one Members. Within six weeks that Committee prepared and presented two Reports; but the approaching close of the Session precluded any further step at that time.

Parliament met again in November the same year. Yet, during that short interval, the affairs of the Company had greatly altered for the worse. So low had their credit sunk with the Bank of England, that they found it necessary to apply to the First Lord of the Treasury for a loan of at least a million sterling. The Minister received their application coldly, and said that he should leave it to the decision of Parliament. Accordingly, at the very commencement of the new Session, Lord North moved for, and carried, a Secret Committee of thirteen Members to be chosen by ballot, and to take into their consideration the whole state of the Company's affairs. At the same time he agreed that the Select Committee of the preceding Session should be revived.

The Directors, trembling at the prospect of inquiry by others, and eager, if they could, to stifle or suppress it by an inquiry of their own, had already passed a Resolution, to send out to India, at their sole expense, a new batch of Supervisors. But the alertness of the Secret Committee defeated this manœuvre. Within ten days a report to the House of Commons pointed out that the step designed by the Directors might prove a serious obstacle in the way of Parliament, and recommended therefore that Parliament should interpose to arrest it. A Bill was accordingly brought in, to restrain, for a limited time, the East India Company from appointing Supervisors in India. To this measure the Directors and their friends in the House offered all the opposition in their power. Burke, who was then upon their side, went so far as to exclaim, "Shame upon such proceedings! Here is an end to confidence and public faith!" With better reason and more temper, Lord North disclaimed all grounds of personal hostility. "It is our wish," he said, "to make the East India Company a great and glorious Company, and settle it upon a permanent foundation."* Under such patronage the Bill was passed by large majorities.

This Bill, however, could only be deemed, as a lawyer might have termed it, an arrest of judgment. Later during the same Session, in the spring of 1773, Lord North proposed and carried through, against all gainsayers, his own measure of reform. This, after it had passed, was commonly called the Regulating Act. In the first place, he granted to the Company a loan of 1,500,000*l.* for four years, and relieved them from the annual payment to the State of 400,000*l.* On the other hand, the Company was restrained from making any greater dividend than six per cent. until the loan should

* Parl. Hist. vol. xvii. pp. 561. and 567.

be repaid, or any greater dividend than eight per cent. until the public should have some participation in the profits. It was then enacted, that instead of annual elections of the whole number of Directors at the India House, six should go out of office each year, and none keep their seats longer than four years. At the same time, the qualification for a vote in each proprietor was raised from 500*l.* to 1000*l.*, with more votes in proportion, up to four, to each proprietor of a larger sum.

In India, the Act provided that the Mayor's Court of Calcutta should be restricted in its jurisdiction to petty cases of trade, and that in its place should be constituted a Supreme Court, to consist of a Chief Justice, and three Puisne Judges, appointed by the Crown. The Governor of Bengal was henceforth to have authority over the other Presidencies, as Governor-General of India, but was himself to be controlled by his Council. In that Council, as previously, he was entitled only to a single or, in case of equality, a casting vote. It was proposed that these nominations should be made by Parliament, and continue for five years; after which they should revert to the Directors, but subject to the approbation of the Crown. In the progress therefore of the Bill through the Commons, the Members of the new Council were expressly named, so as to become a part of the enactment. Warren Hastings, who a year before had assumed the administration of Bengal, was appointed the first Governor-General. Another of the new Council, Richard Barwell, was already at his post; the new Members to be sent from England were General Clavering, the Hon. Colonel Monson, and Philip Francis.

Another clause of Lord North's Bill remitted the drawback on the East India Company's Teas — a step so little regarded at its outset, but so momentous in its consequences, and which has been fully treated in another place.* The Directors at the time were but little gratified with this boon, or any other, when compared with the curtailment of their previous powers. They declared, in a petition to the House, that they would rather forego the loan which they had solicited, than endure the con-

* See vol. v. of the Author's History of England, p. 318. ed. 1853.

ditions which the Minister imposed. But their late misgovernment had been such as to render, in Parliament at least, their adherents few and their lamentations disregarded.

In the course of these proceedings, both before the Committees and within the House, many a shaft was let fly at Lord Clive. Besides the public wrongs of which he stood accused, there was also, it may be feared, a feeling of personal envy at work against him. His vast wealth became a more striking mark for calumny when contrasted with the financial embarrassments of the Directors in whose service he had gained it. And his profusion, as ever happens, offended far more persons than it pleased. He had bought the noble seat of Claremont from the Duchess Dowager of Newcastle, and was improving it at lavish cost. He had so far invested money in the smaller boroughs that he could reckon on bringing into Parliament a retinue of six or seven friends and kinsmen.* Under such circumstances the Select Committee, over which Burgoyne presided, made Clive their more especial object of attack. They drew forth into the light of day several transactions certainly not well formed to bear it, as the forgery of Admiral Watson's signature, and the fraud practised on Omichund. But at the same time they could not shut out the lustre of the great deeds he had performed. Clive himself was unsparingly questioned, and treated with slight regard. As he complains, in one of his speeches: "I, their hum-"ble servant, the Baron of Plassey, have been examined "by the Select Committee more like a sheep-stealer than "a Member of this House!" And he adds, with perfect truth: "I am sure, Sir, if I had any sore places about "me they would have been found: they have probed me "to the bottom; no lenient plasters have been applied to "heal; no, Sir, they were all of the blister kind, pre-"pared with Spanish flies, and other provocatives!"

On this and some other occasions Clive spoke in his own defence in a frank and fearless spirit, with great energy of language, and, it would seem, with great effect

* Letter to Mr. Call, January 19. 1768. Malcolm's Life, vol. iii. p. 219.

upon the House. He was likewise happy in the friendship and assistance of Mr. Wedderburn, then Solicitor-General. It was in May, 1773, that the charges against him, till then vague and undefined, were brought forward as a vote of censure by Burgoyne. To the Government it became an open question. The Attorney-General spoke strongly on the side of the accusers. The Solicitor-General conducted the defence. A great number of placemen and King's Friends took the part of Clive, while the Prime Minister, Lord North, walked into the lobby against him. In the result, the first Resolutions of Burgoyne, alleging certain matters of fact that could scarcely be denied, were carried. But the next, which charged Lord Clive by name with having abused his powers, and set an evil example to the servants of the public, did not pass. At length, as the dawn was slowly breaking on the last of these long and stormy, and in many parts confused, debates, the House agreed almost unanimously to some words which Wedderburn moved: "That Robert Lord Clive did at the same time render "great and meritorious services to his country."

Such a vote might perhaps be deemed almost a verdict of acquittal. Certainly, at least, it showed a wise reluctance to condemn. It closed the whole case, and Clive had no further Parliamentary attack to fear. But the previous taunts and injuries appear to have sunk deep into his haughty mind. Nor was a life of ease, however splendid, congenial to his active temper. In his sumptuous halls of Claremont, or beneath the stately cedars of his park, he was far less really happy than amidst his former toils and cares, on the tented plains of the Carnatic or in the council-chambers of Bengal. Moreover, through the climate of the tropics, his health was most grievously impaired. He had to undergo sharp and oft-recurring spasms of pain, for which opium only could afford him its treacherous and transitory aid. At length, in November 1774, at his house in Berkeley Square, this great man, for such he surely was, fell by his own hand. He was not yet fifty years of age; and the contest in North America was just then beginning to hold forth to him a new career of active exertion,—a new chaplet of honourable fame.

To the last, however, he appears to have retained his serene demeanour, and the stern dominion of his will. It so chanced, that a young lady, an attached friend of his family, was then upon a visit at his house in Berkeley Square, and sat, writing a letter, in one of its apartments. Seeing Lord Clive walk through, she called to him to come and mend her pen. Lord Clive obeyed her summons, and taking out his penknife fulfilled her request; after which, passing on to another chamber, he turned the same knife against himself. This tale, though traditional, has a high contemporary voucher. It was related by the Earl of Shelburne, afterwards the first Marquis of Lansdowne, to the person from whom I received it.

CHAPTER IV.

(CHAP. LXVIII. OF THE HISTORY.)

WARREN HASTINGS, the first Governor-General of India, was born in 1732. He was sprung from a branch, or rather, as they alleged, the main stem, of the great old house of Hastings, from which in another line the Earls of Huntingdon descend. But at the time of little Warren's birth, his branch was fast decaying; and Daylesford, its ancient seat in Worcestershire, was already sold. It was only through the kindness of a kinsman that he obtained his education at Westminster School; and when that relative died he was shipped off at seventeen as a Writer to Bengal. He was noticed by Lord Clive as a man of promise. Under Mr. Vansittart he had much more opportunity to shine. Thus, through the various gradations of the Civil Service at that time, he sped with credit and success. Having married, but become a widower, he returned to England in 1765. But four years afterwards he was again sent forth as second in the Council of Madras; and early in 1772 he proceeded to a far higher, and, as it proved, more lasting post, as first in the Council of Bengal.

Spare in form and shrunk in features, with a mild voice and with gentle manners, Warren Hastings might seem to a casual observer as wanting in manly firmness. It is remarkable that, on his appointment as Governor of Bengal, Lord Clive deemed it right to warn him against this, as he imagined, the weak point of his character. "I "thought,"—thus writes Lord Clive from England,—"I "discovered in you a diffidence in your own judgment and "too great an easiness of disposition, which may subject "you insensibly to be led where you ought to guide." * Never was an error more complete. Among the many

* Letter, August 1. 1771. Life by Malcolm, vol. iii. p. 260.

qualities, good and evil, which distinguished Hastings through the thirteen years of his eventful rule, there was none more marked and striking than his unvarying determination, and resolute fixedness of purpose. With but few partakers of his councils, and, perhaps, none of his full confidence, he formed his purpose singly, and, once formed, adhered to it as to the compass of his course;—regarding as nought delay of time, or variety of means, or change of instruments, so long as the aim was kept in view and by degrees attained.

One strong instance of this tenacity of purpose is recorded by Hastings himself in the chit-chat of his later years. He was telling of a streamlet which skirts the domain of Daylesford, and also the village of Churchill, his dwelling-place in childhood, and which thence flows onwards to join the Isis at Cotswold. "To lie beside the "margin of that stream and muse, was," said Mr. Hastings, "one of my favourite recreations; and there one bright "summer's day, when I was scarcely seven years old, I "well remember that I first formed the determination to "purchase back Daylesford. I was then quite dependent "upon those who were themselves scarcely raised above "want; yet somehow or other the child's dream, as it "did not appear unreasonable at the moment, so in after "years it never faded away. God knows there were "times in my career, when to accomplish that or any "object of honourable ambition, seemed to be impossible, "but I have lived to accomplish this." *

Indeed it may be said of Hastings, that tenacity of purpose was not merely the principal feature of his character, but the key and main-spring of the rest. It made him, on the one hand, consistent and courageous, and with views of policy far beyond the passing hour; not easily perplexed by doubts or cast down by reverses; and worthy in all respects the inscription beneath his portrait, as it hangs to this day in the council-chamber of alcutta: MENS ÆQUA IN ARDUIS. On the other hand, it

* Memoirs of Warren Hastings, by the Rev. G. R. Gleig, vol. i. p. 9. ed. 1841. In this work the comments on each transaction are those of a zealous advocate for Hastings, but it contains many extracts, judiciously made, and of great value, from Hastings's private correspondence.

gave him a certain hardness and insensibility of heart; it made him, on several great occasions in his long career, callous to the sufferings which his policy inflicted, and careless of the means by which his policy might be pursued. He was firm, it may be added, in all his friendships and attachments, but few men have ever been more rancorous and unforgiving.

It was one among the merits of Hastings, that he had made himself thoroughly acquainted, not only with the literature, but also with the temper and feelings, of the nations which he came to rule. Their languages he spoke with ease and fluency; their prejudices, whether of religion or of race, he was ever, unless impelled by some state-necessity, studious not to wound. By such means he was at all times, whether in his triumphs or in his hours of danger and distress, a favourite with the native tribes of Hindostan — a favourite, moreover, at a period when in most cases they had little or no sympathy for the island-strangers. Bishop Heber was told by one of his Mussulman attendants, that he well remembered the time when all black people ran away from a white face; and when the appearance of a single European soldier struck a whole village with affright. "They used "to them now," he added, "they know they no harm do!"*

It was not merely Oriental knowledge that Hastings had acquired. At Westminster School he had deeply embued his mind with classic lore. "What! lose Warren "— lose the best scholar of his year!" had the Head-Master, Dr. Nichols, cried with generous spirit, when the boy's appointment for Bengal was first announced to him. "That will not do at all. Let him remain, and he "shall go on with his education at my charge."† Highly cultivated minds are often wanting in strength; and strong minds are as often wanting in high cultivation; so often, indeed, that in many cases the strength and the cultivation may, I fear, be deemed not only distinct but even in some degree repugnant to each other. But with Hastings, as with intellects of the highest order, they were well and happily combined. Through the long

* Bishop Heber's Journal, June 24. 1824.

† Memoirs by Gleig, vol. i. p. 13.

course of his despatches, more especially the later ones, his graceful and flowing sentences, so sustained in their equal dignity, so devoid of mere rhetorical glitter, and despising or seeming to despise all ornaments but such as the argument itself supplies and needs, seem worthy to be, and in India have often been, a model for state-papers.

At Westminster School little Warren was in the same class with Impey, who afterwards pursued the profession of the law, and, under the Regulating Act of 1773, was sent forth as Sir Elijah, and Chief Justice, to Bengal. It was on Impey, as we shall see hereafter, that the fortunes of Hastings more than once depended. Another of his boyish playmates was the poet Cowper. It is worthy of remark — if a short digression may be here allowed me — how often great and famous houses misunderstand the true sources of their fame. Of all the long line of Hastings, from that Danish Sea King of whom they claim descent, down to that Marquis, best known perhaps as Earl of Moira, who in our own age worthily upheld their ancient name, no one has filled so large a space in the eyes of men as the first Governor-General of India. Thus also, without disparagement to an upright and accomplished Chancellor, it may be said that of all the Cowpers the author of "The Task" is the foremost; since thousands and tens of thousands who never even heard of the statesman, have delighted in the strains of the poet. Yet neither Cowper, in his secluded toils for fame, nor Hastings when battling with his rivals for the administration of an empire, appear to have received the slightest notice or token of approval from their noble kinsmen. Neither the Earl Cowper, nor yet the Earl of Huntingdon of those days, so far as can be traced, at any time expressed at Olney or at Calcutta the least desire to establish a friendly correspondence, or obtain an authentic likeness. Thus at present, as I believe, no contemporary portrait of the greatest of the Cowpers is shown at Panshanger. None of the greatest of the Hastings is shown at Castle Donington.

When in the year 1772 Hastings first assumed the administration of Bengal, he found the whole country weighed down by the effects of the recent famine and depopulation. The greatest praise, perhaps, of his able rule, is the simple fact that scarce any trace of these effects appears in the succeeding years. He enforced a new system in the land revenue founded on leases for five years; a system far indeed from faultless, yet the best, probably, which at that period could be framed. Under that system nearly the same amonnt of income was collected from the far diminished numbers with less, it would seem, of pressure than before. For the accumulating debt and financial embarrassment of the Company more than the common resources seemed to be required. These Hastings strove hard to supply, not always, as will presently be shown, by the most creditable means. At the same time, to the great and manifest advantage of the natives, he put an end to the oppressive tax or duty levied upon marriages. As one of the results of his system of revenue-collection, he established, with signal good effect, district courts for the administration of justice, and district officers to maintain the public peace. Within a few months the provinces were in a great measure cleared of the DECOITS or gangs of thieves, and other prowling marauders. These and such like measures of reform, or of public policy, were carried through by Hastings amidst numerous objections in his council and incessant calls upon his time. Thus at the close of his first half year, he writes to a familiar friend: "Here I am "with arrears of months, and some of years, to bring up; "with the courts of justice and offices of revenue to set "a going; with the official reformation to resume and "complete; . . . . . with the current trifles of the day, "notes, letters, personal applications; every man's busi-"ness of more consequence than any other, and complain-"ants from every quarter of the province hallooing me "by hundreds for justice as often as I put my head out of "window, or venture abroad!"*

Among the earliest acts of Hastings, in Bengal, was one for which, right or wrong, he was in no degree responsible. It arose from the peremptory and positive commands of the Directors at home. Mahomed Reza Khan had now for seven years held his great office, at

* Letter to Josias Dupré, October 8. 1772.

Moorshedabad, as NAIB DEWAN, or chief Minister of the finances. During that time he had perhaps committed faults; he had certainly contracted enmities. But the reports against him of embezzlement and fraud in his high functions appear to have arisen mainly through the intrigues of Nuncomar, his disappointed rival. These reports, however, wrought so far on the Court of Directors, that they sent express instructions to Hastings, concurrently with his own appointment, to secure Mahomed Reza Khan, together with his family and his adherents, and to detain them in custody until his accounts should be examined. Hastings, thus at the outset of his power, could not have ventured to disobey such orders, even if his judgment disapproved them. He took his measures accordingly with promptitude and skill. Mahomed Reza Khan was seized in his bed at midnight by a battalion of Sepoys. The same measure was extended to his confederate, Schitab Roy, at that time Governor of Bahar; a chief who, in the recent wars, had fought with signal bravery upon the English side. The two prisoners were carried to Calcutta, where, after many months of postponement and delay, they were brought to trial before a Committee, over which Hastings himself presided. Nuncomar, with a vengeful rancour, such as no time could soften, no calamities subdue, appeared as the accuser of his ancient rival. But no guilt could be proved to call for any further punishment, nor even to justify the harshness already shown. Both prisoners, therefore, were acquitted and set free; Schitab Roy, moreover, being sent back to hold office in Bahar, clothed in a robe of state and mounted on a richly caparisoned elephant, as marks of honour and respect.*

Nuncomar throve as little in his hopes of ambition as in his projects of revenge. Hastings had meanwhile been effecting a complete change in the former system. It was not merely that he arrested the Minister, he abolished the office. He put an end to the scheme of double government at Moorshedabad and at Calcutta,

* See a note by Professor Wilson, correcting some errors both of fact and date in Mr. Mill (History of India, vol. iii. p. 545., ed. 1840).

transferring to the latter city and to the servants of the Company the entire machinery of state affairs. An empty pageant only was left at the former capital, still decked with the name and honours of Nabob. That Nabob, the heir of Meer Jaffier, was now an infant. On that plea, Hastings took occasion to reduce the yearly allowance granted by the Company from 320,000*l.* to half that sum. To alleviate in some degree the disappointment that was gnawing at the heart of Nuncomar, his son Rajah Goordas, was appointed Treasurer of the young Prince's Household. The guardianship of the young Prince himself was bestowed, not on his own mother, but on another lady of his father's Haram — the Munny Begum, by title and name. This last choice afforded at a later period strong grounds for complaints and cavils against Hastings. Why, it was asked, in such a country, where the female sex is held in so slight esteem, select any woman for that charge; and if any, why overlook a parent's rightful claim? There was nothing in the life or character of the Munny Begum to entitle her to any especial trust; she had been a dancing girl, and as such only had attracted the favour of the old Nabob. But on the other hand, it is to be observed, that her appointment, when proposed by Hastings to the Members of the Council, obtained from them a full and unanimous approval. They state in their Minutes on the subject: "She is said to have acquired a great ascendant over the "spirit of the Nabob, being the only person of whom he "stands in any kind of awe, — a circumstance highly "necessary for fulfilling the chief part of her duty, in "directing his education and conduct which appear to "have been hitherto much neglected." There is another reason, which, in the midst of the Moorshedabad arrests, had probably still more weight with Hastings, but which he reserves for a private letter to the Secret Committee of Directors, namely, that the Munny Begum was "the "declared enemy" of Mahomed Reza Khan. *

* Minutes of Council, July 11. 1772. See also in Mr. Gleig's Memoirs, the letter of Hastings to Dupré, of January 6. 1773. When Hastings writes to the young Nabob, he calls the Munny Begum "the rightful head of his family," and adds, that "she

External affairs also claimed the early care of Hastings. Shah Alum, the Emperor, in name at least, of Hindostan, had more than once endeavoured, but in vain, to prevail upon the English to assist him in expelling the Mahrattas. Finding that alone he could not attack these invaders of his patrimony with the smallest prospect of success, he took the opposite part, and threw himself into their arms. He was received at first with every token of respect and homage, and led back in triumph to his ancestral seat of Delhi. Soon, however, and of course, a quarrel ensued between them, when he found himself no more than a prisoner and a puppet in the hands of his new allies. They compelled him to sign an edict, transferring to them the districts of Allabahad and Corah, which had been bestowed upon him by Lord Clive. But here Hastings interposed. He determined not merely on resuming the districts of Allabahad and Corah, but on discontinuing all further yearly payments to Shah Alum. Breach of faith on this account became, at a later period, one of the charges brought against him. Yet, surely, there were some strong grounds both of justice and of policy in favour of the course which he pursued. We had wished to support the Emperor while he remained independent, or dependent only on ourselves; we might cease to support him whenever he resigned himself to our inveterate foes, and was preparing to turn our own gifts into arms against us.

The districts of Corah and Allabahad were promptly occupied by English troops. As our territory, however, stood at that time there was little or no temptation to annex them. It was computed that the expenses of maintaining them at so great a distance would exceed the utmost revenue they could bring. It was therefore the wish of Hastings to yield them for a stipulated sum to the adjacent State of Oude. He repaired to the city of Benares to confer in person with the Nabob Visier. There, in September, 1773, a treaty was agreed upon between them; the Nabob Visier undertaking to pay for the two districts the sum of fifty Lacs of Rupees.

"stands in the place of his deceased father." It is plain from thence, however strange, that the Nabob's own mother was held as an inferior.

But — alas for the fair fame not only of Hastings, but of England! — another and a weightier question was then decided at Benares. The Rohillas, a tribe of Afghan blood, had earlier in that century, and as allies of the Mogul, descended into the plains of Hindostan. They had obtained for their reward that fertile country which lies between the Ganges and the mountains on the western boundary of Oude. That country bore from them the name of Rohilcund. It had been earned by their services, and it was flourishing under their dominion. Of late there had sprung up a difference between them and their neighbours of Oude, with respect to some pecuniary stipulations which the Rohillas contracted and were backward to discharge. On that ground, Sujah Dowlah had a plea for war against them — a plea certainly plausible, and perhaps just. His real aim, however, was not the settlement of their account, but rather the entire subjugation of their race. He had little hope that his rabble of the plains would stand firm against the hardier offspring of the northern mountaineers. Therefore he applied to the English Governor for the aid of English bayonets; and this request came before Hastings at a time when the Bengal treasury was weighed down with heavy debts, and when nevertheless the letters from the Court of Directors were calling on him in the most earnest terms for large remittances. The Indian prince wanted soldiers, and the English chief wanted money, and on this foundation was the bargain struck between them. It was agreed that a body of the Company's troops should be sent to aid the Nabob Visier in the conquest of the Rohilla country; that the whole expense of these troops while engaged upon that service should be borne by him; and that when the object was accomplished he should pay to the English a farther sum of forty Lacs of Rupees.

Not many months elapsed before these stipulations were fulfilled. In April, 1774, an English brigade under Colonel Champion invaded the Rohilla districts; and in a hard-fought battle gained a decisive victory over the Rohilla troops. Exactly half a century afterwards an English Bishop, on his first Visitation progress, found the whole scene still fresh in the traditions of the country.

It was described to him how Hafiz, the Rohilla chief, an aged warrior, with a long grey beard, remained at last almost alone on a rising ground, in the heat of the fire, conspicuous by his splendid dress and stately horse, waving his hand, and vainly endeavouring to bring back his army to another charge; till, seeing that all was lost, he waved his hand once more, gave a shout, and galloped forwards to die, shot through and through, upon the English bayonets. The Nabob Visier applied for the body of Hafiz, that it might be cut in pieces and his grey head be carried on a pike about the country. But the English Colonel, with a nobler spirit, caused it to be wrapped in shawls and sent with due honour to his kinsmen. The other Afghan chiefs submitted, excepting only one, Fyzoola Khan, who continued his resistance, and was enabled at length to obtain some terms of peace from the Visier. Throughout this conflict, nothing could be more dastardly than the demeanour of the troops of Oude. They had slunk to the rear of the armies; they had kept aloof from the fight; and it was only after the battle was decided, that they came forward to plunder the camp, and despoil the dead and dying. Many an indignant murmur was heard from the British ranks: "We have the honour of the day, and these banditti, "these robbers, are to have the profit!"* Nor was this all. The Visier and his soldiery next applied themselves to wreak their fury on the vanquished, and to lay waste with sword and fire the rich plains of Rohilcund. No terms whatever had been made by Hastings for the more humane and merciful conduct of the war; and Colonel Champion, in his private letters to the Governor, might well avow his fear that, although we stood free from all participation in these cruel deeds, the mere fact of our having been silent spectators of them, would tend, in the minds of the whole Indian people, to the dishonour of the English name.

The case of Hastings as to the Rohillas — a case at the best a bad one — was farther injured by the indiscretion of his friends. Some of them afterwards pleaded for him

* Letter from Colonel Champion to Warren Hastings, April 24. 1774.

in the House of Commons, that the Rohillas were not among the native possessors of the soil in India, but only an invading tribe of foreign lineage and of recent conquest. With just indignation, Mr. Wilberforce exclaimed, "Why, what are we but the Rohillas of Bengal?"* But Hastings himself took better ground. Besides the pecuniary advantages, on which no question could exist, he had political arguments to urge in vindication of his treaty. It was of paramount importance to us to form a close alliance with Oude; and, on forming an alliance with that State, we had a full right to espouse its quarrels; nor could its frontier be made compact and defensible without the expulsion of the Rohillas, who, after all, even in their own districts, formed but a small minority of the entire population, and whose cause was in no degree supported by their Hindoo subjects. Statements of this kind, certainly specious, and even in some part true, but as certainly, I think, inadequate for vindication, had much weight at a later period with many able and upright men—as for example with Lord Grenville. But they did not even for a moment mislead the Prime Minister at the time of the transaction. "As soon"—thus, in 1786, spoke Lord North in the House of Commons—"as soon as I was apprised of the facts of "the Rohilla war, I thought the conduct of Mr. Hastings "highly censurable; and I sent to the Court of Directors, "urging them to combine with me for his recall."†

It was at the close of the Rohilla war, in October, 1774, that there anchored in the Ganges the ship which brought from England the expected Members of the Council and the Judges of the Supreme Court. Of the three new Councillors, Francis was by far the youngest; but his more shining and ardent spirit gave him a great ascendancy over Clavering's and Monson's. He came—there is little risk in affirming—determined to find fault; ready, whatever might befal, to cavil and oppose. The

* Speech in the House of Commons, June 2. 1786.

† Parl. Hist. vol. xxvi. p. 45. In the same debate (p. 54.) Mr. W. W. Grenville "was ready to avow his opinion that he thought "the war was perfectly just as well as politic." For the true state of Rohilcund in 1774, see a note by Professor Wilson upon Mill. (Hist. vol. iii. p. 575.)

very first despatch which he and his two colleagues addressed to the Directors, is filled with complaints that sufficient respect had not been paid them; that no guard of honour had met them on the beach; that the batteries of Fort William, in their salute, instead of twenty-one guns as they expected, had fired only seventeen. The same punctilious and resentful temper attended them in their deliberations. Of the five who met in Council, the old servants of the Company, Hastings and Barwell, stood together; on the other side were arrayed, as though in military order, the General, the Colonel, and the late War-Office Clerk. Thus they formed a majority upon every question that arose; thus, from the very first they wrested the whole power of the Government and all substantial patronage from the hands of Hastings.

So eager were these gentlemen to taste the sweets of power, that Hastings found some difficulty in prevailing upon them to pause even for a single day. With scarce time to read the Minutes, with none at all to inquire or reflect, they began to act. They ordered the English brigade to march back from Rohilcund, whatever might be then the condition of that province. They recalled, with every token of disgrace, Mr. Middleton, the confidential friend of Hastings, and by him appointed the Resident in Oude. They insisted, that even the most private of Mr. Middleton's letters should be laid before them. On these points Hastings, as he was bound, was not slow in appealing to Lord North. He observes most justly, that the new Councillors, even though they might condemn the whole policy and direction of the Rohilla War, ought rather, if they desired to establish future harmony, and to maintain the credit of the government free from inconsistency, to have afforded to their Governor-General the means of receding, without fixing a mark of reprobation on his past conduct, and without wounding his personal consequence at the Court of Oude. And Hastings adds: "Had they acted on such concilia-"tory principles, I should, if I know my own heart, have "cheerfully joined in whatever system they might after-"wards think fit to adopt; not pretending in such a case "to set my judgment against the will of the majority;

"but it was not to be expected that I should subscribe "implicitly to a direct censure of myself." *

In his more familiar letters, the Governor-General thus in strong colours paints the scene: "General "Clavering is, I verily believe, a man of strict honour, but "he brought strong prejudices with him. . . . Colonel "Monson is a sensible man, but received his first im-"pressions from Major Grant. . . . As for Francis, "I shall say nothing of him." A few months later, when the animosities had darkened, Hastings writes: "The "General rummages the Consultations for disputable "matter with old Fowke. Colonel Monson receives, and "I have been assured, descends even to solicit, accusa-"tions. Francis writes." †

Confident in their absolute majority, the three new Councillors pursued their course of rashness, or, as Hastings terms it, frenzy. On the decease of Sujah Dowlah, and the succession of his son Asaph-ul-Dowlah as Nabob Visier, they passed a preposterous vote that the treaties which had been signed with the former should be considered as personal and as having ended with his life. They unsettled for a time the whole administration, both financial and judicial, of Bengal. Still more mischievous was their meddling in the case of Bombay, then first under the recent Act reduced to a subordinate Presidency. They rebuked its Council, and they reversed its policy; and, in utter ignorance of its affairs, took new measures for entangling it in the differences of the several Mahratta chiefs. Meanwhile their power seemed so unquestionable, and their hostility to Hastings so clear, that many of his personal enemies began to brood over projects of revenge as certain of attainment. Two Englishmen of the name of Fowke came forward to charge him with corruption. The Rance, or Princess, of Burdwan, with her adopted son, sent in a similar complaint. But foremost of all in rancour as in rank was Nuncomar. He put into the hands of Francis a paper

* Letter to Lord North, December 4. 1774.

† Letters to Mr. Palk and to Colonel Maclean of December, 1774, and March 25. 1775. Memoirs of Hastings, by Gleig, vol. i. pp. 477. and 516.

containing several heavy accusations against Hastings; above all, that he had taken a bribe for dismissing without punishment Mahomed Reza Khan; and this paper was produced by Francis at the Council-Board.

Long and fierce were the discussions that ensued. The Governor-General did not shrink from the investigation of his conduct, but he insisted, and surely with perfect right, that the Members of the Council should form themselves into a Committee for that purpose, and after receiving whatever evidence they pleased, transmit it for adjudication either to the Supreme Court of Justice at Calcutta, or to the Directors at home. On the other hand the majority maintained, that even while sitting as a Council they might proceed to the trial of their chief. They desired in consequence, that Nuncomar should be called in to confront the Governor-General. "Before "the question is put," says Hastings in his Minute, "I declare that I will not suffer Nuncomar to appear "before the Board as my accuser. I know what belongs "to the dignity and character of the first member of this "administration. I will not sit at this Board in the "character of a criminal. Nor do I acknowledge the "members of this Board to be my judges." But the majority still persevering, the Governor-General rose, declared the meeting dissolved, and left the room with Barwell in his train. The remaining members voted that the meeting was not dissolved, named Clavering as chairman, and called in Nuncomar. He came, and according to the custom of all false accusers, spoke much upon his own integrity, and the absence of every motive save a sense of right for the charge which he had made. And he ended by producing a new letter on which to found another charge. This letter purported to come from the Munny Begum, expressing the gratitude she felt to the Governor-General for her appointment, and adding, that as a token of her gratitude she had presented him with two Lacs of Rupees. "This letter," wrote Hastings, "is a gross forgery, and I make no doubt "of proving it." *

In this state of the transactions, Hastings thought

* To Colonel Maclean, March 25. 1775.

himself entitled to allege, that Nuncomar, Mr. Fowke, and some others were guilty of a conspiracy against him. On this ground he began legal proceedings against them in the Supreme Court. The Judges after a long examination of the case directed Nuncomar and Fowke to give bail, and bound over the Governor-General to prosecute them.

Of a sudden, however, and only a few weeks afterwards, a more serious blow was aimed at Nuncomar by another hand. He was arrested at the suit of a native merchant named Mohun Persaud, and, like any other man accused of felony, was thrown into the common gaol. The charge against him was that he had forged a bond five years before. On that charge, the Supreme Court not then existing, he had been brought to trial before the Mayor's Court of Calcutta, but was released through the authority which at that time Hastings exerted in his favour. The suit had, therefore, been suspended, but not concluded. It was now revived before a higher and more independent tribunal, established expressly with a view to such cases; and it was revived at the very earliest lawful time after the necessary documents had been transferred to the new Court. So opportune was this prosecution for the interests of the Governor-General, and so suspicious the coincidence of time, that Hastings has ever since been suspected and arraigned as the real mover in the business. Yet, besides the presumption on his side to be drawn from the regular conduct of the suit, there is surely some weight in a fact which many writers have passed over—that in the proceedings before the Supreme Court, Hastings solemnly deposed, upon his oath, that he had never directly or indirectly countenanced or forwarded the prosecution for forgery against Nuncomar.*

The new Members of the Council showed the utmost resentment at the prosecution, but found themselves

* See the Memoirs of Sir Elijah Impey, by his Son, p. 83. ed. 1846. In that work, and in a note upon Mill, by Professor Wilson (vol. iii. p. 644.), the argument as to the regular renewal of the suit at the earliest opportunity will be found more fully and particularly stated.

wholly powerless to stem it. Their fierce representations to the Judges proved in vain. They could only send complimentary messages to Nuncomar in his prison, and grant additional favours to his son. The trial came on, in due time, before a Jury composed of Englishmen, when the charge of forgery was established to their entire satisfaction, and a verdict of Guilty was returned. One of the Judges, Sir Robert Chambers, the friend of Dr. Johnson, had proposed to try the prisoner on an earlier and a milder statute, inflicting no capital penalty; but Chambers is stated to have been convinced by, and most certainly he acquiesced in, the arguments against it. The sentence of death on Nuncomar was pronounced by Sir Elijah Impey as the chief, and apparently with the full concurrence of his colleagues. According to the Letters Patent by which the Supreme Court was constituted, the Judges had power to grant a reprieve from execution, provided they gave their reasons, and until the King's pleasure could be known. That power of reprieve, however, they did not see cause to exert on this occasion. Thus the law was left to take its course. On the 5th of August, 1775, the Rajah Nuncomar, at that time seventy years of age, and the head of the Brahmins of Bengal, was led forth to the gallows, and hanged; while Clavering and his two friends, with impotent rage, shut themselves up within their houses, and while an immense concourse of Hindoos looked on in wonder and affright.

For his share in these proceedings the Chief Justice has been arraigned even more severely than the Governor-General. It was Hastings — thus cries Burke in his ardent and sometimes overflowing zeal — it was Hastings who murdered Nuncomar by the hand of Sir Elijah Impey! The personal friendship which had subsisted between them since their schoolboy days was urged as strong presumption of a guilty compact. For this argument, as levelled at one of the Judges, it became convenient to overlook entirely the existence of the other three. Thus Impey, who had but acted jointly, was arraigned alone. At length the surmises and suspicions against him assumed a more definite form. At the close of 1787 a member of the House of Commons, Sir Gilbert Elliot, moved for his impeachment mainly on this ground. Then Sir Elijah was permitted to appear at the Bar, and to speak in his own defence. He showed, to the perfect satisfaction of by far the greater part of those who heard him, that his behaviour through the trial had been wholly free from blame. And as to the proposal of Sir Robert Chambers, — "It was a proposal," said he, "I speak "positively for myself, that I should, and I believe the "other Judges would, have been glad to have concurred "in. . . . . But that both the Statutes could stand together, and that it was optional in the Court to choose "the Statute which it liked best, I thought impossible "on clear principles of Law."

But this was not all. Why, asked Sir Elijah, on behalf of his colleagues and himself, why were they to be censured for not having stayed the execution? By the Letters Patent they were required to give their reasons for any rèspite. What reasons, then, could they have given in the case of Nuncomar? Were they to allege his high rank, his long experience, or his priestly character? These, if rightly viewed, were only aggravations of his crime. Or were they to state that his crime, as any other act of forgery or perjury, was, in the eyes of the people of Bengal, a common and a slight offence?* It might be answered, that for that very reason it was needful to make a solemn and severe example. Yet now, when dispassionately viewed, these arguments against a respite seem more specious than solid, or at least are overborne by still weightier considerations. It is a most essential principle, whenever the penalty of death is to be inflicted, that the popular feeling should keep pace with the established law, lest, instead of horror at the crime, we produce only compassion for the criminal. In the age of Impey, however, this great principle was, even in England, by no means fully acknowledged or acted upon, and by that principle, therefore, Impey must not be too rigorously tried. On the whole, so far as the denial of a respite is concerned, we may think that his decision was

* Even half a century later we find in the Indian Journal of Bishop Heber, "Perjury is dreadfully common, and very little "thought of." (Furreedpoor, July 26. 1824.)

erroneous, but have no grounds whatever for asserting that his motive was corrupt. *

The execution of Nuncomar, although it may not have been connected with any step of Hastings, was certainly auspicious to his interests. The Hindoos could make no nice distinctions, such as the case required, between political and judicial authority. They looked only to the one broad fact that one of their chief men had stood forth to accuse the Governor-General, and that within a few weeks of his accusation that chief man had died upon the gallows. From that moment all the other natives shrank from any further charges against Hastings. From that moment, in their eyes, he recovered a large portion of his power. But it should be added, in justice to his memory, that throughout his long administration, he attracted, in a high degree, their love as well as fear. The English in India also were nearly all upon his side. Hastings, they saw, was familiar with their wants and wishes, and profoundly versed in their affairs. On the other hand they had slight confidence in either Clavering or Monson ; and they had quickly taken fire against the War Office Clerk, who, in all respects ignorant of India, was yet seeking to impose upon it, with peremptory violence, every crotchet of his brain. He had not been many weeks at Calcutta ere he obtained the common surname of " King Francis," or " Francis the First."

The arrogance of Francis, both then and afterwards, was, indeed, almost boundless. It is only, as I conceive, his consciousness of the authorship of Junius that can in any degree explain, though not excuse it. How else

* A very interesting account of the demeanour and the death of Nuncomar, and of its effects upon the Hindoo population, was produced by Sir Gilbert Elliot in 1788, and printed in the Annual Register for that year (p. 177). It was said to be written by Mr. Macrabie, who was the Sheriff present at the execution, and it has been followed by nearly all the later writers. But Mr. Impey, in the Memoirs of his father (see p. 111., and also p. 285.), gives some strong grounds for questioning its authenticity. It was not heard of until after more than twelve years, when it was produced for a merely party purpose, by the far from scrupulous hands of Philip Francis, the brother-in-law of Macrabie; and some of the particulars it states are " directly contradicted by contemporary accounts " upon legal evidence."

does it seem possible that fifteen years later, when that great man, Edmund Burke, was in the zenith of his fame, he should be addressed as follows, in a private letter from Philip Francis? — "Once for all, I wish you would let "me teach you to write English." And then follows, in the same letter, a striking sentence, not inferior perhaps to any in Junius; it most felicitously applies to writings the same principle acknowledged to be true of wood and stone: — "Why will you not allow yourself to be per-"suaded that polish is material to preservation?" *

Another point in the character of Francis — well according with what we may presume of the author of the reply to Junia † — was his taste for profligate amours. It was from these, at a somewhat later period, that arose the personal and bitter estrangement between himself and Sir Elijah Impey. By means of a ladder of ropes, Francis had one night climbed into the chamber of Mrs. Grand, a lady of Scottish birth, the wife of a Calcutta Barrister. After he had remained there for three-quarters of an hour an alarm was given, and Francis descending in haste from the apartment of the lady was seized at the foot of the ladder by the servants of the husband. Hereupon an action was brought by Mr. Grand against Mr. Francis in the Supreme Court of Calcutta. It was usual for the Judges of that Court to assess the damages in civil actions without the intervention of a Jury. Sir Elijah Impey in this case fixed the sum to be awarded at fifty thousand rupees. Yet, in the opinion of his colleague, Sir Robert Chambers, and still more strongly, no doubt, in the opinion of Francis himself, a lesser sum would have sufficed; since, however suspicious the ladder of ropes and the nocturnal visit, no positive act of guilt was proved. Up to that time the Chief Justice and the Member of Council at Calcutta had been on civil, nay familiar terms, but from this transaction may be dated the commencement of the active and persevering

* Letter of November 3. 1790, as printed in Burke's Correspondence, vol. iii. p. 164.

† Of that letter Junius immediately afterwards became ashamed; and he desired Mr. Woodfall to throw doubts on its authenticity. (Note of Sept. 10. 1769.) It is omitted from the earlier editions, but will be found in the publication of 1812. (Vol. iii. p. 218.)

animosity with which Francis ever afterwards continued to pursue Sir Elijah Impey. Mr. Grand succeeded in obtaining a divorce, and Mrs. Grand took refuge with Francis, by whom, however, she was soon afterwards forsaken. She returned to Europe as the companion of another gentleman, Mr. William Macintosh; and, by a far more surprising turn of Fortune, closed her adventurous career as the wife of a celebrated foreign statesman, Prince Talleyrand.*

The news of the divisions in the Council at Calcutta appears to have greatly perplexed the Directors at home. For some time they endeavoured, but with little good effect, to hold a middle course. We find, in November, 1775, the King write as follows to Lord North: "The "East India Directors in their despatch manifestly wish "to hurt neither Hastings nor his adversaries, and there-"fore will most probably disoblige both." Lord North himself, however, was deeply impressed with the iniquity of the Rohilla war. He regretted, that under the Regulating Act there was no power during the first five years to recall the Governor-General without an Address to that effect from the Company to the Crown. "Send us "that Address"—such was his advice to his friends in the Direction; and accordingly after the annual elections in the spring of 1776, a strong effort was made. In the Court of Directors the numbers were nearly even; there were eleven votes for the recall of Hastings, and ten against it. The minority appealed to a Court of Proprietors, where the struggle was renewed. On that occasion the agent of Hastings in London, Colonel Maclean, reckoned up in some dismay the hostile force which not only "the Chairs" but the Government poured in. He saw mingling with the merchants and the City-men no less than forty-nine Peers, Privy Councillors, and men in

* Memoirs of Sir Elijah Impey, by his son, p. 173., and the unpublished biography of Mr. Charles Macintosh, as quoted in the Quarterly Review, No. CLXVII. p. 70. Perhaps it may be thought that Sir Robert Chambers, in his view of this transaction, judged rather according to the Mahomedan law, which in every such case requires the testimony of four eye-witnesses. See the Moslem Annals of Abulfeda (p. 71.), and the Decline and Fall of Gibbon, who calls this "a law of domestic peace." (Vol. ix. p. 326.)

office; at their head a Minister of the Crown, Lord Sandwich. The debate continued till near midnight. A motion for adjournment was made, and the opponents of Hastings prevailed in that division; but a Ballot on the main question being demanded for another day, the motion for his recall was negatived by a majority of upwards of one hundred.

Lord North was greatly incensed at this defeat. He let fall some angry expressions; or, at least, some such were ascribed to him by the zeal of partisans. The two Houses should be called together before Christmas; there should be another India Bill; the Calcutta government must be new modelled; the Company must be restricted to its trade. These vague threats wrought too far upon Colonel Maclean. He believed his patron in risk of a Parliamentary dismissal, or, perhaps, a Parliamentary censure. He was scared instead of being re-assured by the dangers which he had surmounted; and thought only how to shrink from the dangers to come. He had in his possession a private letter, written by Hastings a year and a half before, in which Hastings announced his resolution of resigning if he should not find his measures supported and approved. In another letter, two months afterwards, Hastings had most clearly revoked that resolution.* Nevertheless, Colonel Maclean in October, 1776, thought himself sufficiently empowered to tender to the Court of Directors the resignation of the Governor-General. The Directors, eager to be relieved from their embarrassment, made little difficulty. They accepted the resignation, and, with the connivance of the Crown, named one of their own body, Mr. Edward Wheler, to the vacant place in the Council of Bengal.

But meanwhile the state of that Council had wholly changed. In September, 1776, Colonel Monson had died. By his decease, and by the means of his own casting

* The two letters of Hastings, addressed to Colonel Maclean and another agent, and dated March 27. and May 18. 1775, are published at full length by Mr. Gleig in Hastings's Memoirs. The terms of the second letter are quite explicit. "I now retract the resolution "communicated to you separately in my letters of the 27th of "March." Compare with these documents the Article of Charge (No. ix.), by Mr. Burke.

vote, the full powers of Government fell back into the hands of the Governor-General. With his usual fixedness of purpose he now resumed his former policy and reappointed his old friends. Above all, after a short delay, "Nat Middleton" (for so he fondly calls him), became once more the Resident in Oude. "The first act "of my authority," said Hastings, "might justly be for "the retrieval of the first wound which was given to it." Since his Five Years' Settlement of the land-revenue was now drawing to a close, he gave orders for another valuation, to be conducted solely under his own control. In spite of the strenuous opposition of Clavering and Francis, he created a new office for that object. At the same time his mind was brooding over a vast scheme for the complete ascendancy in India of the English name—a system of subsidiary alliance with native princes, and, above all, with the Nabob of Oude and the Nizam,—a system which it was left to his successors to unfold and to pursue. In all these contemplations of coming empire it is remarkable how deep and far-sighted were his views. Thus, at a time when scarce any other statesman bestowed a thought or care upon the martial race that dwelt along the banks of the Five Rivers, we find Hastings clearly discern and dread their increasing greatness. We find him in one of his Minutes refer with some anxiety to "the nation or religious sect of the Seiks," and desire some occasion "of blasting the growth of a "generation whose strength might become fatal to our "own." *

Such were the schemes that Hastings was maturing, when, in June, 1777, a packet-ship from England anchored in the Hooghly, and all Calcutta was startled with the news that the Governor-General had resigned; that his resignation was accepted; and that the government was transferred to other hands. No man was more astonished at these tidings than the Governor-General himself. He declared that Colonel Maclean had far, very far, exceeded his instructions. But he afterwards said, that nevertheless he should have felt himself bound by

* Minute, December 4. 1784. See Burke's Articles of Charge, No. xviii. sec. 24.

the acts of his agent, had not General Clavering attempted to seize the government by force. Clavering never asked whether the offer of resignation was acknowledged as authentic. He never asked whether — as was in fact the case, and as had been expressly stipulated with the Directors and with Lord North — the precise time for the resignation was to be left to the choice of Hastings. Without question or parley, he, in his own name, summoned a Council, to which Francis came, and at which Clavering took the usual oath as Governor-General. As such also he sent his Persian interpreter to Hastings with a letter, requiring him to deliver the keys of the fort and treasury. Meanwhile, in another chamber, Hastings took the chair with Barwell by his side, and declared himself determined to maintain his just authority until further orders should arrive. Then it was that the attachment of his countrymen stood Hastings in good stead. Had there been, as was feared, an appeal to arms, there seems little question that all, or nearly all, would have ranged themselves upon his side. Seeing this, the opposite party agreed, though unwillingly, to his proposal; that they should ask, and should abide by, the opinion of the Judges of the Supreme Court. This was no season for delay; the case being thus referred to the Judges, they met the same evening, and continued all night in anxious deliberation. At four the next morning Sir Elijah reported their unanimous judgment, that the resignation of Hastings was invalid, and the assumption of power by Clavering illegal. Thus was the Governor-General enabled to maintain his ground. On this occasion he justly felt that his all had been at stake. Writing at the time he says: "If I am gone, and Clavering in "possession, they may prove what they will against me, "even rape and murder." And a few years later we find him mention Impey as "a man to whose support I was "at one time indebted for the safety of my fortune, "honour, and reputation." *

* Memoirs by Gleig, vol. ii. p. 255. Mr. Gleig does not give the exact date of this last letter, but from the context it appears to have been written early in the year 1780. I can by no means agree with those who conceive that it alludes to the case of Nuncomar.

But Hastings was not content with his success on this occasion. He endeavoured to pursue it with a degree of violence and indiscretion scarcely less than his rival had displayed. He prevailed on Barwell to concur in a Resolution that General Clavering, by attempting to usurp the functions of Governor-General, had surrendered and resigned both his place in Council and his office as Commander in Chief of the Indian forces. Against this flagrant abuse of victory Clavering and Francis remonstrated in vain. Now, in their turn, they appealed to the Judges of the Supreme Court. Sir Elijah Impey, in the name of his brethren, pronounced it as their unanimous decision, that the Council had no legal power to remove one of its members or declare his seat vacant. This salutary mediation between two vehement adverse parties—these alternate checks to the excesses of each—seem to me to do honour to Sir Elijah's impartial sense of justice, and serve to disprove the charge brought against his conduct at this juncture, as though, for some corrupt purpose of his own, he had been a mere instrument and puppet in the hands of Hastings.

In this struggle the temper of Clavering—a frank, plain soldier—had been grievously chafed. Only a few weeks afterwards, in August, 1777, he sickened and died. At a later period his friend Mr. Francis thus portrays his character: "He was a strict, rigid man; "not, as some thought, cruel, but rigid, even to prudery, "as I have sometimes told him, when I have seen him "refuse little offerings of fruit and flowers, that certainly "did not come within the legal prohibition of presents."*

It is said, that the last appearance in public of the dying man was, after much solicitation, as a guest at his rival's wedding-feast. Not many days before General Clavering expired, Warren Hastings married Marian Imhoff. † The first husband of this lady was a German by birth, a Baron by title, a miniature painter by profession. Hastings had first met them eight years before,

* Speech in the House of Commons, Feb. 26. 1788.

† "A native, we have somewhere read, of Archangel," says Mr. Macaulay of this lady. (Essays, vol. iii. p. 339.) The precise authority for that statement appears to be the contemporary translator of the Seir Mutakhareen. (Vol. ii. p. 476. note.)

on embarking in England for Madras, when he found them passengers with him on board the "Duke of Grafton." The Baroness was in a high degree graceful and engaging; the Baron, at least in equal measure, needy and intent on gain. Between the fair Marian and Hastings an attachment soon arose; an attachment which, like all his feelings, whether of love or hate, was calm, but deep-rooted, and most stedfast; an attachment which appears to have continued without cloud or change for well nigh fifty years. A kind of Council was held between the lady, her husband and her lover. It was agreed that advantage should be taken of the looseness of the marriage-tie in Northern Germany; that the Baroness, with the Baron's full consent, should commence a suit for a divorce in the law-courts of Franconia; that meanwhile they should continue to dwell together; and that, on obtaining the desired release, Hastings should make the Baroness his wife, adopting for his own her two children by the Baron. It may well be supposed, that in this negotiation the pecuniary interests of Imhoff himself were not forgotten. Some years elapsed before the requisite formalities could be gone through in the Franconian Courts; but at length, in the summer of 1777, the sentence of divorce reached India; the Baroness became Mrs. Hastings, and the Baron returned to Europe with wealth far greater than his skill in portrait painting could have gained. *

These transactions, which may be considered as belonging only to private life, were at a later period drawn into the public scene. When Hastings himself returned to Europe, when his conduct had become the mark for Parliamentary speeches and Parliamentary impeachments, his enemies were never weary of descanting on the dangerous fascinations of his wife. She was accused of receiving presents in India: she was accused of making presents in England. Her favourable reception at St.

* It appears from the letters of Goethe to Madame de Stein, as first published in 1848, that Imhoff, on his return to Europe, married one of Madame de Stein's sisters, and was often seen in the Weimar circles. When he died, in 1788, Goethe, who had discerned his character, goes so far as to say: *Deine Schwester wird auch einsehen lernen, dass er zu ihrem glück gestorben sei.* (See vol. iii. p. 308.)

James's increased the Opposition rage. Through her it was endeavoured to aim an insidious blow against the consort of the Sovereign. What other ground, it was malignantly asked, except some sordid interest, some share in the plundered "wealth of Ormus and of Ind," could propitiate towards the relict of Mr. Imhoff the most pure and spotless of Queens? All the satirical poems of that period teem with such attacks.*

In the council-chamber of Bengal the decease of General Clavering was nearly balanced by the arrival of Mr. Wheler. The new member took part, in most cases, against the Governor-General with Francis. But, besides that he showed himself a far less acrimonious opponent, the power of the casting-vote still left on every question the practical ascendancy in the hands of Hastings.

From the supreme government of India let us pass to the subordinate-Council of Madras. There, though on a smaller scale, dissension had grown to a still more formidable height. Some years since a war had been waged against the petty kingdom of Tanjore. The Rajah, one of the Mahratta princes, had been taken prisoner and deposed. The territory had been seized and transferred to the Nabob of Arcot. At home the Directors, after no small amount of wavering, had disapproved these measures. They despatched peremptory orders to restore, without loss of time, the Rajah to his throne. Moreover, they sent out to the chief place at Madras a personal friend of the Rajah, the former Governor, Pigot, who had recently been raised to an Irish peerage. Thus from the first moment of his landing again on Indian ground, Lord Pigot found himself in direct opposition to the leading members of his Council. He did, however, proceed to Tanjore and reinstate the Rajah. But on his return he saw a formidable combination leagued against him; at its head Mahomed Ali, the Nabob of Arcot.

* Thus in the Political Eclogues:

"O'er Mornington French prattle holds command;
"Hastings buys German phlegm at second-hand."

And in the Rolliad we are invited to a description of "the ivory "bed which was lately presented to Her Majesty by Mrs. Hastings."

Mahomed Ali, the old ally of the English, and maintained in his dominion by their means, had not, as was expected, fixed his residence in any of his own palaces or cities. Abandoning all appearance of state, he dwelt in a common country-house, near the suburbs of Madras. There he was ever intriguing and caballing with several of the Company's servants. They would supply him with money at any sudden call, and well knew how to make such loans most highly advantageous to themselves. Foremost among these usurers stood Mr. Paul Benfield, a man to whom Burke's eloquence has given immortal fame,—if fame indeed it should be called! For, as the misdeeds of Verres will live for ever in the glowing denunciations of Cicero, so has the genius of Burke poured its imperishable lustre over the whole tortuous track of the Madras money-lenders, and rescued from oblivion the "Debts of the Nabob of Arcot."*

Paul Benfield was of humble birth and of no patrimony. He had filled a small place in the Company's service at a salary of a few hundred pounds a year, and was chiefly conspicuous for keeping the finest carriages and horses at Madras. His ostentatious habits of expense did not seem consistent with any large accumulation of wealth. To the public surprise he now brought forward a claim on the Nabob, for money lent to the amount of 162,000*l.*, besides another claim on individuals in Tanjore to the amount of 72,000*l.* For the whole of this enormous sum he held assignments on the revenues and standing crops in Tanjore; and he pleaded that his interest ought not to be affected by the reinstatement of the Rajah. The Nabob, when consulted on the matter, at once admitted and confirmed the claim. In this case Lord Pigot might well suspect collusion. He might also reasonably question the right of the Nabob to make any such assignments in Tanjore. The majority of his Council, however, were inclined to favour these demands, and there ensued a long train of angry altercations. At length the issue was taken on a side-point of small importance—the desire of Lord Pigot to appoint Mr. Russel, one of his own friends, as Resident at Tanjore. Finding

* See his great speech of Feb. 28. 1785.

himself out-voted, Lord Pigot first set the dangerous example—so soon to recoil upon himself—of overstepping the bounds of law. He assumed that the Governor was an integral part of the Council; that he was not bound by the majority against him, and might refuse to carry out any decision in which he had not concurred. The opposite doctrine was maintained, no less vehemently, by the other members. Upon this an arbitrary order from Lord Pigot declared them suspended from their functions; and they, in return, concerted measures for his arrest. The commander of the forces, Sir Robert Fletcher (the same who, in Bengal, had been cashiered), was at that time ill; but the second in command, Colonel Stuart, was upon their side. On the 24th of August, 1776, the Colonel passed the greater part of the day, in company or in business, with Lord Pigot; he both breakfasted and dined with him as his familiar friend, and was driving in the carriage with him when, according to the Colonel's previous orders, the carriage was surrounded and stopped by troops. His Lordship was then informed that he was their prisoner. As such he was forthwith conveyed to St. Thomas's Mount. There he was left in an officer's house, with a battalion of artillery to guard him, while all the powers of Government were assumed and administered by his opponents in the Council.

This violent act of the Council of Madras against their Governor, produced, at a later period, a keen discussion in the House of Commons. Admiral Pigot declared, on that occasion, that his brother had been offered a bribe amounting to 600,000*l.* in English money, only to defer, and that for a short and specified time, the reinstatement of the Rajah of Tanjore. On the other hand, Mr. Stratton, one of the members of the Council who had ordered the Governor's arrest, said it was a fact well known, that Lord Pigot might have had his liberty again in three days, had he chosen to accept it.*

In the Courts of Directors and Proprietors there appeared upon this subject the usual fluctuation. There was, however, a better reason for it, in a case where beyond all doubt neither party had been free from blame.

* Debate in the House of Commons, April 16. 1779.

At length it was agreed that the members of the Council who had concurred in this arrest should be recalled; and on their return they became liable, under Resolutions of the House of Commons, to a trial and a fine. At the same time a commission was prepared under the Company's seal, by which Lord Pigot was restored to his office; but he was directed within one week to give up the Government to his successor, and embark for England. By these means it was intended to avoid a triumph, or the appearance of a triumph, to either side. But long before these orders could be received in India, Lord Pigot was beyond the reach of any human sentence. After eight months of confinement he died at St. Thomas's Mount.

Early in 1778 the government of Madras was assumed by Sir Thomas Rumbold. He might avoid dissensions with his Council, but on other grounds he incurred, and not unjustly, the censure of the Court of Directors. In less than three years we find him utterly dismissed from their service. He was accused of tyranny to the Chiefs of the Northern Circars, of injustice to the Nizam, of arrogance to Hyder Ali. Nor did even his personal character stand clear from all reproach. It was proved that, during his two years of government, he was enabled to remit to London more than three times the amount of his legal salary.* In the Session of 1782 a Bill of Pains and Penalties against him for breaches of public trust was brought in by Mr. Dundas; but ceased to attract attention, or to be actively pressed, amidst the Ministerial changes that ensued. Well might Mr. Fox observe, however: "If the Bill should be lost for want of attendance, that would not clear the character of Sir "Thomas Rumbold."

* Second Report of the Committee of Secrecy, 1781. Sir Thomas alleged, in reply, that he had at the time property of his own in India; and this was proved by the evidence and accounts of his attorney, Mr. Price. But, on making full allowance for these, says Professor Wilson, "there still remains a considerable sum to be "accounted for, to explain the large amount of his remittances to "England." (Note to Mill's Hist. vol. iv. p. 151., and another, p. 172.)

CHAPTER V.

(CHAP. LXIX. OF THE HISTORY.)

In the last two chapters we have traced the progress of our Eastern empire when not assailed, nor even threatened, by any European enemy. The scene is now about to change. That war which, commencing in North America, troubled not England only but also France and Spain, cast its baleful shadows to the Mexican seas on the one side, and to the shores of Coromandel on the other. Then it was that the experience, the energy, the high statesmanship of Hastings were signally displayed. Then it was, that the value of his services was felt even by his adversaries in Downing Street or Leadenhall. Lord North, to his honour, laid aside all party resentment. As he afterwards stated in the House of Commons, he knew the abilities of Mr. Hastings, and felt that this was not the time for any change in the government of India.* Thus, when the period of Five Years fixed by the Regulating Act had expired, the Governor-General was quietly and without a struggle re-appointed.

At the beginning of 1778, the tidings were already rife among the native races, that YENGHI DUNIA, or New World, as they called America, had broken loose from the country of the COOMPANY SAHIB.† Already might they hear the rising sounds of exultation from the rival settlements of Chandernagore and Pondicherry. But the first sign or symptom that reached Hastings of French cabals in India came from the Mahratta States. These had grown to greatness in the decline of the Mogul empire and risen on its ruins, but had since been weakened

* Speech, June 1. 1786. Parl. Hist. vol. xxvi. p. 46.

† Seir Mutakhareen, vol. iii. p. 332.

by dissensions of their own. Among themselves, as in the venerable monarchy from the ruins of which they had sprung, there was a wide line between the real and the rightful exercise of power. The lineal heir of Sivajee, the true Sovereign in name, had become a mere state-prisoner in the palace of Sattara. The actual authority was vested in a great magistrate, or chief of the Council, who was called the Peshwah, and who held court with regal state at Poonah. Through a strange anomaly that Ministerial office descended by hereditary right, and sometimes therefore devolved upon a minor. The Peshwah, besides his own or the Rajah of Sattara's dominions, always claimed, and occasionally exercised, a kind of feudal supremacy over the other Mahratta principalities that lay scattered in the wide expanse between the hill-forts of Mysore and the waters of the Ganges. First among them were the houses of Scindiah and of Holkar; the Guicowar, who ruled in Guzerat; and the Bonslah, or Rajah of Berar, a scion of the line of Sivajee. All these Mahratta chiefs, in common with their subjects, held the Brahmin faith; in that respect, as in some others, forming a remarkable contrast to the race of the Mahomedan conquerors beside them, as the Nizam and the Visier. The mean origin of the first Mahratta freebooters is denoted even in the hereditary titles of their princes; the Guicowar, for example, signifies only the cow-herd. It is denoted also by the simple and abstemious habits which they long preserved. A Mussulman historian, the contemporary of Warren Hastings, describes the most powerful Mahratta ruler of his time, as living only on the food of the poorest peasant —on black bread made of Badjrah, unripe mangoes, and raw red pepper. "Let the reader," says the more refined Mahomedan, "guess the taste of the whole nation by "this sample of its chiefs. And although," he adds, "they have come to command kingdoms and to rule over "empires, they are still the beggars they have been. "Go to any of them, from the lowest clerk to the Mi-"nister of State, and the first words which you shall "hear from them are always these:—'What have you "'brought for me?—Have you brought anything for "'me?' and should any man go empty-handed to them, "they would strip him of his turban and coat, and then "recommend him devoutly to Almighty God!"*

Between the chiefs at Poonah and the Presidency of Bombay there had been in former years some intricate negotiations and some desultory wars. The English had obtained possession of the island of Salsette, which, so lately as 1750, the Mahrattas had wrested from the Portuguese. They had also given shelter to a deposed and exiled Peshwah named Ragoba, or Ragonaut Row, who still carried on a cabal, and kept up a party, at home. Such was the posture of affairs when the Governor-General was startled by the tidings that a French ship had anchored in one of the Mahratta ports, and that a French agent had set out for Poonah. This Frenchman proved to be the Chevalier de St. Lubin, an adventurer who had formerly taken some part in the intrigues of the Presidency of Madras, and who had now obtained from his own government a clandestine commission to treat with the Mahrattas. It was reported to Hastings, that already they had agreed to his terms, and consented to yield to the French the port of Choul, on the coast of Malabar. "War is now inevitable," said Hastings to his Council; "let us then be the first to strike a blow!" In this suggestion he was, as usual, supported by Barwell, and, as usual, opposed by Francis and Wheler, but, as usual also, his casting-vote prevailed. It was resolved, that a division of the Bengal army should be sent across the Jumna, and march through Bundelcund upon the Peshwah's country. Orders were sent to the Council of Bombay to enter into a concert of measures with Ragoba, and strive by all means to forward his pretensions. At the same time the Governor-General commenced an active negotiation, and sought to form a close alliance with another claimant to a principal place among the Mahratta chiefs—with Bonslah, the ruler of Berar.

It has been questioned, how far in these dealings with the Mahrattas, Hastings acted strictly in good faith.

* Seir Mutakhareen, vol. iii. p. 228. The word *Gai* or *Gao*, which lies at the root of *Guicowar*, when combined with *rus* (the Latin *ros*), forms the poetical name which the Hindoos give to milk; *gaorus*, or cow-dew.

Certainly, at least, he is entitled to the praise, at a most difficult crisis, of energy and skill. The news of the disaster at Saratoga, far from damping his spirit, only animated his endeavours. "If it be really true"—thus he spoke to his Council—"that the British arms and influence "have suffered so severe a check in the Western world, "it is the more incumbent on those who are charged "with the interests of Great Britain in the East to ex-"ert themselves for the retrieval of the national loss."* Only a few days after the Governor-General had thus spoken—only a few weeks after the British troops had marched—the further intelligence which the policy of Hastings had anticipated came. On the 7th of July, a letter from Mr. Baldwin, the Consul of England at Cairo, brought the news to Calcutta, that in the month of March preceding, war had been proclaimed both in London and in Paris. Not an hour did Hastings lose. "On the "same day," he says, "we wrote to the Governor of Fort "St. George, to prepare for the immediate attack of "Pondicherry; and we set them an example on the 10th, "by the capture of Chandernagore."†

Pondicherry was invested by Sir Hector Munro, at the head of the Madras army. It yielded, after a brave resistance, and an engagement off the coast, between the French and English squadrons. Then the French retained nothing in India but Mahé, a small fort and settlement on the coast of Malabar; and this also was reduced by the English from Madras, in the course of the ensuing spring. Meanwhile, in Bengal, the zeal of Hastings had directed the most active measures of defence. Several further batteries were raised along the river. Several armed cruizers were equipped. Stores for three months, both of ammunition and victuals, were laid up in Fort William. Nine new battalions of Sepoys were enrolled. A demand for three battalions more was made upon the Rajah of Benares, and was agreed to, the Rajah being regarded as a feudatory prince, and required to contribute

* Declaration in Council, June 22. 1778. Burke's Articles of Charge, xx.

† To Laurence Sulivan, Esq., August 18. 1778. Memoirs by Gleig, vol. ii. p. 203.

his share to the burthens of the war. The artillery was reinforced by recruits from the native Lascars; while the Europeans at Calcutta, to the number of one thousand, were enrolled as Militia in case of need. "Mr. Francis" — thus writes the Governor-General to a private friend — "affects to regard our means as insufficient, our "resources as already exhausted, a French invasion as "impending, and the country incapable of resistance. I "am, for my own part, confirmed in my opinion, that the "French, if they ever attempt the invasion of Bengal. "must make their way to it by an alliance with one of "the powers of the country; and the only power with "which that can be at present effected is the Mahratta."

To this Mahratta expedition, therefore, the eyes of Hastings were anxiously turned. At first it was far from prospering. The commanding officer, Colonel Leslie, instead of pursuing his march after he had crossed the Jumna, loitered during four months, without the least necessity, in the plains of Bundelcund. His recall was unanimously voted in the Council-chamber at Calcutta, and was only anticipated by tidings of his death. His successor, Colonel Goddard, was an excellent and enterprising officer. He advanced at once into Berar. But further delays ensued in consequence of successive revolutions at the Court of Poonah. To await the effects of these, orders to halt were sent to Colonel Goddard from the Council of Bombay. Perhaps, however, their real object was to clutch the expected credit for themselves, since before the close of the year they sent forth an expedition of their own. That body of troops exceeded 4000 in number; it was accompanied by Ragoba; and the principal officer who served in it was Colonel Egerton. But by a most infelicitous arrangement, the superintendence and control of the expedition was vested by the Council in a travelling Committee; or, in other words, field-deputies, according to the former precedents of Holland.

On climbing the Ghauts or passes and entering the Mahrattas' territory, Colonel Egerton was not joined, as Ragoba had encouraged him to hope, by any chief of importance, nor by any considerable number of adherents. On the contrary, he saw around him irregular troops of hostile cavalry, retiring as he advanced, but active and successful in cutting off his supplies. His own movements at this juncture were sufficiently deliberate: only eight miles in eleven days. In January, 1779, he had reached a point within sixteen miles of Poonah. There he found an army assembled to oppose him, and the Committee-men, losing courage, made up their minds to a retreat. A retreat was begun accordingly that night, and continued until the next afternoon, when, at a place called Wargaum, the English found themselves surrounded and hemmed in. One brave subaltern, Captain Hartley, offered to cut his way through, and to carry back the little army to Bombay, declaring that he could rely upon his men. His superior officers, on the other hand, deemed any such attempt chimerical, and determined to seek their safety in negotiation. The terms required for their unmolested passage were hard indeed, yet, hard though they were, could not be disputed unless by arms. It was agreed that all the acquisitions gained by the English from the Mahrattas, since the peace of 1756, should be restored. It was further agreed, that the person of Ragoba should be given up, not indeed to the Poonah chiefs, but to Scindiah.

In mitigation of this last ignominious clause we may observe that, even previously, Ragoba, seeing the ill plight of the English army, and despairing of its safe return by force of arms, had declared his own intention of surrendering himself to Scindiah, as to a mediator and umpire rather than an enemy. Already for some days had he been in correspondence with that chief. The Committee felt, therefore, the less scruple in consenting to his surrender when required as a stipulation of their treaty. Yet, in spite of some such extenuating circumstances, the convention of Wargaum may justly be regarded as the most discreditable to the arms of England ever framed since they had first appeared on Indian soil. To the English, in all three Presidencies, it seemed like a Saratoga in miniature. To the French partisans throughout India it gave a bolder spirit and a louder tone. It combined, if not the whole Mahratta empire, yet several more of the Mahratta chiefs against us. It revived the hopes, and disclosed the animosity, both of the Nizam and Hyder Ali; but on the mind of the Governor-General it had no effect. As ever, that was firm and fearless. He refused to alter his plans: he refused to recall his troops. On the contrary, he at once directed Goddard to advance. General Goddard (for to that higher rank was he speedily promoted) justified the confidence of Hastings by his energy and skill. In his campaign of that year, and of the following, he, in great measure, retrieved and worthily maintained the honour of the British arms. At one time we see him reduce by storm the fort of Ahmedabad; at another time, by a siege, the city of Bassein. On another occasion he appears gaining a victory over the entire force, 40,000 strong, of Scindiah and Holkar combined. Meanwhile Ragoba had found early means to escape from the hands of Scindiah, and took shelter in Surat. Thus the advantages to the Mahrattas from the day of Wargaum proved fleeting and short-lived.

In a hilly district lying to the south of Agra, and bearing, at that time, the name of Gohud, Hastings waged war upon a smaller scale. With the Hindoo prince, or Rana, of that district he had concluded an alliance. The Rana being, in consequence, attacked by the Mahrattas, applied to his confederates in Bengal; and a small body of troops, under Captain Popham, was sent to his support. Not merely did Captain Popham, with little assistance from the Rana, clear Gohud from its invaders, but he carried the war into some of the Mahratta country; he besieged and reduced the city of Lahar; and he gained renown throughout the East when he took, by escalade, a rock-fortress which was deemed impregnable — the "castled crag" of Gwalior.*

In these and his other military measures Hastings was not left to rely upon his own unassisted judgment. At the first outbreak of the war with France the Cabinet

* The strength of this rock-fortress appears at all times to have filled the Gwalior troops with overweening confidence. So lately as 1843, we find the Resident at Gwalior report them as "vauntingly "declaring that they are come out to resist the further advance of "the Governor-General, and to make the British force recross the "Chumbul!" (Letter of Colonel Sleeman, Dec. 25. 1843. Gwalior Papers, p. 151.) Only four days afterwards, the great battle of Maharaj-poor corrected this slight misapprehension.

of London had determined to send back to the Indian service the most illustrious of its veterans; the same who had led the charge at Wandewash, and received the keys of Pondicherry. Sir Eyre Coote, invested with a two-fold rank as commander of the forces and as member of the Council, arrived at Calcutta in March 1779. He had no disposition to ally himself with Francis, or intrigue against Hastings; yet he gave nearly as much trouble to the latter as ever had Francis himself. The lapse of almost twenty years since his last successes had not been without effect, either on his body or his mind. He had become less active in his movements, and more fretful in his temper. A love of gain had grown up side by side with his love of glory; and strongly impressed with his own great merits, he was ever prone to deem himself slighted or neglected. It required constant care in Hastings to avoid or to explain away any causes of offence between them, while at the same time the Governor-General was striving to obtain for him a large increase to his allowances from the Nabob of Oude, or other less obvious quarters. These additional allowances to Sir Eyre Coote were urged, at a later period, as additional charges against Hastings himself, although he had never sought to derive from them the smallest selfish advantage, and was only zealous — too zealous it might be — to carry out his public objects by the helpmates or by the instruments, which he had not chosen, but which a higher authority assigned him.*

Neither from Sir Eyre, nor yet from Wheler, at this juncture, did Francis obtain more than occasional support — far distant from the constant concurrence of Clavering and Monson. He found, also, that by his unavailing course of opposition, all his humbler partisans were shut out from every share of patronage and power. At this juncture, therefore, he showed some readiness to relax in his hostility. On the other part, Hastings likewise had several strong motives to desire reconcilement. He wished to rid himself of a daily-recurring obstruction.

* See Burke's Articles of Charge, xvi. sect. 36., &c. Before the close of 1779, we find Hastings thus write of Sir Eyre:—"My letters "have been all friendly to him; his to me all petulant and suspicious; "I know not why or for what. I bear with him, and will bear, for I "am lost if he abandons me." (Memoirs by Gleig, vol. ii. p. 242.)

He wished to release his friend Barwell, who had amassed a large fortune, and who was eager to return with it to England, but who had promised to remain in India, so long as his help was needed. Under these circumstances, early in the year 1780, an engagement was concluded, according to which Francis proposed to desist from systematic opposition, and to acquiesce in all the measures for the prosecution of the Mahratta war, while Hastings undertook to appoint Mr. Fowke, and some other adherents of Francis, to certain lucrative posts. On the faith of this agreement, and with the full consent of Hastings, Barwell embarked for Europe. But, only a few weeks afterwards, the old dissension at the Council-Board burst forth anew. The immediate cause was the expedition in Gohud. Hastings alleged that this was only a branch of his Mahratta war; Francis, on the contrary, maintained that this was a separate object, to which he was not pledged, and which he might freely oppose. The Governor-General, on this occasion, lost, or laid aside, his customary calmness, and in reply to a Minute of his rival, placed on record, in Council, the following words:—"I do not trust to Mr. Francis's promises of "candour, convinced that he is incapable of it. I judge "of his public conduct by his private, which I have "found to be void of truth and honour." After such expressions Hastings may be justly charged with the entire blame of the scandal which ensued. When the Council broke up, Francis drew the Governor-General into another chamber, and read to him a challenge; it was accepted by Hastings, and they met on the day but one after—on the morning of the 17th of August. It was between five and six o'clock, and the sun had not yet fully risen on the sacred river and the boundless plain; but there was already the stir of life among the dusky races of Bengal. "I am ashamed," thus afterwards wrote Hastings, "to have been made an actor in this "silly affair; and I declare to you, upon my honour, that "such was my sense of it at the time that I was much "disturbed by an old woman whose curiosity prompted "her to stand by as a spectatress." He adds: "A scene "so little comprehended by the natives of this part of "the world. attracted others of the same stamp from the "adjacent villages to partake in the entertainment."* With surprise indeed they must have gazed. None of their own most barbaric rites—neither the zealot who rushes forward to be crushed by the car of Juggernaut, nor the widow compelled to share the funeral pile of her dead lord, nor the worshipper of Siva, deeming that he gains the favour of the idol if he sheds the blood of an innocent wayfarer—none of these, when first beheld, could have more greatly amazed the island-strangers than were the Hindoos to see two members of that Council, sent over for their governance, engage in single combat, according to certain fancied rules: each seeking, as he would explain it, not to destroy the other, but only to clear himself; each taking a careful aim at his antagonist, yet each ready, should he see that antagonist fall, to express a generous sympathy, and to staunch, to the utmost of his power, the wound which he had made.

Hastings and Francis fired at nearly the same instant; Hastings was unharmed, but Francis was shot through the side. He was conveyed to an adjacent house, where the surgeons found, that although his wound was severe, his life was not in danger. In the course of the same day Hastings sent his secretary with a message to the sick man, expressing his concern, and offering to call upon him when his health should be sufficiently restored. Francis coldly acknowledged the civility, but said, that after what had passed, the Governor-General and himself could meet only at the Council-Board. There accordingly they did meet for some weeks more; but early in the next December Francis gave up his office and returned to England. In taking that step, he did no more than fulfil an intention which, finding his influence wholly declined, he had formed even in the preceding year. At that time his position and his purpose were delineated, as follows, by his chief: "Francis is miserable; and is weak enough to declare it, in a manner "much resembling a passionate woman whose hands are "held to prevent her from doing mischief. He vows he "will go home in November, but I do not believe that "his resolution is so fixed as he pretends."†

* To L. Sulivan, Esq., August 30. 1780.
† Ibid., April 18. 1779.

Dissension with Francis, however fierce, was no novelty to Hastings. But during the same period he had to wage a painful warfare with a former friend—Sir Elijah Impey. In the Regulating Act of 1773 the limits between the judicial and political powers which it instituted had not been duly defined. Thus it happened, that on several points in practice the Supreme Court came to clash with the Supreme Council. Moreover, the new Judges had gone out with overstrained ideas of their rights and privileges. They would scarcely acknowledge any co-ordinate authority for which they could find no precedent in Westminster Hall. "Who"—thus on one occasion spoke Mr. Justice Le Maistre—"who are the Provincial Chief and Council of Dacca? "They are no Corporation in the eye of the law. A "man might as well say that he was commanded by the "King of the Fairies as by the Council of Dacca; be-"cause the law knows no such body."* On these principles it happened that the most cherished customs and feelings, both of the Hindoos and of the Mussulmans, were often set at nought. It was impossible for the Governor-General to view their resentment with indifference or without an effort at redress. The consequent dissension between the Supreme Court and the Supreme Council for a long time only smouldered. At last, in the beginning of 1780, it burst into open flame. The immediate cause was the progress of a suit which had been brought against a wealthy landholder, the Rajah of Cossijurah, by Cossinaut Baboo his agent at Calcutta, when the Judge issued a writ to sequester his lands and goods. For this object an armed band, consisting of sixty men and commanded by a Serjeant of the Court, was despatched to Cossijurah. The Rajah, with a just apprehension of the terrors of the law, had already fled from his house. Nevertheless it was forcibly entered by the gang of bailiffs; nor did they even shrink from breaking open the ZENANA, or the women's chambers, ever held sacred in the East amidst the worst barbarities of war. The servants of the Rajah stood at the threshold

* Appendix No. 9. to the Report of the Committee of 1781; and note to Mill's History of India, vol. iv. p. 317.

ready to resist, so far as they could resist, what they deemed the dishonour of their master, but some of them were wounded and the rest beaten back and overborne. Nor was this all. It was alleged by the Rajah, that not only had his Zenana been forced and his property plundered, but his place of worship also had been stripped of its ornaments, and his collection of revenue been prevented.

When these tidings reached Calcutta, the Governor-General, supported on this one occasion by his Council's unanimous assent, took, as was his duty, effectual measures of redress. A circular was issued to the landholders of Bengal explaining that, unless in certain specified cases, they owed no obedience to the mandates of the Supreme Court. Upon this, all patience and all prudence departed from Sir Elijah Impey and his brother Judges. Even the most violent steps did not seem to them too strong. They cast into prison Mr. North Naylor, the Company's attorney, merely because, as he was bound to do, he had obeyed the orders of the Council. They caused a summons to be served on every member of the Council requiring him to appear at their bar, and to answer for his public acts. Hastings and the other members refused to obey the call. The Judges pronounced the refusal to be "a clear contempt of His Majesty's law and of his Courts." It is difficult to say to what extremities—scarcely short of civil war—this collision might have grown, had not Cossinaut, no doubt on some secret inducements held out to him by the Governor-General, suddenly dropped his actions at law; thus depriving the Judges of all present materials upon which their wrath could build.

The immediate case might thus be dealt with, but a more permanent remedy was needed. With this view, the fertile brain of Hastings devised another scheme. Under the Act of 1773 there were certain judicial powers which belonged to the Supreme Council as a tribunal of appeal from some of the provincial Courts, but which the Supreme Council had neither sufficient time, nor yet sufficient knowledge, to exert. Hastings proposed that these powers should be henceforth vested in a Judge appointed by the Governor and Council, and removable at their pleasure, and that this newly appointed Judge should be no other than the Chief Justice of the Supreme Court. Such was the scheme which, in September 1780, Hastings laid before his colleagues in the Government, and which, in spite of strenuous opposition from Francis and from Wheler, was carried through. To Francis, who almost immediately afterwards returned to England, there only remained the spiteful satisfaction of spreading far and wide among his friends and the public at home the charge, that the Chief Justice had been bribed from a course of opposition by a new salary of 8,000*l.* a year.

It must be owned, that whenever there has been strife between two persons, and whenever that strife is ended by the one accepting from the other a post of honour and of profit, we shall seldom err in casting heavy censure on the character of one or both. In this case, however, there are several circumstances of alleviation or defence which were not known to, or not weighed by, the public at the time, but which demand the careful consideration of a later age. In the first place, there appears no inconsistency in the course pursued on this occasion by Sir Elijah Impey. His proceedings on the suit of Cossinaut were already closed. On the general question, he had struggled and protested against that portion of judicial power claimed by the members of the Supreme Council; he was bound therefore to be satisfied, when those members, of their own accord, divested themselves of that judicial power, and transferred it to judicial hands. No complaint, however slight, of his reconciliation could surely have been raised had any other judge but himself been named to the new post. Impey would have done far better to decline it, yet it does not follow, that in accepting it his motives were all of a sordid kind. In his secret letters to his nearest kindred some weeks afterwards, while, adverting to the great additional labour which he had consented to discharge, he declares that he did so — "in the hope that I may be able to convert "these courts which, from ignorance or corruption, have "hitherto been a curse, into a blessing. No pecuniary "satisfaction has been offered or even mentioned to me." *

* Sir Elijah Impey to his brother in England, November 12. 1780.

Thus he had taken the duty without any promise of reward, although in the same private letter we find him frankly acknowledge—"but I do not imagine it is in-"tended that my trouble is to go unrecompensed." Some weeks afterwards the Council did accordingly determine that a salary, not, as was said, of eight thousand, but of five thousand pounds a year, should be attached to the new office. * Then, however, Sir Elijah stated, that he should refuse to accept any part of this money until the opinion of the Lord Chancellor had been asked and obtained from England. There are still extant the regular vouchers of the sums paid to the Chief Justice in pursuance of the Council's order, and paid back by him to the Company's account. And in point of fact, neither then nor at any time afterwards was a single rupee of this new salary received for his own use by Sir Elijah Impey. †

The Mahratta campaign, and the altercations with Francis and with Impey, however burthensome to Hastings, were not, at this time, his only, nor yet his greatest, care. Another and more pressing danger rose in view. Hyder Ali, the mighty sovereign of Mysore, had observed with much displeasure, the British expedition to Mahé. On several lesser points also he had been most imprudently thwarted and chafed by Sir Thomas Rumbold at Madras. With his usual energy of character, he made few complaints, but actively matured his plans. He saw that the opportunity was favourable; that the English were now entangled in a difficult war with the Mahrattas, and that a French armament was soon expected on the coast of Coromandel. He drew together an army which amounted, or at least which popular terror magnified, to 90,000 men. These forces, though wild and savage, were not wholly wanting in European discipline; they had been trained, in part, by good officers from France, and

* Minutes of the Revenue Council, December 22. 1780.

† See the facts of the case, and the documents to prove it, set forth at full length in the Memoirs of Impey, by his son, pp. 209—229. And again, pp. 256—263. The reader should be, of course, on his guard against the writer's bias, and should judge only from the documents themselves.

they drew into the field, with competent artillerymen, one hundred pieces of artillery.

Besides these resources of skill and of experience, there were other expedients which stand in glaring contrast to the former, but which, in the opinion of the Sovereign of Mysore, were not less conducive to success. He gave orders that, in all the temples of his capital, there should be performed, with the utmost solemnity, the mysterious rite of the JEBBUM. It is singular that both Hyder and his son Tippoo (the one at least a nominal, and the other a zealous, Mussulman) appear to have held implicit faith in the Hindoo forms of superstition which are denoted by that word. The forms are of various kinds. Sometimes, to obtain the end which the prince desires, the Brahmins stand up to their breasts in water, beating the water with their hands, and howling forth their incantations. Sometimes, with the same view, a snake of the Cobra Capella kind is suspended by the tail from the roof of the apartment, while incense is burned at a fire kindled immediately below. In all these ceremonies, the presence of salt was deemed as unlucky as the spilling it in England.*

The Government of Madras was, almost to the last, unconscious of its danger. Early in April 1780, Sir Thomas Rumbold had sailed for England, congratulating himself, in the final Minute he recorded, that all was tranquil, and that no disturbance of the calm was to be feared. His successor, Mr. Whitehill, was a man wholly unequal to the charge. Almost the same might be said of Sir Hector Munro, the commander of the forces; for either age or climate had dealt hardly with the hero of Buxar. Thus the English chiefs were nearly taken by surprise, when, in the height of summer, the horsemen of Mysore, the vanguard of Hyder's army, came dashing down the passes that lead from their wild hills. This was the invasion which some years afterwards

* See Colonel Wilks's South of India, vol. ii. p. 254. note. Our own superstition as to salt-spilling has, in all probability, an Eastern origin. But there is a curious passage in Cervantes, showing that at one time in Spain it was confined to members of a single noble family—the Mendozas. (Don Quixote, ch. 58. vol. vi. p. 154. ed. Paris 1814.)

was described with so much glowing eloquence by Burke. This was the "black cloud that hung for a while on the "declivities of the mountains." This was the "menacing "meteor which blackened all the horizon until it sud- "denly burst, and poured down the whole of its contents "upon the plains of the Carnatic."*

At the approach of Hyder's army, the frontier-posts, held by Sepoys, surrendered wiih but slight resistance; and his onward progress was marked by fire and the sword. From the summit of St. Thomas's Mount the people of Madras could see, on the horizon, columns of dark smoke ascend from the burning villages. The ladies and the children (and may we not include some gentlemen?) were filled with terror and affright. Their gay villas around the city were forsaken, while the narrow space behind the cannon of Fort St. George was thronged. In the field there were already some not wholly inconsiderable forces. Sir Hector Munro had above five thousand men, and Colonel Baillie above three. Some active and useful aid to these forces was expected from the constant ally of England, the Nabob of Arcot. A Mussulman noble, sent by that potentate, did accordingly arrive, with great ceremony, at Sir Hector's camp. He said to Munro that he was ordered, by Mahomed Ali, to attend him, but had no powers given him to procure either provisions or intelligence — the only two things needed. "As I wanted neither a valet nor a cook," says the General, "I told the gentleman I would dis- "pense with his services!"†

Had Baillie and Munro at once combined their forces, as they might and should, it seems probable, from the much larger number of Europeans in their ranks, that they might have stood firm against all the armies of Mysore. But their torpor, or perhaps their jealousy, delayed them, and thus enabled Hyder to assail them singly, while yet only a few miles asunder. On the 10th of September the troops of Baillie were overwhelmed and cut to pieces. A similar fate might have befallen Munro

* Speech on the Nabob of Arcot's debts, February 28. 1785. The first germ of this fine passage lies perhaps in the κινδυνον ωσπερ νεφος of Demosthenes περι του στεφανου.

† Wilks's South of India, vol. ii. p. 268.

had he not saved himself by a precipitate retreat towards Mount St. Thomas, first casting his artillery into the tanks, and relinquishing his baggage and stores. Thus only the walled towns remained to the English: all the open country was, or would be, Hyder's.

A swift-sailing ship, despatched for the express purpose, brought these ill tidings to Calcutta on the 23rd of the same month. On no occasion, either before or since, were the genius, the energy, the master-spirit of Hastings more signally displayed. In a single day he framed a new system of policy, renouncing his late favourite schemes, and contemplating only the altered state of public affairs. In his own words—"All my "hopes of aggrandising the British name and enlarging "the interests of the Company, gave instant place to the "more urgent call to support the existence of both in "the Carnatic; nor did I hesitate a moment to abandon "my own views for such an object. The Mahratta war "has been, and is yet, called mine. God knows why. I "was forced into it. It began with the acts of others "unknown to me. I never professed any other design "but to support the Presidency of Bombay, if it had "succeeded in the plans which it had formed, or to pro-"tect and save them if they failed. . . . . . Perhaps the "war with Hyder may be, in like manner, called my "war."*

On the 25th the council met. The Governor-General proposed, that a treaty not merely of peace but of alliance should be tendered to the Mahrattas, yielding the main points at issue in the war; that every soldier available in Bengal should at once be shipped off to Madras; that fifteen Lacs of Rupees should without delay be despatched to the same quarter; that Sir Eyre Coote, as alone sufficient, should be requested to assume the chief command against Mysore; and that the powers allowed to the Supreme Presidency by the Act of 1773 should be strained to the utmost, by superseding Mr. Whitehill, the new and incapable Governor of Fort St. George. Francis, whose hatreds were as usual much stronger than his patriotism, raised his voice almost for

* Letter to L. Sulivan, Esq., October 28. 1780.

the last time in India to declare, that he would have sent only one half of the money and none of the troops. Nevertheless, the proposals of Hastings were carried through, and Sir Eyre Coote obeyed the honourable call to the scenes of his past glory. In the first days of November he landed at Madras. No sooner had he taken his seat in Council, than he produced the document from Hastings suspending Mr. Whitehill. That gentleman, though taken by surprise, attempted some faint demur, but, the majority of the Council acquiescing, he was compelled to retire, and the member next in seniority succeeded to the Chair.

Hyder Ali, since his great successes over Baillie and Munro, had reduced the fort of Arcot, and was besieging Wandewash and Vellore. But the arrival of the new commander and of the reinforcements from Bengal struck his mind with awe. He raised the siege of both places when, in January 1781, he saw Coote take the field, though still with most scanty forces and inadequate supplies. Sir Eyre, apprehensive of a rising among the French so lately subdued, next marched south and encamped on the Red Hills of Pondicherry. Later in the season he advanced to Porto Novo, a haven some forty miles further to the southward. There, on the 1st of July, he succeeded in bringing Hyder to a battle. He had only between eight and nine thousand men to oppose to the myriads of Mysore. Yet such was the ascendancy of European valour and European skill, that after six hours of conflict Hyder's forces fled in utter disarray, leaving on the field several thousand dead and wounded, while upon the side of the English the loss scarcely exceeded four hundred men.

Hyder himself had watched the progress of the battle from a small eminence, seated cross-legged on a stool. Amazed at his own reverses, he could scarce believe his eyes; and when some of his followers suggested that it was time to move, he answered them only by a torrent of abuse. At last, a groom who had long served him and was, in some sort, a privileged man, boldly seized his master's feet and forced on his slippers; exclaiming as he thus equipped him for flight: "We will beat them to-"morrow; in the meanwhile mount your horse!" Hyder took the counsel, and was quickly beyond the reach of danger.

The victory at Porto Novo was not left unimproved by Coote. He turned, and with good effect, towards Wandewash, which was again besieged. "Wandewash is safe"—thus he wrote to the Government of Madras—"it being the third time in my life I have had the "honour to relieve it." Hyder then fell back to what he deemed a lucky spot, as it certainly was a strong position; the very ground on which, in the preceding year, he had defeated Baillie. There, on the 27th of August, he engaged in another battle with Sir Eyre. In this action, to which a neighbouring village gave its name of Pollilore, the ground was so unfavourable to the English, that Sir Hector Munro, who commanded the first line, could not forbear a remonstrance to his chief. "You "talk to me, Sir, when you should be doing your duty!"—such was the stern reply; a reply which, rankling in the mind of Munro, caused him to retire from active service to Madras, and from thence next year to England.* The results of Pollilore were far less decisive, and purchased by much heavier sacrifice than those of Porto Novo; yet still, at the close, the flight of Hyder from his chosen ground left to Coote, undoubtedly, both the honour and the advantage of the day. The open country was recovered; and the Carnatic was saved.

From Calcutta the Governor-General had lost no time in commencing a negotiation for peace with the Mahrattas. But this was long protracted by the number of their chiefs, and the intricacy of the relations between them; and it was not till the spring of 1782 that the treaties were finally concluded at Salbye. Meanwhile, the entire strain of the war, both with Poonah and Mysore, fell upon the Presidency of Bengal, from which, nevertheless, large remittances were still expected by the Directors and Proprietors at home. Under these pressing circumstances, Hastings was compelled to seek new

* Sir Hector survived till 1806, dying quietly at his seat in Ross-shire. (Ann. Regist. for that year, p. 366.) Some years before, his son, a young officer serving in Bengal, was killed by a Royal tiger, "which," says an eye-witness, "rushed into the jungle with him 'with as much ease as I could lift a kitten!" (Ibid. 1793, p. 31.)

sources of supply. He thought himself entitled to call for aid from the great feudatories or vassals of his power, and, above all, from Cheyte Sing, the Rajah of Benares.

Benares — a city of above half a million of inhabitants, pent up in narrow alleys, through none of which a wheel-carriage could pass — may be regarded as the centre and the capital of the Hindoo superstitions. The Ganges, though everywhere revered as holy, is yet deemed more holy at Benares than at any other portion of its course. Every man, say the Brahmins, who dies in the sacred city, and is cast into the sacred stream, is sure of acceptance on high — even though he may have committed enormous crimes, and even though he may have been an eater of beef! The only other requisite condition is, that he should be bountiful "to the poor "Brahmins." Long flights of steps, ever crowded with pious bathers, are here seen in downward succession to the stream. Here, the temples are many and magnificent. From each of these discordant strains of music, such as the Hindoos love, resound. The bulls devoted to Siva, tame and familiar as mastiffs, walk lazily up and down the narrow streets. The monkeys, sacred to Hunimaun, that divine ape who, as the Brahmins assure us, was the conqueror of Ceylon, are not less numerous, clinging to all the roofs and little projections of the temples, thrusting, as they chatter, their heads and hands into every fruiterer's shop, or snatching the food from the children at their meals. Hideous acts and attitudes of penance are displayed on every side by religious mendicants disfigured alike by nature and by skill, — by chalk, — by cow-dung, — by disease, — while, on the contrary, a never-failing income is derived from the concourse and the charity of the wealthier pilgrims.*

The city and district of Benares formed a small state, ruled by a Hindoo prince, but tributary to the Mussul-

* Bishop Heber's Diary (vol. i. pp. 371—400. ed. 1828) contains a most animated and picturesque description of Benares, from which the particulars of mine are drawn. As he passed through the holy places, the Bishop complains of the vast number of garlands which in compliment were hung around his neck; "until at last," he says, "I looked more like a sacrifice than a Priest!"

mans of Oude. In 1774, however, the Nabob of Oude, in a treaty with the English, yielded to them all his rights upon Benares; and since that time Cheyte Sing, the Rajah, had punctually transmitted his tribute to Calcutta. It has been contended, that beyond the exact payment of this stipulated sum Cheyte Sing owed nothing to the English. On the contrary, Hastings held, that the Company, like other suzerains, might, in extraordinary perils, claim from its vassals some extraordinary aid. At the outbreak of the Mahratta war in 1778, I have already shown how the Governor-General exacted from Benares three new battalions of Sepoys. The first demand was only for one year, but as the war went on it was annually renewed. Cheyte Sing murmured and remonstrated in vain. At last, according to the fashion of the East, he thought to put an end to further requisitions by offering to Hastings for his own use a present of two Lacs of Rupees. The conduct of Hastings in this transaction is not quite clear. He took the money, and for a time concealed it both from the Bengal Council and from the Directors at home. After some interval, however, he placed it to the Company's account, and sternly intimated to the Rajah, that the five Lacs required for the Sepoys must be paid as before — adding shortly afterwards one Lac more as a fine for evasion and delay.*

In referring to this case, it should be borne in mind that Cheyte Sing was known to be rich, and supposed to be ill-affected. Notwithstanding all his pleas of poverty, he had certainly amassed considerable treasure. He had done his best to foment and aggravate the dissensions in the Council in the time of Clavering; and at that time showed a disposition to take part against Hastings. It

* The points against Hastings in this affair are wrought out in full relief by Burke in his Articles of Charge (iii. and viii.), and the explanations by Hastings himself (in 1782 and 1785) can scarcely be thought conclusive. But great attention is due to the judgment passed by Professor Wilson in his Notes upon Mill (vol. iv. p. 373.): "It appeared in evidence, that Hastings communicated all the circum-"stances relating to this present to the Accountant-General who re-"ceived the money, &c. It is undeniable, therefore, that Hastings "never intended to appropriate this money to his own use. (See the Minutes of Evidence, 1155. 2747.)

may be, without want of charity, presumed that, besides the public exigencies, Hastings was likewise in some measure swayed by a feeling of revenge. New demands upon Cheyte Sing were now poured in so thick and fast as to show a predetermination of driving him to refusal and resistance, and thence to ruin. The Rajah, at last, seriously alarmed, tendered as a peace-offering the sum of 200,000*l.* But Hastings declared that he would be content with nothing short of half a million.

Such was the critical state to which this question had grown in the summer of 1781. Then, the designs of Hastings upon Benares, as also some others which he had in view for Oude, seemed to need his personal presence and direction. Besides himself, there was remaining only one member of the Council, Mr. Wheler. That gentleman was prevailed upon to delegate his authority to his chief; and thus armed with the full powers of the Council, the Governor-General set out for the north-western provinces. He travelled with little of pomp or state, and even beyond the frontier with only a few score of Sepoys. Indeed, it well deserves attention, that the greatest of the English in India — the rulers whose sway over the minds of the natives has been strongest — did not resort to, or rely upon, those pageantries in which the natives are supposed to take delight. There is a remarkable testimony to that effect, as to both Clive and Hastings, from a Frenchman by birth, and a Mussulman by adoption, who had resided in India during a long course of years. He states, that he well remembers, in 1755, the magnificence of M. de Bussy and the other French chiefs in the Deccan. He states, that Bussy always wore a dress of rich brocade, with embroidered hat and shoes; his table, always in plate, was served with three, often with four courses; he sat upon a kind of throne, with the arms of his King in relief; and, whenever he stirred from home, he was mounted on an elephant, preceded by a band of musicians, singing his feats of chivalry, and followed by two head-Chobdars, reciting his eulogium! On the contrary, continues the Frenchman, "Colonel Clive always wore his regimentals in the "field, was always on horseback, and never in a palan-"quin; he had a plentiful table, but no ways delicate, "and never more than two courses. He used to march "mostly at the head of the column, with his aides-de-"camp, or was hunting at the right and left. Governor "Hastings always wore a plain coat of English broad-"cloth; and never anything like lace or embroidery. His "whole retinue a dozen of horse-guards; his throne a "plain chair of mahogany, with plenty of such thrones "in the hall; his table sometimes neglected; his diet "sparing and always abstemious; his address and deport-"ment very distant from pride and still more so from "familiarity."*

The Governor-General arrived at Benares on the 14th of August, 1781. Cheyte Sing had gone forth many miles to meet him, with every mark of honour, and with the humblest professions of respect. Nay, on entering the Governor's pinnace, he even took off his turban and laid it on the lap of Hastings—a symbol to denote his unlimited submission. Hastings, with whom mere forms had little weight, received all these compliments with coldness. He sternly refused a visit from the Rajah in Benares, and next morning sent to him the Resident, with a paper of complaints and demands. These Cheyte Sing attempted to explain or evade. Without further parley, Hastings put him under arrest; sending two companies of Sepoys to guard him as a prisoner in his palace.

"The Rajah"—such was the report of the English Resident to Hastings—"submitted quietly to the arrest; "and assured me that, whatever were your orders, he was "ready to obey." But not such were the feelings of his people. It was no light thing for an European chief to seize the person of a Hindoo Prince in the very sanctuary and stronghold of the Hindoo superstitions. The multitude gathered in the streets, confident in their growing numbers. They might also expect some aid from the holy bulls, or the not less holy apes, that they saw around them. From outcries and threats, they quickly passed to blows. By a strange neglect the two companies of Sepoys round the palace had come without ammunition;

* Note by the first translator of the Seir Mutakhareen, vol. iii. p. 150. ed. Calcutta, 1789.

consequently they were soon overpowered. Two other companies sent for their support were surrounded and cut to pieces in the narrow alleys. Hastings had then left, for his own protection, no more than fifty men. With these he barricaded the house in which he had taken up his residence, but could not, long together, have maintained it against a mob which he describes as "about "two thousand, furious and daring from the easy success "of their last attempt."—"Cheyte Sing," he adds, in a more private letter, "had me at his mercy at Benares "if the wretch had known his advantage."*

Happily for Hastings, the thought which at this time was uppermost in Cheyte Sing's mind was not for victory or vengeance, but only for escape. In the midst of the confusion, he made his way from his palace by a secret postern, which opened to the Ganges. The bank was precipitous, but he was let down, as from a wall, by a line of his attendants' turbans tied together; and, finding a boat, was rowed over to the opposite shore. There he was quickly joined by his principal adherents from the city of Benares, and he began to muster troops. Still, however, it was mainly to a reconciliation that his wishes turned. He addressed to the Governor-General a petition, abounding with apologies for the past, and offers of allegiance for the future.

Through all the storm that raged around him the equable mind of Hastings was never for a moment stirred. So far from making any concession to Cheyte Sing, he did not even vouchsafe him a reply. He carefully refrained from spreading any superfluous alarm by his communications either with Bengal or Oude. Yet his pen was not idle. He wrote to the nearest officers within the British territory to require aid. He wrote to Mrs. Hastings, whom he had left at Monghir, to inform her of his safety. And lastly—with the same perfect calmness and self-command as when seated quietly in his chamber at Calcutta, or beneath his garden-trees at Allipore—he wrote to the agent charged to treat with the Mahratta chiefs, giving him such detailed instructions as by the last advices that negotiation needed. The sure convey-

* To Major Scott, January 1. 1782. Memoirs by Gleig, vol. ii. p. 420.

ance of these letters was now no easy task; but here again the fertile mind of Hastings was ready with a scheme. Having reduced them to the smallest compass, and rolled them into pieces of quill, he intrusted them to some well-tried HIRCARRAHS, or Hindoo messengers, who, by his orders, taking out their ear-rings, concealed them in their ears. Thus did these men pass safely and without detection through the hostile throng.

Meanwhile, although the chief part of the insurgents had left Benares, and joined the prince beyond the river, the position of Hastings in the city continued full of peril. Not only was the insurrection general through the district of Benares; it was spreading through great part of the misgoverned state of Oude; it was threatening even the British province of Bahar. New passions began to ferment, and new hopes to rise. Cheyte Sing himself, instead of further pleas for mercy, was beginning to dream of conquest and revenge. Hastings and his small band, even though reinforced by some recruits, and by the boatmen who had brought them to Benares, could no longer hope to maintain themselves as a mere vanguard in the midst of foes. He set forth from the city by night, yet not unobserved, the rabble hooting him as he rode along with a jingling rhyme, not yet forgotten in Benares.* Unassailed, however, on this occasion, except in words, he made his way successfully to the rock-fortress of Chunar. There he was quickly joined by a protecting force; at its head the brave and enterprising Major Popham, the conqueror of Gualior. Against such troops, and such a chief, the rabble of Cheyte Sing, now swelled to forty thousand, could not stand. The Hindoo

"Hat' hee pur howdah, ghore pur jeen
"Juldee bah'r jata Sahib Wârren Husteen!"

"Horse, elephant, howdah, set off at full speed,
"Ride away my Lord Warren Hastings!"

"It is a nursery rhyme which is often sung to children (at Benares)," says Bishop Heber. (Journals, vol. i. p. 438. ed. 1828.) Both the Bishop and another eminent writer of our own day appear to be in error when they consider this a song in praise of Hastings instead of in triumph over him. See a note to Impey's Memoirs of Sir Elijah, p. 234.

prince was utterly routed and driven from his states. One of his kinsmen was in his stead named Rajah of Benares, but his yearly tribute was raised to forty Lacs of Rupees, and he became on all points a mere stipendiary and subject of the English, soon to be removed, as he had been appointed, by their sovereign will. Nothing was left to Cheyte Sing beyond the fortress of Bidgegur, which held his treasure, and which the princess his mother defended. After a siege of several weeks the place was reduced by Major Popham. The treasure — after all Cheyte Sing's pleas of utter poverty, at the commencement of the contest — was found to exceed in value 250,000*l.* But it did not, as Hastings hoped, go to replenish the coffers of Bengal; it was seized by the army as prize. The fault here lay mainly in the Governor-General himself; in his own hasty letters and own inconsiderate expressions, during the heat of the siege.

On reviewing the whole of this transaction, which in the impeachment of Hastings formed the great Benares charge, we find its real facts utterly distorted by the ardour of both sides. While Fox and Burke, in urging it, allege the vilest motives and most heinous crimes, not even the shadow of an indiscretion is allowed by Mr. Nicholls, or by Major Scott. Between the two extreme parties, thus fiercely warring upon Indian affairs, there arose a great Minister, free from any party-trammels with either. The judgment of Mr. Pitt, expressed, for the first time, in his speech of June, 1786, was formed, as he states, after a long and laborious study of the question. On nearly all points he approved the course of Hastings. He maintained that the Governor-General was entitled to consider Cheyte Sing as a feudatory prince, and to call upon him for extraordinary aid. He maintained that Cheyte Sing had shown contumacy in refusing such aid; and that, in punishment of his contumacy, Hastings had good right to impose on him a fine. "But," continued Mr. Pitt, "in fining the Rajah 500,000*l.* for "a mere delay to pay 50,000*l.*, which 50,000*l.* he had "actually paid, Mr. Hastings proceeded in an arbitrary, "tyrannical manner, and was not guided by any principle "of reason and justice. This proceeding destroyed all "relation and connection between the degrees of guilt "and punishment; . . . . . that punishment was utterly "disproportionate and shamefully exorbitant."* These weighty words did not merely at that time prevail — did not merely, then, in fact, decide the great question of the day — Impeachment or no Impeachment; but they are now, as I conceive, confirmed and ratified by the voice of History. It is on that point, and that point alone, in the Benares Charge, the exorbitancy of the fine, that the voice of History may pronounce Hastings to have erred, no doubt led astray by his personal resentment and rancour against Cheyte Sing. An objection has indeed been raised to Mr. Pitt's discriminating censure, as though it were not adequate to support a vote of condemnation, since the question of a larger or a lesser fine can be no more than a difference in degree. Yet what is it but a difference in degree, that with children, for example, separates the chastisement which the legislator praises from that which he is bound to punish — the chastisement which aims at correction from the chastisement tending to maim and to deform? Not far dissimilar, surely, is the relation of a liege-lord to his vassals, where the duty of protection goes side by side with the right of control.

If Hastings could have felt remorse — a feeling almost alien from his nature — he might have felt it when he found his aim in all this violence, the treasure at Bidgegur, diverted by his soldiers from the public uses which he had designed. But he only turned with the keener energy to his projects upon Oude. We have seen how, in 1775, Sujah Dowlah was succeeded, as Nabob and Visier, by his son Asaph ul Dowlah. One of the first acts of the new prince was to remove the seat of his government from Fyzabad to the rising city of Lucknow.† There remained, however, as sojourners in the palace of Fyzabad, the grandmother of the young Sovereign, and also his mother, the widow of Sujah Dowlah. These aged ladies were called the Begums or princesses of Oude.‡

* Parl. Hist. vol. xxvi. p. 111.

† Hamilton's East India Gazetteer, vol. ii. p. 132.

‡ "*Begum* is a title of Turkish origin and the feminine of *Beg*, "which signifies Prince, both in Tartary and Turkey, but means no "more than a trooper, both in Persia and in India." (Note to the Seir Mutakhareen, vol. i. p. 297.)

They had kept possession of Sujah Dowlah's treasure, amounting, it was said, to upwards of 3,000,000*l*. They had also vast Jaghires, and maintained a princely state. On the other hand, Asaph ul Dowlah showed himself so careless and so prodigal, that he soon grew poor. Wholly given up to the most disgraceful vices, and lavishing his own Crown lands upon his minions, he neglected the welfare and aroused the resentment of his people. To secure himself from the effects of that resentment, and of his neighbours' warlike enterprises, he had asked the help of a British brigade. It had been most readily granted by Hastings, who foresaw that it would reduce him to the rank of a dependent prince, and who added the condition that the Visier should defray its entire cost and charge. Under these circumstances, it was not long before the Visier's payments fell into arrear. He earnestly pleaded for the withdrawal of the troops or for the remission of the money, at the very time when the Governor-General was bending his whole thoughts on the possible means of obtaining some further aid.

On planning his north-western journey, Hastings had determined that as soon as he had closed the affairs of Benares, he would take in hand those of Oude, and repair in person to Lucknow. His visit was anticipated by the eagerness of Asaph ul Dowlah, who came forth beyond the frontier to meet him. The Governor-General and the Visier passed several days together in the rock-fortress of Chunar. There it was that Hastings first unfolded his grand scheme for the relief of both. He proposed that Asaph ul Dowlah should resume the domains which he had improvidently granted, and also those which his father had bequeathed. But it was not merely in this manner that the Begums were to be despoiled. Another part of the scheme was to wring from them the larger portion of their treasure, the money thus accruing to be accepted by the English in liquidation of the arrears which they claimed from Oude.

In this plan of Hastings for despoiling the princesses he had not even the merit of original invention. The idea was so simple and easy, that it had long since occurred, without prompting, to the mind of the Visier. He had at various times obtained from his mother and his grandame sums amounting to 630,000*l*. Against the last of these payments they had struggled to the utmost of their power. Nor did they yield until the Visier at last agreed to a treaty pledging himself on no account or pretence to make any further demand upon them; and to this treaty they had obtained the guarantee of the Council of Bengal, through the ascendancy at that time, of Clavering and Monson, and contrary to the wish of Hastings. Thus, then, the faith of the English Government was clearly pledged against the very course which an English Governor was attempting to pursue.

Let it not be thought, however, that Hastings wanted (did ever an oppressor want?) pleas for his oppression. First he might allege, with some show of reason, that according to the Mahomedan law, the treasure of the late Visier belonged, of right, not to the widow, but to the son. Next he might point to the depositions of numerous witnesses, that upon the news of the outbreak in Benares some retainers of the two Begums had stirred up insurrection in Oude. It so happened that Sir Elijah Impey was at this very time engaged in a tour through the upper provinces — a tour which he had undertaken partly for recreation and health, and partly, as was his duty, to inspect the local courts. He now offered Hastings to proceed to Lucknow, and receive the depositions of these witnesses in regular form. The offer was gladly accepted, and the depositions were accordingly received. From these it might, perhaps, be clear that some of the Begums' people had been concerned in the late disturbance; but there was no proof whatever to show that they had acted by the order, or even with the knowledge, of the aged ladies. Above all it is to be borne in mind that no opportunity was ever allowed the princesses to be heard in their own defence. Yet it was upon such wholly one-sided testimony that Hastings mainly relied for his own justification. "Let this," he wrote to a friend in London, "let this be an answer to the men of virtue who may "exclaim against our breach of faith, and the inhumanity "of dealing war against widows, princesses of high birth, "and defenceless old women — These old women had "very nigh effected our destruction." *

* To L. Sulivan, Esq., February 21. 1782.

It was in September, 1781, that the Governor-General and the Visier signed a treaty at Chunar, according to the terms which the former had proposed. Then they parted. Hastings followed in the train of his victorious troops to Benares, and from thence returned to Bengal, while Asaph ul Dowlah wended back his way to Oude. With the assistance of Mr. Middleton, the English Resident at his Court, he prepared to carry into effect his stipulations. But, in resuming the grants of land, he had to encounter the most vehement remonstrances, both from his mother and his minions. His heart was moved by some touch of pity or of shame. Even Mr. Middleton, though the devoted friend, or, to speak more truly perhaps, the humble servant, of the Governor-General, faltered at the long course of exaction that lay before him. Hastings alone was, as ever, unbending, cold, and hard. He sternly reminded the Visier of their plighted compact. He bade, in the most peremptory terms, the Resident proceed on his instructions. "If you," he added, "cannot "rely on your own firmness, I will free you from these "charges; I will myself proceed to Lucknow; I will myself undertake them." *

Thus spurred on, both the Visier and the Resident, though wincing, began to move. The Jaghires of the two princesses were forcibly resumed. The city and palace of Fyzabad, in which they dwelt, were surrounded and reduced by a body of British troops. Still, however, the Begums would not part with any portion of their hidden treasure. The difficulty was how to discover or lay hands upon it without profaning, as the races of the East conceive, the sacred bounds of the Zenana. It was resolved to arrest and confine two aged Eunuchs, the heads of the household, and the principal Ministers of the princesses. These men were cast into prison, and loaded with irons; and, on finding them obdurate, an order was issued in January, 1782, that until they yielded they should be debarred from all food. This order, to the shame and opprobrium not only of himself and his employer, but even of the English name in India, bore

* Letter, December 25. 1781. Burke's Articles of Charge, IV. sec. 12.

the signature — I am pained to own it — of Nathaniel Middleton.

To the pangs of hunger the aged Ministers gave way, and within two days agreed to disburse the sum which was then required. But that sum was only a part of the whole demand. To extort the rest other most rigorous measures were employed. The two prisoners were removed from Fyzabad to Lucknow. The weight of their irons was increased; torture was threatened, and perhaps inflicted; certain it is, at least, that every facility was granted by the British Assistant Resident to the officers of the Visier, who were sent for that purpose to the prison-house. Meanwhile at Fyzabad the palace-gates of the princesses continued to be strictly guarded. Food was allowed to enter, but not always in sufficient quantities for the number of the inmates, so that the Begums might be wrought upon by the distress of their attendants. "The melancholy cries of famine," says a British officer upon the spot, "are more easily imagined than described." Thus, through the greater part of 1782, severity followed severity, and sum was exacted after sum. The Ministers were not set free, nor the princesses relieved from duresse until after there had been obtained from them treasure exceeding in amount one million sterling. Notwithstanding all their pleas of poverty — pleas perfectly justifiable in the face of such oppression — there was still remaining in their hands property to the value of at least one million more.

It has been urged, yet surely without good reason, that for these acts of barbarity the Visier upon the spot, rather than the Governor-General at a distance, should be held responsible. It has also been contended, that they were no necessary consequence of the original scheme, as framed at Chunar, for despoiling the Dowagers of Oude. And, as regards that scheme, the later apologists of Hastings, discarding for the most part the flimsy pretexts which he put forward at the time, prefer to take their stand on the broad ground that large supplies of money were absolutely needed for the prosecution of the war; and that we should have lost India if we had not plundered the Begums. Certainly, in one respect at least, Hastings may deserve to be far distinguished above the long line of robber-magistrates in story — from Verres the prætor, down to Monsieur Rapinat.* He plundered for the benefit of the State, and not for his own. His main thought was ever, that he had a great empire to save — and he did save it. Yet, with all due appreciation of his object, and with all due allowance for his difficulties, his conduct to the princesses of Oude appears to me incapable of any valid vindication, and must be condemned as alike repugnant to the principles of justice and humanity.

Rumours of abuses in India — of wrangling Councils, rapacious Governors, unjust judges, and unnecessary wars — had for some time past already crossed the seas to England. Lord North, sore pressed on other questions, had no motive for resisting, and did not resist, inquiry upon these. In the course of 1781, he agreed to or proposed the appointment of two Committees of the House of Commons; the one "Select," to consider the state of the administration of justice in Bengal; the other "Secret," to investigate the causes of the war in the Carnatic. The first Committee had for Chairman General Richard Smith, a member of the Opposition; and among its most zealous and untiring members was Edmund Burke. The second, on the contrary, was presided over by a member of the Government — Henry Dundas, at that time Lord Advocate of Scotland. Each Committee presented several able Reports, and collected a great mass of important evidence. Neither Committee showed any tenderness to Hastings. All the worst points in his administration, and, above all, his war with the Rohillas, were unsparingly dragged to light. Impey also was severely censured for his acceptance of the new judicial

* Of Rapinat, who was Commissioner of the Directory in Switzerland, it is said by M. Michaud in the Supplement to the Biog. Univ.: "Il dut une grande célébrité beaucoup plus à la bizarrerie de son "nom qu'à ses déprédations, qui au fond ne furent pas plus considér- "ables que celles de tant d'autres." Here is one of the epigrams against him, which may at least deserve to be ranked with the *hog's broth* quibble—the *Jus Verrinum*—of Cicero:

> "Un pauvre Suisse que l'on ruine
> "Desire fort qu'on expliquat,
> "Si Rapinat vient de rapine
> "Ou bien rapine de Rapinat!"

office created by the Council of Bengal. The case of both of these high functionaries was brought before the House of Commons at nearly the same time, but, as will presently be seen, with very different results.

In May, 1782, General Smith moved an Address to the King, praying that His Majesty would recall Sir Elijah Impey "to answer to the charge of having accepted "an office granted by, and tenable at the pleasure of, "the servants of the East India Company, which has a "tendency to create a dependence in the Supreme Court "of Judicature upon those over whose actions the said "Court was intended as a control." This Address appears to have been carried without either division or debate. In the July following Sir Elijah was accordingly summoned home by a letter from the Secretary of State, Lord Shelburne. He returned to England, but several years elapsed before that or any other charge against him came to be publicly preferred.

In April, 1782, the main results of the knowledge gathered in the Secret Committee upon Indian wars and Indian policy were unfolded to the House by Mr. Dundas in a lucid and most able speech of three hours. It was then, perhaps, more than on any previous occasion, that he fully showed or saw acknowledged the mastery of debate which he so long retained. A few weeks later he moved a more specific Resolution against Hastings, purporting that it was the duty of the Court of Directors to remove the Governor-General, he "having, in sundry "instances, acted in a manner repugnant to the honour "and policy of this nation." The Rockingham Ministry, urged forward by the fiery vehemence of Burke, gave their support to this Resolution; and no other considerable party in Parliament opposed it. The Court of Directors also, in compliance with its terms, soon afterwards voted an Order of Recall. But when in the October following that Order of Recall came before the Court of Proprietors, the scene was wholly changed. A large majority of the Proprietors showed themselves the steady friends of Hastings. They observed that the wish of only one of the branches of the Legislature had no claim on their obedience; and that the law, as it then stood, gave the right of removing a Governor-General, not to the House of Commons, nor yet to the Ministers of the Crown, but solely to the Court of Directors, subject to their own control. Under these circumstances — deeming the abilities of Hastings essential to the administration of affairs in India — encouraged also in their views on seeing that since the Parliamentary proceedings Lord Rockingham had died, and Burke seceded from office — they resolutely rescinded the Order of Recall. They were the better able to pursue an independent course on this occasion, since in 1781 Lord North had passed an Act extending their Constitutional powers for a period of ten years.

Thus was Hastings upheld at his post; thus might his energies still maintain the varying fortunes of the war in the Carnatic. To that war he continued to apply most strenuously all the men and all the money he could raise His public-spirited endeavours were well seconded by those of the new Governor of Fort St. George, Lord Macartney, who had gained some reputation by negotiating a treaty of commerce with Russia, and who mainly on that ground had been appointed to Madras. Lord Macartney brought out from England the news of the Declaration of War against the Dutch; and it became one of his first objects to reduce the settlements which they possessed on the coasts of Coromandel and Ceylon. But he found unexpected difficulties, from the failing health and froward temper of Sir Eyre Coote. That brave old veteran, suffering about this very time from a stroke of palsy, was ever imagining that he was insulted, and declaring that he would resign. It was requisite — thus wrote Lord Macartney at the time — "to court him like "a mistress and to humour him like a child." Hopeless of co-operation from the General in chief, the Governor resolved to act on his own resources. He called out the Militia of Madras, and, putting himself at their head, reduced the Dutch factories at Sadras and Pulicat. Next he fitted out a more considerable expedition against the more important settlement of Negapatam; and he prevailed upon Sir Hector Munro to accept the command, Sir Hector being then on ill terms with Sir Eyre, and waiting at Madras for a passage to England. In November, 1781, Negapatam was accordingly besieged and taken, several thousand Dutch troops, after a resolute resistance, being made prisoners on this occasion. Inspirited by that exploit, a body of 500 men was put on board the fleet, and sent to the attack of Fort Ostenburg and Trincomalee, in the island of Ceylon. This service, also, was no less successfully performed, but was much more than counterbalanced by the disaster which, in February 1782, befel another British detachment in the district of Tanjore. There Colonel Brathwaite, at the head of 100 Europeans and 1,800 Sepoys, found himself surrounded and surprised by an army of Mysore, under Hyder's son Tippoo and M. Lally. He and his men fought most bravely, but at last were overpowered by superior numbers; and all either cut to pieces or taken captive and consigned to the dungeons of Seringapatam.

In the same month of February, 1782, the armament from France, so long expected, appeared off the coast of Coromandel. Its command had devolved on De Suffren, one of the best seamen whom his country can boast. He had been trained in the Order of the Knights of Malta, who at this time conferred upon him the high rank of their BAILLI. Ready, bold, and enterprising, of most active habits although of most unwieldy size, he was likewise never wanting in judgment or in skill. Already, on his outward voyage, he had fought a pitched battle with an English squadron at Porto Praya, in one of the Cape de Verd Islands. By his prompt arrival at the Cape of Good Hope he had secured that colony against the same squadron for his new allies the Dutch. In India it was one of his first cares to land at Porto Novo 2,000 French soldiers whom he had on board, to form, with their countrymen already serving, an auxiliary force to the armies of Mysore. These troops being joined by Tippoo, flushed as he was then with his triumph over Colonel Brathwaite, they proceeded in conjunction to invest Cuddalore, a seaport town between Porto Novo and Pondicherry. Having to encounter only a feeble garrison of 400 men, they easily prevailed in their attack; and Cuddalore, thus wrested from the English, became of great importance to the French, both as a place of arms and as a harbour, during the whole remainder of the war.

It so chanced, that at the very time when the armament from France appeared in the Indian seas, the British fleet in that quarter was seasonably reinforced by several new ships from England. M. de Suffren and Sir Edward Hughes, the two Admirals here opposed to each other, were antagonists well matched, both for skill and intrepidity. In the period between February, 1782, and June, 1783, no less than five pitched battles were fought between them. In these their force was very nearly equal, with only a slight superiority on most occasions on the side of the French.* But in none of these was any decisive advantage gained by either party. The English might constantly prefer a slight and nominal claim to the honours of the day; yet, in truth, these honours belonged to all the brave men who were here contending. No ship of war was captured; no overwhelming loss of men was achieved; and, in turning to the best account the results of every action, De Suffren showed a far superior skill, especially in the retaking Trincomalee and the relieving Cuddalore.

The arrival of the French auxiliaries to the forces of Mysore was, in a great measure, counterbalanced by the peace which at this time Hastings concluded with the Mahratta states. Thus, the English could continue to wage, on no unequal terms, the war in the Carnatic until, in December, 1782, it received a new turn from the illness and death of Hyder Ali. This event was concealed as long as possible, to afford time for Tippoo, who was then upon the coast of Malabar, to return and claim in person the allegiance of the people and the troops. But when the intelligence did at last reach Calcutta, it fired anew the energies of Sir Eyre Coote. Weak health had compelled the failing veteran, after one more battle with Hyder at Arnee, to withdraw from the field in the Carnatic, and sail back to his Council-chambers of Bengal. Now, however, he felt, or he fancied, his strength in some

* Thus, in the second action (April, 1782), "the English line "consisted of eleven ships, carrying 732 guns, and the French of "twelve, carrying 770." In the third action, however (July, 1782), the English ships were eleven, and the French eleven also; the English guns 732, and the French 706. (Wilks's South of India, vol. ii. p. 383. and 395.)

degree restored; and he was eager to measure swords against the new Sultan. For this purpose he embarked in an armed vessel which carried out supplies of money to Madras. This, towards the close of its voyage, was chased for two days and two nights by some French ships of the line. During all this time the General's anxiety kept him constantly on deck. The excessive heat by day, the unwholesome dews at night, wrought sad havoc on his already wasted frame; and thus, although the ship with its pecuniary treasure escaped from its pursuers, its most precious freight could not be permanently saved. Sir Eyre Coote expired in April, 1783, only two days after he had landed at Madras.

Tippoo during this time had returned to the coast of Malabar. There he had to wage war against General Mathews and a body of troops from Bombay set free by the peace with the Mahrattas. The English General at first had great successes, reducing both Bednore and Mangalore. But the appearance of the Sultan at the head of 50,000 men changed the scene. Mathews was besieged in Bednore and taken prisoner with all his Europeans. Being accused, though unjustly, of a breach of faith, he was put in irons, and sent in the strictest duresse with many of his comrades to Seringapatam, there to perish in the dungeons of the tyrant.

At Madras the command of the forces, in the absence of Sir Eyre, had devolved, though far less adequately, on General Stuart. That officer, in the spring of 1783, commenced operations against the French in Cuddalore, who had lately received from Europe some considerable reinforcements under M. de Bussy. The lines in front of the town, which Bussy had well fortified, and which he no less valiantly defended, were assailed by Stuart with more of intrepidity than skill. The fleets also, on both sides, hastened to the scene of action; and at the close of June some decisive engagements were expected, both by sea and land, when suddenly the tidings came that the preliminaries of peace between France and England had been signed at Versailles. By that compact Pondicherry and the other settlements of France in India, as they stood before the war, were to be restored. The French took possession accordingly, but, on the other hand, they recalled their detachment serving under Tippoo in Malabar, and prepared to sail back with their armament to France.

Tippoo then remained alone. He had set his heart on adding lustre to his arms by reducing in person the stronghold of Mangalore, but, having achieved that object in the autumn of 1783, he was no longer disinclined to treat with the English upon the footing of a mutual restitution of all conquests made since the commencement of the war. Thus was peace restored through all the wide extent of India, and thus did the administration of Hastings, which endured until the spring of 1785, close, after all its storms, with scarce a cloud upon its sky.

Glancing back for a moment to the rise and progress of our Eastern empire, from the first victory of Clive till the final retirement of Hastings, we must feel that it was stained by several acts that we have reason to deplore. The true foundation, or at least the true security, of our just and beneficent rule in India was that system of double government which the genius of Mr. Pitt devised. With every drawback however, it may be said, and not merely of the later period, that the sway even of the worst of the foreign governors was better than the sway even of the best of the native princes. The people of Hindostan might sometimes see a neighbouring tribe, like the Rohillas, assailed by the English without any show of right; they might sometimes see one of their own chiefs foully dealt with or despoiled, as was the case with Omichund; yet still they felt that, among themselves, the poor man was protected from harm. They had no longer to fear the annual inroads of the Mahratta horsemen through the teeming rice-fields of Bengal. They had no longer to fear that even those handfuls of rice which the enemy had spared might be snatched from them by the first man in office who passed along—by any minion, however base, of their own Sultan or Soubahdar. Viewing these things, they were disposed to regard the great English chiefs with gratitude, as most mild and equitable rulers. While in England, Clive and Hastings were commonly railed against as tyrants, in India they were commonly extolled as benefactors. Already was there growing up in the Indian people that feeling — far more fully unfolded at the present period — that feeling on which the permanence of our Eastern empire, if permanent it be, must mainly rest — that feeling which, to give one homely instance of it, led two villagers, when they did not deem a stranger nigh them, thus to commune with each other. "A good rain this for the bread," said the one. "Yes," was the answer, "and a good government, under which "a man may eat bread in safety!"*

The future destinies of India, so far as human eye can scan them, are all surely fraught with the fairest hopes. Everywhere in that country has victory crowned our arms. The last of our rivals on the Sutlege has utterly succumbed before us. Yet our security from the perils of war has in no degree, as I conceive, made us neglectful of the arts of peace. The desire to do our duty by that high and solemn trust has never yet been so earnestly felt amongst us; it pervades, it animates, all parties in the country. Taught by gradual experience, our system of government has been improved, and is still improving. High ability is trained both at Addiscombe and Haileybury for the objects both of administration and defence. In India lines of railway are beginning to span the boundless plains. The great want of the country and the climate, Irrigation, a want too long unheeded by the English rulers, has at length attracted their anxious care. With cultivation thus quickened by our wealth and directed by our skill, we may trust that in another age, the supplies of Tea within our own dominions may be such as to rival, perhaps even to supersede, the produce of the provinces of China. We may trust that the supply of Cotton for our looms may become the largest from that region which gave to Cotton its first name in the Western world.† Above all, we may indulge a well-grounded

* Conversation overheard by Archdeacon Corrie. See Bishop Heber's Journal, vol. ii. p. 33. ed. 1828.

† "Superior pars Egypti, in Arabiam vergens, gignit fruticem "quem aliqui Gossipium vocant, plures *Xylon*, et ideo lina inde acta "*Xylina*. Parvus est, similemque barbatæ nucis defert fructum," &c. (Plin. Hist. Nat. lib. xix. c. i.) On this passage Colonel Wilks observes: "The term *Xylon* was certainly not derived from "the Arabs, who name the plant *Kuttun* (cotton), but it bears a close

confidence that advancement in knowledge and in morals may here keep pace with the progress of prosperity, and that as the fouler Hindoo superstitions already pale before the growing light of day, so that God, in his own good time, and in the measure of his own appointed Revelation, may, even to this long benighted people, make himself clearly and fully known.

"resemblance to the common Indian pronunciation of Ceylon; as "muslin from Moosul and calico from Calicut, the emporia from which "these substances became known in the west." (South of India, vol. iii. p. 20.)

THE END.

ALBEMARLE STREET, LONDON.
January, 1859.

MR. MURRAY'S

GENERAL LIST OF WORKS.

ABBOTT'S (REV. J.) Philip Musgrave; or, Memoirs of a Church of England Missionary in the North American Colonies. Post 8vo. 2*s*. 6*d*.

ABERCROMBIE'S (JOHN, M.D.) Enquiries concerning the Intellectual Powers and the Investigation of Truth. *Fifteenth Edition*. Fcap. 8vo. 6*s*. 6*d*.

——— Philosophy of the Moral Feelings. *Tenth Edition*. Fcap. 8vo. 4*s*.

——— Pathological and Practical Researches on the Diseases of the Stomach, &c. *Third Edition*. Fcap. 8vo. 6*s*.

ACLAND'S (REV. CHARLES) Popular Account of the Manners and Customs of India. Post 8vo. 2*s*. 6*d*.

ADDISON'S WORKS. A New Edition, with a New Life and Notes. By Rev. WHITWELL ELWIN. 4 Vols. 8vo. *In Preparation*.

ADOLPHUS'S (J. L.) Letters from Spain, in 1856 and 1857. Post 8vo. 10*s*. 6*d*.

ÆSCHYLUS. (The Agamemnon and Choephorœ.) Edited, with Notes. By Rev. W. PEILE, D.D. *Second Edition*. 2 Vols. 8vo. 9*s*. each.

ÆSOP'S FABLES. A New Translation. With Historical Preface. By Rev. THOMAS JAMES, M.A. With 100 Woodcuts, by JOHN TENNIEL and J. WOLF. *26th Thousand*. Post 8vo. 2*s*. 6*d*.

AGRICULTURAL (THE) JOURNAL. Of the Royal Agricultural Society of England. 8vo. 10*s*. *Published half-yearly*.

AMBER-WITCH (THE). The most interesting Trial for Witchcraft ever known. Translated from the German by LADY DUFF GORDON. Post 8vo. 2*s*. 6*d*.

ARABIAN NIGHTS ENTERTAINMENT. Translated from the Arabic, with Explanatory Notes. By E. W. LANE. *A New Edition*. Edited by E. STANLEY POOLE. With 600 Woodcuts. 3 Vols. 8vo. 42*s*.

ARTHUR'S (LITTLE) History of England. By LADY CALLCOTT. *Eighteenth Edition*. With 20 Woodcuts. Fcap. 8vo. 2*s*. 6*d*.

AUNT IDA'S Walks and Talks; a Story Book for Children. By a LADY. Woodcuts. 16mo. 5*s*.

AUSTIN'S (SARAH) Fragments from German Prose Writers. With Biographical Notes. Post 8vo. 10*s*.

——— Translation of Ranke's History of the Popes of Rome. *Third Edition*. 2 Vols. 8vo. 24*s*.

B

ADMIRALTY PUBLICATIONS; Issued by direction of the Lords Commissioners of the Admiralty:—

1. A MANUAL OF SCIENTIFIC ENQUIRY, for the Use of Officers in H.M. Navy and Travellers in General. By Various Hands. *Third Edition, revised.* Woodcuts. Post 8vo.

2. AIRY'S ASTRONOMICAL OBSERVATIONS MADE AT GREENWICH. 1836 to 1847. Royal 4to. 50*s.* each.

——— ASTRONOMICAL RESULTS. 1848 to 1856. 4to. 8*s.* each.

3. ——— APPENDICES TO THE ASTRONOMICAL OBSERVATIONS.

1836.—I. Bessel's Refraction Tables.
II. Tables for converting Errors of R.A. and N.P.D. into Errors of Longitude and Ecliptic P.D. } 8*s.*
1837.—I. Logarithms of Sines and Cosines to every Ten Seconds of Time.
II. Table for converting Sidereal into Mean Solar Time. } 8*s.*
1842.—Catalogue of 1439 Stars. 8*s.*
1845.—Longitude of Valentia. 8*s.*
1847.—Twelve Years' Catalogue of Stars. 14*s.*
1851.—Maskelyne's Ledger of Stars. 6*s.*
1852.—I. Description of the Transit Circle. 5*s.*
II. Regulations of the Royal Observatory. 2*s.*
1853.—Bessel's Refraction Tables. 3*s.*
1854.—I. Description of the Zenith Tube. 3*s.*
II. Six Years' Catalogue of Stars. 10*s.*

4. ——— MAGNETICAL AND METEOROLOGICAL OBSERVATIONS. 1840 to 1847. Royal 4to. 50*s.* each.

——— MAGNETICAL AND METEOROLOGICAL RESULTS. 1848 to 1855. 4to. 8*s.* each.

5. ——— ASTRONOMICAL, MAGNETICAL, AND METEOROLOGICAL OBSERVATIONS, 1848 to 1854. Royal 4to. 50*s.* each.

6. ——— REDUCTION OF THE OBSERVATIONS OF PLANETS, 1750 to 1830. Royal 4to. 50*s.*

7. ——— ——— LUNAR OBSERVATIONS. 1750 to 1830. 2 Vols. Royal 4to. 50*s.* each.

8. BERNOULLI'S SEXCENTENARY TABLE. *London*, 1779. 4to.

9. BESSEL'S AUXILIARY TABLES FOR HIS METHOD OF CLEARING LUNAR DISTANCES. 8vo.

10. ——— FUNDAMENTA ASTRONOMIÆ: *Regiomontii*, 1818. Folio. 60*s.*

11. BIRD'S METHOD OF CONSTRUCTING MURAL QUADRANTS. *London*, 1768. 4to. 2*s.* 6*d.*

12. ——— METHOD OF DIVIDING ASTRONOMICAL INSTRUMENTS. *London*, 1767. 4to. 2*s.* 6*d.*

13. COOK, KING, AND BAYLY'S ASTRONOMICAL OBSERVATIONS. *London*, 1782. 4to. 21*s.*

14. EIFFE'S ACCOUNT OF IMPROVEMENTS IN CHRONOMETERS. 4to. 2*s.*

15. ENCKE'S BERLINER JAHRBUCH, for 1830. *Berlin*, 1828. 8vo. 9*s.*

16. GROOMBRIDGE'S CATALOGUE OF CIRCUMPOLAR STARS. 4to. 10*s.*

17. HANSEN'S TABLES DE LA LUNE. 4to. 20*s.*

17. HARRISON'S PRINCIPLES OF HIS TIME-KEEPER. PLATES. 1767. 4to. 5*s.*

18. HUTTON'S TABLES OF THE PRODUCTS AND POWERS OF NUMBERS. 1781. Folio. 7*s.* 6*d.*

19. LAX'S TABLES FOR FINDING THE LATITUDE AND LONGITUDE. 1821. 8vo. 10*s.*

ADMIRALTY PUBLICATIONS—*continued.*

20. LUNAR OBSERVATIONS at GREENWICH. 1783 to 1819. Compared with the Tables, 1821. 4to. *7s. 6d.*

22. MASKELYNE'S ACCOUNT OF THE GOING OF HARRISON'S WATCH. 1767. 4to. *2s. 6d.*

21. MAYER'S DISTANCES of the MOON'S CENTRE from the PLANETS. 1822, *3s.*; 1823, *4s. 6d.* 1824 to 1835, 8vo. *4s.* each.

23. ———— THEORIA LUNÆ JUXTA SYSTEMA NEWTONIANUM. 4to. *2s. 6d.*

24. ———— TABULÆ MOTUUM SOLIS ET LUNÆ. 1770. 4to. *5s.*

25. ———— ASTRONOMICAL OBSERVATIONS MADE AT GOTTINGEN, from 1756 to 1761. 1826. Folio. *7s. 6d.*

26. NAUTICAL ALMANACS, from 1767 to 1861. 8vo. *2s. 6d.* each.

27. ———— SELECTIONS FROM THE ADDITIONS up to 1812. 8vo. *5s.* 1834-54. 8vo. *5s.*

28. ———— SUPPLEMENTS, 1828 to 1833, 1837 and 1838. 8vo. *2s.* each.

29. ———— TABLE requisite to be used with the N.A. 1781. 8vo. *5s.*

30. POND'S ASTRONOMICAL OBSERVATIONS. 1811 to 1835. 4to. *21s.* each.

31. RAMSDEN'S ENGINE for DIVIDING MATHEMATICAL INSTRUMENTS. 4to. *5s.*

32. ———— ENGINE for DIVIDING STRAIGHT LINES. 4to. *5s.*

33. SABINE'S PENDULUM EXPERIMENTS to DETERMINE THE FIGURE OF THE EARTH. 1825. 4to. *40s.*

34. SHEPHERD'S TABLES for CORRECTING LUNAR DISTANCES. 1772. Royal 4to. *21s.*

35. ———— TABLES, GENERAL, of the MOON'S DISTANCE from the SUN, and 10 STARS. 1787. Folio. *5s. 6d.*

36. TAYLOR'S SEXAGESIMAL TABLE. 1780. 4to. *15s.*

37. ———— TABLES OF LOGARITHMS. 4to. *3l.*

38. TIARK'S ASTRONOMICAL OBSERVATIONS for the LONGITUDE of MADEIRA. 1822. 4to. *5s.*

39. ———— CHRONOMETRICAL OBSERVATIONS for DIFFERENCES of LONGITUDE between DOVER, PORTSMOUTH, and FALMOUTH. 1823. 4to. *5s.*

40. VENUS and JUPITER: OBSERVATIONS of, compared with the TABLES. *London*, 1822. 4to. *2s.*

41. WALES' AND BAYLY'S ASTRONOMICAL OBSERVATIONS. 1777. 4to. *21s.*

42. WALES' REDUCTION OF ASTRONOMICAL OBSERVATION MADE IN THE SOUTHERN HEMISPHERE. 1764—1771. 1788. 4to. *10s. 6d.*

BABBAGE'S (CHARLES) Economy of Machinery and Manufactures. *Fourth Edition.* Fcap. 8vo. *6s.*

———— Ninth Bridgewater Treatise. 8vo. *9s. 6d.*

———— Reflections on the Decline of Science in England, and on some of its Causes. 4to. *7s. 6d.*

———— Views of the Industry, the Science, and the Government of England, 1851. *Second Edition.* 8vo. *7s. 6d.*

BAIKIE'S (W. B.) Narrative of an Exploring Voyage up the Rivers Quorra and Tshadda in 1854. Map. 8vo. 16*s.*

BANKES' (GEORGE) STORY OF CORFE CASTLE, with documents relating to the Time of the Civil Wars, &c. Woodcuts. Post 8vo. 10*s.* 6*d.*

BASSOMPIERRE'S Memoirs of his Embassy to the Court of England in 1626. Translated with Notes. 8vo. 9*s.* 6*d.*

BARROW'S (SIR JOHN) Autobiographical Memoir, including Reflections, Observations, and Reminiscences at Home and Abroad. From Early Life to Advanced Age. Portrait. 8vo. 16*s.*

——— Voyages of Discovery and Research within the Arctic Regions, from 1818 to the present time. Abridged and arranged from the Official Narratives. 8vo. 15*s.*

——— (SIR GEORGE) Ceylon; Past and Present. Map. Post 8vo. 6*s.* 6*d.*

——— (JOHN) Naval Worthies of Queen Elizabeth's Reign, their Gallant Deeds, Daring Adventures, and Services in the infant state of the British Navy. 8vo. 14*s.*

——— Life and Voyages of Sir Francis Drake. With numerous Original Letters. Post 8vo. 2*s.* 6*d.*

BEES AND FLOWERS. Two Essays. By Rev. Thomas James. Reprinted from the "Quarterly Review." Fcap. 8vo. 1*s.* each.

BELL'S (SIR CHARLES) Mechanism and Vital Endowments of the Hand as evincing Design. *Sixth Edition.* Woodcuts. Post 8vo. 7*s.* 6*d.*

BENEDICT'S (JULES) Sketch of the Life and Works of Felix Mendelssohn Bartholdy. *Second Edition.* 8vo. 2*s.* 6*d.*

BERTHA'S Journal during a Visit to her Uncle in England. Containing a Variety of Interesting and Instructive Information. *Seventh Edition.* Woodcuts. 12mo. 7*s.* 6*d.*

BIRCH'S (SAMUEL) History of Ancient Pottery and Porcelain: Egyptian, Assyrian, Greek, Roman, and Etruscan. With 200 Illustrations. 2 Vols. Medium 8vo. 42*s.*

BLUNT'S (REV. J. J.) Principles for the proper understanding of the Mosaic Writings, stated and applied, together with an Incidental Argument for the truth of the Resurrection of our Lord. Being the HULSEAN LECTURES for 1832. Post 8vo. 6*s.* 6*d.*

——— Undesigned Coincidences in the Writings of the Old and New Testament, an Argument of their Veracity: with an Appendix containing Undesigned Coincidences between the Gospels, Acts, and Josephus. *Sixth Edition.* Post 8vo. 7*s.* 6*d.*

——— History of the Church in the First Three Centuries. *Second Edition.* 8vo. 9*s.* 6*d.*

——— Parish Priest; His Duties, Acquirements and Obligations. *Third Edition.* Post 8vo. 7*s.* 6*d.*

——— Lectures on the Right Use of the Early Fathers. *Second Edition.* 8vo. 15*s.*

——— Plain Sermons Preached to a Country Congregation. *Second Edition.* 2 Vols. Post 8vo. 7*s.* 6*d.* each.

BLACKSTONE'S (Sir William) Commentaries on the Laws of England. A New Edition, adapted to the present state of the law. By R. Malcolm Kerr, LL.D. 4 Vols. 8vo. 42*s.*

——— (The Student's Blackstone:) Being those Portions of the above work which relate to the British Constitution and the Rights of Persons. By R. Malcolm Kerr, LL.D. Post 8vo. 9*s.*

BLAINE (Roberton) on the Laws of Artistic Copyright and their Defects, for Artists, Engravers, Printsellers, &c. 8vo. 3*s.* 6*d.*

BOOK OF COMMON PRAYER. With 1000 Illustrations of Borders, Initials, and Woodcut Vignettes. *A New Edition.* Medium 8vo. 21*s. cloth,* 31*s.* 6*d. calf,* or 42*s. morocco.*

BOSWELL'S (James) Life of Dr. Johnson. Including the Tour to the Hebrides. Edited by Mr. Croker. *Third Edition.* Portraits. Royal 8vo. 15*s.*

BORROW'S (George) Lavengro; The Scholar—The Gipsy—and the Priest. Portrait. 3 Vols. Post 8vo. 30*s.*

——— Romany Rye; a Sequel to Lavengro. *Second Edition.* 2 Vols. Post 8vo. 21*s.*

——— Bible in Spain; or the Journeys, Adventures, and Imprisonments of an Englishman in an Attempt to circulate the Scriptures in the Peninsula. 3 Vols. Post 8vo. 27*s.*, or *Popular Edition* 16mo, 6*s.*

——— Zincali, or the Gipsies of Spain; their Manners, Customs, Religion, and Language. 2 Vols. Post 8vo. 18*s.*, or *Popular Edition,* 16mo, 6*s.*

BRAY'S (Mrs.) Life of Thomas Stothard, R.A. With Personal Reminiscences. Illustrated with Portrait and 60 Woodcuts of his chief works. 4to.

BREWSTER'S (Sir David) Martyrs of Science, or the Lives of Galileo, Tycho Brahe, and Kepler. *Second Edition.* Fcap. 8vo. 4*s.* 6*d.*

——— More Worlds than One. The Creed of the Philosopher and the Hope of the Christian. *Seventh Thousand.* Post 8vo. 6*s.*

——— Stereoscope: its History, Theory, Construction, and Application to the Arts and to Education. Woodcuts. 12mo. 5*s.* 6*d.*

——— Kaleidoscope: its History, Theory, and Construction, with its application to the Fine and Useful Arts. *Second Edition.* Woodcuts. Post 8vo. 5*s.* 6*d.*

BRITISH ASSOCIATION REPORTS. 8vo. York and Oxford, 1831-32, 13*s.* 6*d.* Cambridge, 1833, 12*s.* Edinburgh, 1834, 15*s.* Dublin, 1835, 13*s.* 6*d.* Bristol, 1836, 12*s.* Liverpool, 1837, 16*s.* 6*d.* Newcastle, 1838, 15*s.* Birmingham, 1839, 13*s.* 6*d.* Glasgow, 1840, 15*s.* Plymouth, 1841, 13*s.* 6*d.* Manchester, 1842, 10*s.* 6*d.* Cork, 1843, 12*s.* York, 1844. 20*s.* Cambridge, 1845, 12*s.* Southampton, 1846, 15*s.* Oxford, 1847, 18*s.* Swansea, 1848, 9*s.* Birmingham, 1849, 10*s.* Edinburgh, 1850, 15*s.* Ipswich, 1851, 16*s.* 6*d.* Belfast, 1852, 15*s.* Hull, 1853, 10*s.* 6*d.* Liverpool, 1854, 18*s.* Glasgow, 1855, 15*s.*; Cheltenham 1856, 18*s*; Dublin, 1857, 15*s.*

BRITISH CLASSICS. A New Series of Standard English Authors, printed from the most correct text, and edited with elucidatory notes. Published occasionally in demy 8vo. Volumes.

Already Published.

GOLDSMITH'S WORKS. Edited by PETER CUNNINGHAM, F.S.A. Vignettes. 4 Vols. 30*s*.

GIBBON'S DECLINE AND FALL OF THE ROMAN EMPIRE. Edited by WILLIAM SMITH, LL.D. Portrait and Maps. 8 Vols. 60*s*.

JOHNSON'S LIVES OF THE ENGLISH POETS. Edited by PETER CUNNINGHAM, F.S.A. 3 Vols. 22*s*. 6*d*.

BYRON'S POETICAL WORKS. Edited, with Notes. 6 vols. 45*s*.

In Preparation.

WORKS OF POPE. Edited, with Notes.

WORKS OF DRYDEN. Edited, with Notes.

HUME'S HISTORY OF ENGLAND. Edited, with Notes.

LIFE, LETTERS, AND JOURNALS OF SWIFT. Edited, with Notes, by JOHN FORSTER.

WORKS OF SWIFT. Edited, with Notes. By JOHN FORSTER.

WORKS OF ADDISON. Edited, with Notes. By Rev. W. ELWIN.

BROUGHTON'S (LORD) Journey through Albania and other Provinces of Turkey in Europe and Asia, to Constantinople, 1809—10. *Second Edition*. Maps and Woodcuts. 2 Vols. 8vo. 30*s*.

——————— ITALY: Remarks made in several Visits from the Year 1816 to 1854. 2 vols. Post 8vo.

BUBBLES FROM THE BRUNNEN OF NASSAU. By an Old MAN. *Sixth Edition*. 16mo. 5*s*.

BUNBURY'S (C. J. F.) Journal of a Residence at the Cape of Good Hope; with Excursions into the Interior, and Notes on the Natural History and Native Tribes of the Country. Woodcuts. Post 8vo. 9*s*.

BUNYAN (JOHN) and Oliver Cromwell. Select Biographies. By ROBERT SOUTHEY. Post 8vo. 2*s*. 6*d*.

BUONAPARTE'S (NAPOLEON) Confidential Correspondence with his Brother Joseph, sometime King of Spain. *Second Edition*. 2 vols. 8vo. 26*s*.

BURGHERSH'S (LORD) Memoir of the Operations of the Allied Armies under Prince Schwarzenberg and Marshal Blucher during the latter end of 1813—14. 8vo. 21*s*.

——————— Early Campaigns of the Duke of Wellington in Portugal and Spain. 8vo. 8*s*. 6*d*.

BURGON'S (Rev. J. W.) Portrait of a Christian Gentleman: a Memoir of the late Patrick Fraser Tytler, author of "The History of Scotland." 8vo. *In the Press*.

BURN'S (LIEUT-COL.) French and English Dictionary of Naval and Military Technical Terms. *Third Edition*. Crown 8vo. 15*s*.

BURNS' (ROBERT) Life. By JOHN GIBSON LOCKHART. Fifth *Edition*. Fcap. 8vo. 3*s*.

BURR'S (G. D.) Instructions in Practical Surveying, Topographical Plan Drawing, and on sketching ground without Instruments. *Third Edition*. Woodcuts. Post 8vo. 7*s*. 6*d*.

BUXTON'S (Sir Fowell) Memoirs. With Selections from his Correspondence. By his Son. *Fifth Edition.* 8vo. 16*s.*; or, *Popular Edition.* Post 8vo. 8*s.* 6*d.*

BYRON'S (Lord) Life, Letters, and Journals. By Thomas Moore. *Cabinet Edition.* Plates. 6 Vols. Fcap. 8vo. 18*s.*

——— Life, Letters, and Journals. By Thomas Moore. *Popular Edition.* Portrait and Vignette. One Volume, royal 8vo. 12*s.*

——— Poetical Works. *Library Edition.* Portrait. 6 Vols. Demy 8vo. 45*s.*

——— Poetical Works. *Cabinet Edition.* Plates. 10 Vols. Fcap. 8vo. 30*s.*

——— Poetical Works. *People's Edition.* Portrait and Steel Engravings. Royal 8vo. 9*s.*

——— Poetical Works. *Travelling Edition.* Printed in small but beautifully clear type. Portrait. Crown 8vo. 9*s.*

——— Poetical Works. *Pocket Edition. Containing* Childe Harold; Dramas, 2 Vols.; Tales and Poems; Miscellanies, 2 Vols.; Beppo and Don Juan, 2 Vols. 8 Vols. 24mo. 20*s.* Or, *separately,* 2*s.* 6*d.* Each volume.

——— Childe Harold's Pilgrimage. A New and beautifully printed Edition. Illustrated, with Wood Engravings, from original Drawings by Percival Skelton. Fcap. 4to. 21*s.*

——— Illustrated with 30 Steel Vignettes. Crown 8vo. 10*s.* 6*d.*

BYRON Beauties. Poetry and Prose. A Reading Book for Youth. Portrait. Fcap. 8vo. 3*s.* 6*d.*

CALVIN'S (John) Life. With Extracts from his Correspondence. By Thomas H. Dyer. Portrait. 8vo. 15*s.*

CALLCOTT'S (Lady) Little Arthur's History of England. 18*th Edition.* With 20 Woodcuts. Fcap. 8vo. 2*s.* 6*d.*

CARMICHAEL'S (A. N.) Greek Verbs. Their Formations, Irregularities, and Defects. *Second Edition.* Post 8vo. 8*s.* 6*d.*

CARNARVON'S (Lord) Portugal, Gallicia, and the Basque Provinces. From Notes made during a Journey to those Countries. *Third Edition.* Post 8vo. 6*s.*

CAMPBELL'S (Lord) Lives of the Lord Chancellors and Keepers of the Great Seal of England. From the Earliest Times to the Death of Lord Eldon in 1838. 4*th Edition.* 10 Vols. Crown 8vo. 6*s.* each.

——— Life of Lord Chancellor Bacon. Fcap. 8vo. 2*s.* 6*d.*

——— Lives of the Chief Justices of England. From the Norman Conquest to the Death of Lord Tenterden. *Second Edition.* 3 Vols. 8vo. 42*s.*

——— (George) Modern India. A Sketch of the System of Civil Government. With some Account of the Natives and Native Institutions. *Second Edition.* 8vo. 16*s.*

——— India as it may be. An Outline of a proposed Government and Policy. 8vo. 12*s.*

——— (Thos.) Short Lives of the British Poets. With an Essay on English Poetry. Post 8vo. 6*s.*

CASTLEREAGH (THE) **DESPATCHES**, from the commencement of the official career of the late Viscount Castlereagh to the close of his life. Edited by the MARQUIS OF LONDONDERRY. 12 Vols. 8vo. 14*s*. each.

CATHCART'S (SIR GEORGE) Commentaries on the War in Russia and Germany, 1812-13. Plans. 8vo. 14*s*.

——— Military Operations in Kaffraria, which led to the Termination of the Kaffir War. *Second Edition*. 8vo. 12*s*.

CAVALCASELLE (G. B.) Notices of the Early Flemish Painters; Their Lives and Works. Woodcuts. Post 8vo. 12*s*.

CHANTREY (SIR FRANCIS). Winged Words on Chantrey's Woodcocks. Edited by JAS. P. MUIRHEAD. Etchings. Square 8vo. 10*s*. 6*d*.

CHARMED ROE (THE); or, The Story of the Little Brother and Sister. By OTTO SPECKTER. Plates. 16mo. 5*s*.

CLARENDON (LORD CHANCELLOR); Lives of his Friends and Contemporaries, illustrative of Portraits in his Gallery. By Lady THERESA LEWIS. Portraits. 3 Vols. 8vo. 42*s*.

CLAUSEWITZ'S (CARL VON) Campaign of 1812, in Russia. Translated from the German by LORD ELLESMERE. Map. 8vo. 10*s*. 6*d*.

CLIVE'S (LORD) Life. By REV. G. R. GLEIG, M.A. Post 8vo. 6*s*.

COLERIDGE (SAMUEL TAYLOR). Specimens of his Table-Talk. *Fourth Edition*. Portrait. Fcap. 8vo. 6*s*.

——— (HENRY NELSON) Introductions to the Study of the Greek Classic Poets. *Third Edition*. Fcap. 8vo. 5*s*. 6*d*.

COLONIAL LIBRARY. [See Home and Colonial Library.]

COOKERY (DOMESTIC). Founded on Principles of Economy and Practical Knowledge, and adapted for Private Families. *New Edition*. Woodcuts. Fcap. 8vo. 5*s*.

CORNWALLIS (THE) Papers and Correspondence during the American War,—Administrations in India,—Union with Ireland, and Peace of Amiens. From Family Papers, &c. Edited by CHARLES ROSS. 3 Vols. 8vo. 63*s*.

CRABBE'S (REV. GEORGE) Life, Letters, and Journals. By his SON. Portrait. Fcap. 8vo. 3*s*.

——— and Poetical Works. *Cabinet Edition*. Plates. 8 Vols. Fcap. 8vo. 24*s*.

——— and Poetical Works. *Popular Edition*. Plates. One Volume. Royal 8vo. 10*s*. 6*d*.

CRAIK'S (G. L.) Pursuit of Knowledge under Difficulties. *New Edition*. 2 Vols. Post 8vo. 12*s*.

CURZON'S (HON. ROBERT) Visits to the Monasteries of the Levant. *Fourth Edition*. Woodcuts. Post 8vo. 15*s*.

——— ARMENIA AND ERZEROUM. A Year on the Frontiers of Russia, Turkey, and Persia. *Third Edition*. Woodcuts. Post 8vo. 7*s*. 6*d*.

CUNNINGHAM'S (ALLAN) Life of Sir David Wilkie. With his Journals and Critical Remarks on Works of Art. Portrait. 3 Vols. 8vo. 42*s*.

CUNNINGHAM'S (Allan) Poems and Songs. Now first collected and arranged, with Biographical Notice. 24mo. 2*s*. 6*d*.

——— (Capt. J. D.) History of the Sikhs. From the Origin of the Nation to the Battle of the Sutlej. *Second Edition*. Maps. 8vo. 15*s*.

——— (Peter) London—Past and Present. A Handbook to the Antiquities, Curiosities, Churches, Works of Art, Public Buildings, and Places connected with interesting and historical associations. *Second Edition*. Post 8vo. 16*s*.

——— Modern London. A complete Guide for Visitors to the Metropolis. Map. 16mo. 5*s*.

——— Westminster Abbey. Its Art, Architecture, and Associations. Woodcuts. Fcap. 8vo. 1*s*.

——— Works of Oliver Goldsmith. Edited with Notes. Vignettes. 4 vols. 8vo. 30*s*. (Murray's British Classics.)

——— Lives of Eminent English Poets. By Samuel Johnson, LL.D. Edited with Notes. 3 vols. 8vo. 22*s*. 6*d*. (Murray's British Classics.)

CROKER'S (J. W.) Progressive Geography for Children. *Fifth Edition*. 18mo. 1*s*. 6*d*.

——— Stories for Children, Selected from the History of England. *Fifteenth Edition*. Woodcuts. 16mo. 2*s*. 6*d*.

——— Boswell's Life of Johnson. Including the Tour to the Hebrides. *Third Edition*. Portraits. Royal 8vo. 15*s*.

——— Lord Hervey's Memoirs of the Reign of George the Second, from his Accession to the death of Queen Caroline. Edited with Notes. *Second Edition*. Portrait. 2 Vols. 8vo. 21*s*.

——— Essays on the Early Period of the French Revolution. Reprinted from the Quarterly Review. 8vo. 15*s*.

——— Historical Essay on the Guillotine. Fcap. 8vo. 1*s*.

CROMWELL (Oliver) and John Bunyan. By Robert Southey. Post 8vo. 2*s*. 6*d*.

CROWE'S (J. A.) Notices of the Early Flemish Painters; their Lives and Works. Woodcuts. Post 8vo. 12*s*.

CURETON (Rev. W.) Remains of a very Ancient Recension of the Four Gospels in Syriac, hitherto unknown in Europe. Discovered, Edited, and Translated. 4to. 24*s*.

DARWIN'S (Charles) Journal of Researches into the Natural History and Geology of the Countries visited during a Voyage round the World. Post 8vo. 8*s*. 6*d*.

DAVIS'S (Sir J. F.) China: A General Description of that Empire and its Inhabitants, down to 1857. *New Edition*. Woodcuts. 2 Vols. Post 8vo. 14*s*.

DAVY'S (Sir Humphry) Consolations in Travel; or, Last Days of a Philosopher. *Fifth Edition*. Woodcuts. Fcap. 8vo. 6*s*.

——— Salmonia; or, Days of Fly Fishing. With some Account of the Habits of Fishes belonging to the genus Salmo. *Fourth Edition*. Woodcuts. Fcap. 8vo. 6*s*.

DENNIS' (George) Cities and Cemeteries of Etruria; or, the extant Local Remains of Etruscan Art. Plates. 2 Vols. 8vo. 42*s*.

DOG-BREAKING; the Most Expeditious, Certain, and Easy Method, whether great excellence or only mediocrity be required. By LIEUT.-COL. HUTCHINSON. *Third Edition.* Revised and enlarged. Woodcuts. Post 8vo. 9*s.*

DOMESTIC MODERN COOKERY. Founded on Principles of Economy and Practical Knowledge, and adapted for Private Families. *New Edition.* Woodcuts. Fcap. 8vo. 5*s.*

DOUGLAS'S (GENERAL SIR HOWARD) Treatise on the Theory and Practice of Gunnery. *Fourth Edition.* Plates. 8vo. 21*s.*

——— Treatise on the Principle and Construction of Military Bridges, and the Passage of Rivers in Military Operations. *Third Edition.* Plates. 8vo. 21*s.*

——— Naval Warfare with Steam. Woodcuts. 8vo. 8*s.* 6*d.*

DRAKE'S (SIR FRANCIS) Life, Voyages, and Exploits, by Sea and Land. By JOHN BARROW. *Third Edition.* Post 8vo. 2*s.* 6*d.*

DRINKWATER'S (JOHN) History of the Siege of Gibraltar, 1779-1783. With a Description and Account of that Garrison from the Earliest Periods. Post 8vo. 2*s.* 6*d.*

DRYDEN'S (JOHN) Works. A New Edition, based upon Sir Walter Scott's Edition, entirely revised. 8vo. *In Preparation.*

DUDLEY'S (EARL OF) Letters to the late Bishop of Llandaff. *Second Edition.* Portrait. 8vo. 10*s.* 6*d.*

DUFFERIN'S (LORD) Letters from High Latitudes, being some Account of a Yacht Voyage to Iceland, &c., in 1856. *Fourth Edition.* Woodcuts. Post 8vo. 9*s.*

DURHAM'S (ADMIRAL SIR PHILIP) Naval Life and Services. By CAPT. ALEXANDER MURRAY. 8vo. 5*s.* 6*d.*

DYER'S (THOMAS H.) Life and Letters of John Calvin. Compiled from authentic Sources. Portrait. 8vo. 15*s.*

——— New History of Modern Europe. From the taking of Constantinople by the Turks to the Close of the War in the Crimea. 4 Vols. 8vo. *In Preparation.*

EASTLAKE (SIR CHARLES) The Schools of Painting in Italy. From the Earliest times. From the German of KUGLER. Edited, with Notes. *Third Edition.* Illustrated from the Old Masters. 2 Vols. Post 8vo. 30*s.*

EDWARDS' (W. H.) Voyage up the River Amazon, including a Visit to Para. Post 8vo. 2*s.* 6*d.*

EGERTON'S (HON. CAPT. FRANCIS) Journal of a Winter's Tour in India; with a Visit to Nepaul. Woodcuts. 2 Vols. Post 8vo. 18*s.*

ELDON'S (LORD CHANCELLOR) Public and Private Life, with Selec-tions from his Correspondence and Diaries. By HORACE TWISS. *Third Edition.* Portrait. 2 Vols. Post 8vo. 21*s.*

ELIOT'S (HON. W. G. C.) Khans of the Crimea. Being a Nar-rative of an Embassy from Frederick the Great to the Court of Krim Gerai. Translated from the German. Post 8vo. 6*s.*

ELLIS (MRS.) On the Education of Character, with Hints on Moral Training. Post 8vo. 7*s.* 6*d.*

——— (REV. W.) Three Visits to Madagascar. During 1853,-54, and -56, including a Journey to the Capital, with notices of Natural History, and Present Civilisation of the People. *Fourth Thousand.* Map and Woodcuts. 8vo. 16*s.*

ELLESMERE'S (LORD) Two Sieges of Vienna by the Turks. Translated from the German. Post 8vo. 2*s.* 6*d.*

——— Second Campaign of Radetzky in Piedmont. The Defence of Temeswar and the Camp of the Ban. From the German. st8vo. 6*s.* 6*d.*

——— Life and Character of the Duke of Wellington; a Discourse. Fcap. 8vo. 6*d.*

——— Campaign of 1812 in Russia, from the German of General Carl Von Clausewitz. Map. 8vo. 10*s.* 6*d.*

——— Pilgrimage, and other Poems. Crown 4to. 24*s.*

——— Essays on History, Biography, Geography, and Engineering. 8vo. 12*s.*

ELPHINSTONE'S (HON. MOUNTSTUART) History of India—the Hindoo and Mahomedan Periods. *Fourth Edition.* With an Index. Map. 8vo. 18*s.*

ELWIN'S (REV. W.) Lives of Eminent British Poets. From Chaucer to Wordsworth. 4 Vols. 8vo. *In Preparation.*

ENGLAND (HISTORY OF) from the Peace of Utrecht to the Peace of Versailles, 1713—83. By LORD MAHON. *Library Edition*, 7 Vols. 8vo, 93*s.*; or, *Popular Edition*, 7 Vols. Post 8vo. 35*s.*

——— From the First Invasion by the Romans, down to the 14th year of Queen Victoria's Reign. By MRS. MARKHAM. 98*th Edition.* Woodcuts. 12mo. 6*s.*

——— As IT IS: Social, Political, and Industrial, in the 19th Century. By W. JOHNSTON. 2 Vols. Post 8vo. 18*s.*

——— and France under the House of Lancaster. With an Introductory View of the Early Reformation. *Second Edition.* 8vo. 15*s.*

ENGLISHWOMAN IN AMERICA. Post 8vo. 10*s.* 6*d.*

——— RUSSIA: or, Impressions of Manners and Society during a Ten Years' Residence in that Country. *Fifth Thousand.* Woodcuts. Post 8vo. 10*s.* 6*d.*

ERSKINE'S (CAPT., R.N.) Journal of a Cruise among the Islands of the Western Pacific, including the Fejees, and others inhabited by the Polynesian Negro Races. Plates. 8vo. 16*s.*

ESKIMAUX (THE) and English Vocabulary, for the use of Travellers in the Arctic Regions. 16mo. 3*s.* 6*d.*

ESSAYS FROM "THE TIMES." Being a Selection from the LITERARY PAPERS which have appeared in that Journal. *7th Thousand.* 2 vols. Fcap. 8vo. 8*s.*

EXETER'S (BISHOP OF) Letters to the late Charles Butler, on the Theological parts of his Book of the Roman Catholic Church; with Remarks on certain Works of Dr. Milner and Dr. Lingard, and on some parts of the Evidence of Dr. Doyle. *Second Edition.* 8vo. 16*s.*

FAIRY RING (THE), A Collection of TALES and STORIES for Young Persons. From the German. By J. E. TAYLOR. Illustrated by RICHARD DOYLE. *Second Edition.* Fcap. 8vo.

FALKNER'S (FRED.) Muck Manual for the Use of Farmers. A Treatise on the Nature and Value of Manures. *Second Edition*, with Glossary of Terms and an Index. Fcap. 8vo. 5*s.*

FAMILY RECEIPT-BOOK. A Collection of a Thousand Valuable and Useful Receipts. Fcap. 8vo. 5*s.* 6*d.*

FANCOURT'S (Col.) History of Yucatan, from its Discovery to the Close of the 17th Century. With Map. 8vo. 10*s*. 6*d*.

FEATHERSTONHAUGH'S (G. W.) Tour through the Slave States of North America, from the River Potomac, to Texas and the Frontiers of Mexico. Plates. 2 Vols. 8vo. 26*s*.

FELLOWS' (Sir Charles) Travels and Researches in Asia Minor, more particularly in the Province of Lycia. *New Edition*. Plates. Post 8vo. 9*s*.

FERGUSSON'S (James) Palaces of Nineveh and Persepolis Restored: an Essay on Ancient Assyrian and Persian Architecture. With 45 Woodcuts. 8vo. 16*s*.

——— Handbook of Architecture. Being a Concise and Popular Account of the Different Styles prevailing in all Ages and Countries in the World. With a Description of the most remarkable Buildings. *Fourth Thousand*. With 850 Illustrations. 8vo. 26*s*.

FERRIER'S (T. P.) Caravan Journeys in Persia, Affghanistan, Herat, Turkistan, and Beloochistan, with Descriptions of Meshed, Balk, and Candahar, and Sketches of the Nomade Tribes of Central Asia. *Second Edition*. Map. 8vo. 21*s*.

——— History of the Afghans. Map. 8vo. 21*s*.

FEUERBACH'S Remarkable German Crimes and Trials. Translated from the German by Lady Duff Gordon. 8vo. 12*s*.

FISHER'S (Rev. George) Elements of Geometry, for the Use of Schools. *Fifth Edition*. 18mo. 1*s*. 6*d*.

——— First Principles of Algebra, for the Use of Schools. *Fifth Edition*. 18mo. 1*s*. 6*d*.

FLOWER GARDEN (The). An Essay. By Rev. Thos. James. Reprinted from the "Quarterly Review." Fcap. 8vo. 1*s*.

FORD'S (Richard) Handbook for Spain, Andalusia, Ronda, Valencia, Catalonia, Granada, Gallicia, Arragon, Navarre, &c. *Third Edition*. 2 Vols. Post 8vo. 30*s*.

——— Gatherings from Spain. Post 8vo. 6*s*.

FORSTER'S (John) Historical & Biographical Essays. Contents:—

I. The Grand Remonstrance, 1641.
II. The Plantagenets and the Tudors.
III. The Civil Wars and Oliver Cromwell.
IV. Daniel De Foe.
V. Sir Richard Steele.
VI. Charles Churchill.
VII. Samuel Foote.

2 Vols. Post 8vo. 21*s*.

FORSYTH'S (William) Hortensius, or the Advocate: an Historical Essay on the Office and Duties of an Advocate. Post 8vo. 12*s*.

——— History of Napoleon at St. Helena. From the Letters and Journals of Sir Hudson Lowe. Portrait and Maps. 3 Vols. 8vo. 45*s*.

FORTUNE'S (Robert) Narrative of Two Visits to China, between the years 1843-52, with full Descriptions of the Culture of the Tea Plant. *Third Edition*. Woodcuts. 2 Vols. Post 8vo. 18*s*.

——— Residence among the Chinese: Inland, on the Coast, and at Sea, during 1853-56. Woodcuts. 8vo. 16*s*.

FRANCE (History of). From the Conquest by the Gauls to the Death of Louis Philippe. By Mrs. Markham. *56th Thousand*. Woodcuts. 12mo. 6*s*.

FRENCH (The) in Algiers; The Soldier of the Foreign Legion—and the Prisoners of Abd-el-Kadir. Translated by Lady Duff Gordon. Post 8vo. 2*s.* 6*d.*

GALTON'S (Francis) Art of Travel; or, Hints on the Shifts and Contrivances available in Wild Countries. *Second Edition.* Woodcuts. Post 8vo. 6*s.*

GEOGRAPHICAL (The) Journal. Published by the Royal Geographical Society of London. 8vo.

GERMANY (History of). From the Invasion by Marius, to the present time. On the plan of Mrs. Markham. *Ninth Thousand.* Woodcuts. 12mo. 6*s.*

GIBBON'S (Edward) Decline and Fall of the Roman Empire. *A New Edition.* Preceded by his Autobiography. Edited with Notes by Dr. Wm. Smith. Maps. 8 Vols. 8vo. 60*s.*

——— The Student's Gibbon; Being the History of the Decline and Fall, Abridged, incorporating the Researches of Recent Commentators. By Dr. Wm. Smith. *Sixth Thousand.* Woodcuts. Post 8vo. 7*s.* 6*d.*

GIFFARD'S (Edward) Deeds of Naval Daring; or, Anecdotes of the British Navy. 2 Vols. Fcap. 8vo.

GISBORNE'S (Thomas) Essays on Agriculture. *Third Edition.* Post 8vo.

GLADSTONE'S (W. E.) Prayers arranged from the Liturgy for Family Use. *Second Edition.* 12mo. 2*s.* 6*d.*

GOLDSMITH'S (Oliver) Works. A New Edition. Printed from the last editions revised by the Author. Edited by Peter Cunningham. Vignettes. 4 Vols. 8vo. 30*s.* (Murray's British Classics.)

GLEIG'S (Rev. G. R.) Campaigns of the British Army at Washington and New Orleans. Post 8vo. 2*s.* 6*d.*

——— Story of the Battle of Waterloo. Compiled from Public and Authentic Sources. Post 8vo. 5*s.*

——— Narrative of Sir Robert Sale's Brigade in Afghanistan, with an Account of the Seizure and Defence of Jellalabad. Post 8vo. 2*s.* 6*d.*

——— Life of Robert Lord Clive. Post 8vo. 5*s.*

——— Life and Letters of General Sir Thomas Munro. Post 8vo. 5*s.*

GORDON'S (Sir Alex. Duff) Sketches of German Life, and Scenes from the War of Liberation. From the German. Post 8vo. 6*s.*

——— (Lady Duff) Amber-Witch: the most interesting Trial for Witchcraft ever known. From the German. Post 8vo. 2*s.* 6*d.*

——— French in Algiers. 1. The Soldier of the Foreign Legion. 2. The Prisoners of Abd-el-Kadir. From the French. Post 8vo. 2*s.* 6*d.*

———Remarkable German Crimes and Trials. From the German of Fuerbach. 8vo. 12*s.*

GRANT'S (Asahel) Nestorians, or the Lost Tribes; containing Evidence of their Identity, their Manners, Customs, and Ceremonies; with Sketches of Travel in Ancient Assyria, Armenia, and Mesopotamia; and Illustrations of Scripture Prophecy. *Third Edition.* Fcap 8vo. 6*s.*

GRENVILLE (The) PAPERS. Being the Public and Private Correspondence of George Grenville, his Friends and Contemporaries, during a period of 30 years.—Including his Diary of Political Events while First Lord of the Treasury. Edited, with Notes, by W. J. Smith. 4 Vols. 8vo. 16s. each.

GREEK GRAMMAR FOR SCHOOLS. Abridged from Matthiæ By the Bishop of London. *Ninth Edition*, revised by Rev. J. Edwards. 12mo. 3s.

GREY'S (Sir George) Polynesian Mythology, and Ancient Traditional History of the New Zealand Race. Woodcuts. Post 8vo. 10s. 6d.

GROTE'S (George) History of Greece. From the Earliest Times to the close of the generation contemporary with the death of Alexander the Great. *Third Edition.* Maps and Index. 12 vols. 8vo. 16s. each.

GROSVENOR'S (Lord Robert) Leaves from my Journal during the Summer of 1851. *Second Edition.* Plates. Post 8vo. 3s. 6d.

GUSTAVUS VASA (History of), King of Sweden. With Extracts from his Correspondence. Portrait. 8vo. 10s. 6d.

HALLAM'S (Henry) Constitutional History of England, from the Accession of Henry the Seventh to the Death of George the Second. *Seventh Edition.* 3 Vols. 8vo. 30s.

——— History of Europe during the Middle Ages. *Tenth Edition.* 3 Vols. 8vo. 30s.

——— Introduction to the Literary History of Europe, during the 16th, 17th, and 18th Centuries. *Fourth Edition.* 3 Vols. 8vo. 36s.

——— Literary Essays and Characters. Selected from the last work. Fcap. 8vo. 2s.

——— Historical Works. Containing the History of England,—The Middle Ages of Europe,—and the Literary History of Europe. *Complete Edition.* 10 Vols. Post 8vo. 6s. each.

HAMILTON'S (James) Wanderings in Northern Africa, Benghazi, Cyrene, the Oasis of Siwah, &c. *Second Edition.* Woodcuts. Post 8vo. 12s.

——— (Walter) Hindostan, Geographically, Statistically, and Historically. Map. 2 Vols. 4to. 94s. 6d.

HAMPDEN'S (Bishop) Essay on the Philosophical Evidence of Christianity, or the Credibility obtained to a Scripture Revelation from its Coincidence with the Facts of Nature. 8vo. 9s. 6d.

HARCOURT'S (Edward Vernon) Sketch of Madeira; with Map and Plates. Post 8vo. 8s. 6d.

HART'S ARMY LIST. (*Quarterly and Annually.*) 8vo.

HAY'S (J. H. Drummond) Western Barbary, its wild Tribes and savage Animals. Post 8vo. 2s. 6d.

HEBER (Bishop) Parish Sermons; on the Lessons, the Gospel, or the Epistle, for every Sunday in the Year, and for Week-day Festivals. *Sixth Edition.* 2 Vols. Post 8vo. 16s.

——— Sermons Preached in England. *Second Edition.* 8vo. 9s. 6d.

——— Hymns written and adapted for the weekly Church Service of the Year. *Twelfth Edition.* 16mo. 2s.

——— Poetical Works. *Fifth Edition.* Portrait. Fcap. 8vo. 7s. 6d.

——— Journey through the Upper Provinces of India, From Calcutta to Bombay, with a Journey to Madras and the Southern Provinces. 2 Vols. Post 8vo. 12s.

HAND-BOOK OF TRAVEL-TALK; or, Conversations in English, German, French, and Italian. 18mo. *3s. 6d.*

——— NORTH GERMANY—HOLLAND, BELGIUM, and the Rhine to Switzerland. Map. Post 8vo. 10*s.*

——— SOUTH GERMANY—Bavaria, Austria, S·lzberg, the Austrian and Bavarian Alps, the Tyrol, and the Danube, from Ulm to the Black Sea. Map. Post 8vo. 10*s.*

——— PAINTING—the German, Flemish, and Dutch Schools: From the German of KUGLER. *A New Edition.* Edited by DR. WAAGEN. Woodcuts. Post 8vo. (*In the Press.*)

——— SWITZERLAND—the Alps of Savoy, and Piedmont. Maps. Post 8vo. 9*s.*

——— FRANCE—Normandy, Brittany, the French Alps, the Rivers Loire, Seine, Rhone, and Garonne, Dauphiné, Provence, and the Pyrenees. Maps. Post 8vo. 10*s.*

——— SPAIN—Andalusia, Ronda, Granada, Valencia, Catalonia, Gallicia, Arragon, and Navarre. Maps. 2 Vols. Post 8vo. 30*s.*

——— PORTUGAL, LISBON, &c. Map. Post 8vo. 9*s.*

——— PAINTING—SPANISH AND FRENCH SCHOOLS. By SIR EDMUND HEAD, BART. Woodcuts. Post 8vo. 12*s.*

——— NORTH ITALY—Florence, Sardinia, Genoa, the Riviera, Venice, Lombardy, and Tuscany. Map. Post 8vo. 2 Vols. 12*s.*

——— CENTRAL ITALY—SOUTH TUSCANY and the PAPAL STATES. Map. Post 8vo. 7*s.*

——— ROME—AND ITS ENVIRONS. Map. Post 8vo. 9*s.*

——— SOUTH ITALY—Naples, Pompeii, Herculaneum, Vesuvius, &c. Map. Post 8vo. 10*s.*

——— SICILY. Map. Post 8vo. (*In the Press.*)

——— PAINTING—the Italian Schools. From the German of KUGLER. Edited by SIR CHARLES EASTLAKE, R. A. Woodcuts. 2 Vols. Post 8vo. 30*s.*

——— ITALIAN PAINTERS: (A SHORT BIOGRAPHICAL DICTIONARY OF.) With a Chart. Post 8vo. 6*s.* 6*d.*

——— GREECE—the Ionian Islands, Albania, Thessaly, and Macedonia. Maps. Post 8vo. 15*s.*

——— TURKEY—MALTA, ASIA MINOR, CONSTANTINOPLE, Armenia, Mesopotamia, &c. Maps. Post 8vo.

——— EGYPT—Thebes, the Nile, Alexandria, Cairo, the Pyramids, Mount Sinai, &c. Map. Post 8vo. 15*s.*

——— SYRIA AND PALESTINE; the Peninsula of Sinai, Edom, and the Syrian Desert. Maps. 2 Vols. Post 8vo. 24*s.*

——— INDIA.—Part 1. Bombay and Madras. Map. 2 Parts. Post 8vo.

——— DENMARK—NORWAY and SWEDEN. Maps. Post 8vo. 15*s.*

——— RUSSIA—THE BALTIC AND FINLAND. Maps. Post 8vo. 12*s.*

HANDBOOK OF LONDON, PAST AND PRESENT. Alphabetically arranged. *Second Edition.* Post 8vo. 16*s.*

——— MODERN LONDON. A Guide to all objects of interest in the Metropolis. Map. 16mo. 5*s.*

——— ENVIRONS OF LONDON. Including a Circle of 30 Miles round St. Paul's. Maps. Post 8vo. (*In preparation.*)

——— DEVON AND CORNWALL. Maps. Post 8vo.

——— WILTS, DORSET, AND SOMERSET. Map. Post 8vo.

——— KENT AND SUSSEX. Map. Post 8vo. 10*s.*

——— SURREY, HANTS, and the Isle of Wight. Maps. Post 8vo. 7*s.* 6*d.*

——— WESTMINSTER ABBEY—its Art, Architecture, and Associations. Woodcuts. 16mo. 1*s.*

——— CATHEDRALS OF ENGLAND. Post 8vo. *In Preparation.*

——— PARIS. Post 8vo. (*In Preparation.*)

——— FAMILIAR QUOTATIONS. Chiefly from English Authors. *Third Edition.* Fcap. 8vo. 5*s.*

——— ARCHITECTURE. Being a Concise and Popular Account of the Different Styles prevailing in all Ages and Countries. By JAMES FERGUSSON. *Fourth Thousand.* With 850 Illustrations. 8vo. 26*s.*

——— ARTS OF THE MIDDLE AGES AND RE-naissance. By M. Jules Labarte. With 200 Illustrations. 8vo. 18*s.*

HEAD'S (SIR FRANCIS) Rough Notes of some Rapid Journeys across the Pampas and over the Andes. Post 8vo. 2*s.* 6*d.*

——— Descriptive Essays: contributed to the "Quarterly Review." 2 Vols. Post 8vo. 18*s.*

——— Bubbles from the Brunnen of Nassau. By an OLD MAN. *Sixth Edition.* 16mo. 5*s.*

——— Emigrant. *Sixth Edition.* Fcap. 8vo. 2*s.* 6*d.*

——— Stokers and Pokers; or, the London and North-Western Railway. Post 8vo. 2*s.* 6*d.*

——— Defenceless State of Great Britain. Post 8vo. 12*s.*

——— Faggot of French Sticks; or, Sketches of Paris. *New Edition.* 2 Vols. Post 8vo. 12*s.*

——— Fortnight in Ireland. *Second Edition.* Map. 8vo. 12*s.*

——— (SIR GEORGE) Forest Scenes and Incidents in Canada. *Second Edition.* Post 8vo. 10*s.*

——— Home Tour through the Manufacturing Districts of England, Scotland, and Ireland, including the Channel Islands, and the Isle of Man. *Third Edition.* 2 Vols. Post 8vo. 12*s.*

——— (SIR EDMUND) Handbook of Painting—the Spanish and French Schools. With Illustrations. Post 8vo.

——— Shall and Will; or, Two Chapters on Future Auxiliary Verbs. *Second Edition, Enlarged.* Fcap. 8vo. 4*s.*

HEIRESS (The) in Her Minority; or, The Progress of Character. By the Author of "Bertha's Journal." 2 Vols. 12mo. 18*s.*

HERODOTUS. A New English Version. Edited with Notes, and Essays. By Rev. G. Rawlinson, assisted by Sir Henry Rawlinson, and Sir J. G. Wilkinson. Maps and Woodcuts. 4 Vols. 8vo. 18*s. each.*

HERVEY'S (Lord) Memoirs of the Reign of George the Second, from his Accession to the Death of Queen Caroline. Edited, with Notes by Mr. Croker. *Second Edition.* Portrait. 2 Vols. 8vo. 21*s.*

HICKMAN'S (Wm.) Treatise on the Law and Practice of Naval Courts Martial. 8vo. 10*s.* 6*d.*

HILLARD'S (G. S.) Six Months in Italy. 2 Vols. Post 8vo. 16*s.*

HISTORY OF ENGLAND AND FRANCE under the House of Lancaster. With an Introductory View of the Early Reformation. *Second Edition.* 8vo. 15*s.*

HOLLAND'S (Rev. W. B.) Psalms and Hymns, selected and adapted to the various Solemnities of the Church. *Third Edition.* 24mo. 1*s.* 3*d.*

HOLLWAY'S (J. G.) Month in Norway. Fcap. 8vo. 2*s.*

HONEY BEE (The). An Essay. By Rev. Thomas James. Reprinted from the "Quarterly Review." Fcap. 8vo. 1*s.*

HOOK'S (Rev. Dr.) Church Dictionary. *Eighth Edition.* 8vo. 16*s.*

——— Discourses on the Religious Controversies of the Day. 8vo. 9*s.*

——— (Theodore) Life. By J. G. Lockhart. Reprinted from the "Quarterly Review." Fcap. 8vo. 1*s.*

HOOKER'S (Dr. J. D.) Himalayan Journals; or, Notes of an Oriental Naturalist in Bengal, the Sikkim and Nepal Himalayas, the Khasia Mountains, &c. *Second Edition.* Woodcuts. 2 vols. Post 8vo. 18*s.*

HOOPER'S (Lieut.) Ten Months among the Tents of the Tuski; with Incidents of an Arctic Boat Expedition in Search of Sir John Franklin. Plates, 8vo. 14*s.*

HORACE (Works of). Edited by Dean Milman. With 300 Woodcuts. Crown 8vo. 21*s.*

——— (Life of). By Dean Milman. Woodcuts, and coloured Borders. 8vo. 9*s.*

HOSPITALS AND SISTERHOODS. By a Lady. Fcap. 8vo. 3*s.* 6*d.*

HOUSTOUN'S (Mrs.) Yacht Voyage to Texas and the Gulf of Mexico. Plates. 2 Vols. Post 8vo. 21*s.*

HOME AND COLONIAL LIBRARY. Complete in 70 Parts.

Post 8vo, 2*s.* 6*d.* each, or bound in 34 Volumes, cloth.

CONTENTS OF THE SERIES.

THE BIBLE IN SPAIN. By GEORGE BORROW.
JOURNALS IN INDIA. By BISHOP HEBER.
TRAVELS IN THE HOLY LAND. By CAPTAINS IRBY and MANGLES.
THE SIEGE OF GIBRALTAR. By JOHN DRINKWATER.
MOROCCO AND THE MOORS. By J. DRUMMOND HAY.
LETTERS FROM THE BALTIC. By a LADY.
THE AMBER-WITCH. By LADY DUFF GORDON.
OLIVER CROMWELL & JOHN BUNYAN. By ROBERT SOUTHEY.
NEW SOUTH WALES. By MRS. MEREDITH.
LIFE OF SIR FRANCIS DRAKE. By JOHN BARROW.
FATHER RIPA'S MEMOIRS OF THE COURT OF CHINA.
A RESIDENCE IN THE WEST INDIES. By M. G. LEWIS.
SKETCHES OF PERSIA. By SIR JOHN MALCOLM.
THE FRENCH IN ALGIERS. By LADY DUFF GORDON.
VOYAGE OF A NATURALIST. By CHARLES DARWIN.
HISTORY OF THE FALL OF THE JESUITS.
LIFE OF LOUIS PRINCE OF CONDE. By LORD MAHON.
GIPSIES OF SPAIN. By GEORGE BORROW.
THE MARQUESAS. By HERMANN MELVILLE.
LIVONIAN TALES. By a LADY.
MISSIONARY LIFE IN CANADA. By REV. J. ABBOTT.
SALE'S BRIGADE IN AFFGHANISTAN. By REV. G. R. GLEIG.
LETTERS FROM MADRAS. By a LADY.
HIGHLAND SPORTS. By CHARLES ST. JOHN.
JOURNEYS ACROSS THE PAMPAS. By SIR F. B. HEAD.
GATHERINGS FROM SPAIN. By RICHARD FORD.
SIEGES OF VIENNA BY THE TURKS. By LORD ELLESMERE.
SKETCHES OF GERMAN LIFE. By SIR A. GORDON.
ADVENTURES IN THE SOUTH SEAS. By HERMANN MELVILLE.
STORY OF BATTLE OF WATERLOO. By REV. G. R. GLEIG.
A VOYAGE UP THE RIVER AMAZON. By W. H. EDWARDS.
THE WAYSIDE CROSS. By CAPT. MILMAN.
MANNERS & CUSTOMS OF INDIA. By REV. C. ACLAND.
CAMPAIGNS AT WASHINGTON. By REV. G. R. GLEIG.
ADVENTURES IN MEXICO. By G. F. RUXTON.
PORTUGAL AND GALLICIA. By LORD CARNARVON.
LIFE OF LORD CLIVE. By REV. G. R. GLEIG.
BUSH LIFE IN AUSTRALIA. By H. W. HAYGARTH.
THE AUTOBIOGRAPHY OF HENRY STEFFENS.
SHORT LIVES OF THE POETS. By THOMAS CAMPBELL.
HISTORICAL ESSAYS. By LORD MAHON.
LONDON & NORTH-WESTERN RAILWAY. By SIR F. B. HEAD.
ADVENTURES IN THE LIBYAN DESERT. By BAYLE ST. JOHN.
A RESIDENCE AT SIERRA LEONE. By a LADY.
LIFE OF GENERAL MUNRO. By REV. G. R. GLEIG.
MEMOIRS OF SIR FOWELL BUXTON. By his SON.

HUME (The Student's). A History of England, from the Invasion of Julius Cæsar. By David Hume; abridged and continued to the Present Time. Woodcuts. Post 8vo. *7s. 6d.* (*Uniform with The Student's Gibbon.*)

HUTCHINSON (Colonel) on Dog-Breaking; the most expeditious, certain, and easy Method, whether great Excellence or only Mediocrity be required. *Third Edition.* Revised and enlarged. Woodcuts. Post 8vo. *9s.*

IRBY AND MANGLES' Travels in Egypt, Nubia, Syria, and the Holy Land, including a Journey round the Dead Sea, and through the Country east of the Jordan. Post 8vo. *2s. 6d.*

JAMES' (Rev. Thomas) Fables of Æsop. A New Translation, with Historical Preface. With 100 Woodcuts by Tenniel and Wolf. *Twenty-sixth Thousand.* Post 8vo. *2s. 6d.*

JAMESON'S (Mrs.) Memoirs of the Early Italian Painters, and of the Progress of Italian Painting in Italy. *Tenth Edition.* With 70 Woodcuts. Fcap. 8vo. *6s.*

JAPAN AND THE JAPANESE. Described from the Accounts of Recent Dutch Travellers. *New Edition.* Post 8vo. *6s.*

JARDINE'S (David) Narrative of the Gunpowder Plot. *New Edition.* Post 8vo. *7s. 6d.*

JERVIS'S (Capt.) Manual of Operations in the Field, for the Use of Officers. Post 8vo. *9s. 6d.*

JESSE'S (Edward) Favorite Haunts and Rural Studies; or Visits to Spots of Interest in the Vicinity of Windsor and Eton. Woodcuts. Post 8vo. *12s.*

——— Scenes and Occupations of Country Life. With Recollections of Natural History. *Third Edition.* Woodcuts. Fcap. 8vo. *6s.*

——— Gleanings in Natural History. With Anecdotes of the Sagacity and Instinct of Animals. *Eighth Edition.* Fcap. 8vo. *6s.*

JOHNSON'S (Dr. Samuel) Life: By James Boswell. Including the Tour to the Hebrides, with Notes by Sir W. Scott. Edited by the late Mr. Croker. *Third Edition.* Portraits. Royal 8vo. *15s.*

——— Lives of the most eminent English Poets. A New Edition. Edited by Peter Cunningham. 3 vols. 8vo. *22s. 6d.* (Murray's British Classics.)

JOHNSTON'S (Wm.) England as it is: Social, Political, and Industrial, in the Middle of the 19th Century. 2 Vols. Post 8vo. *18s.*

JOURNAL OF A NATURALIST. *Fourth Edition.* Woodcuts. Post 8vo. *9s. 6d.*

JOWETT'S (Rev. B.) Commentary on St. Paul's Epistles to the Thessalonians, Galatians, and Romans. With Notes and Dissertations. *Second Edition.* 2 Vols. 8vo.

KEN'S (Bishop) Life. By A Layman. *Second Edition.* Portrait. 2 Vols. 8vo. *18s.*

KEN'S (BISHOP) Exposition of the Apostles' Creed. Extracted from his "Practice of Divine Love." *New Edition.* Fcap. 1*s.* 6*d.*

——— Approach to the Holy Altar. Extracted from his "Manual of Prayer" and "Practice of Divine Love." *New Edition.* Fcap. 8vo. 1*s.* 6*d.*

KING'S (REV. S. W.) Italian Valleys of the Alps; a Tour through all the Romantic and less-frequented "Vals" of Northern Piedmont, from the Tarentaise to the Gries. With Illustrations. Crown 8vo. 18*s.*

KING EDWARD VITH's Latin Grammar; or, an Introduction to the Latin Tongue, for the Use of Schools. 12*th Edition.* 12mo. 3*s.* 6*d.*

——— First Latin Book; or, the Accidence, Syntax and Prosody, with an English Translation for the Use of Junior Classes. *Third Edition.* 12mo. 2*s.*

KNAPP'S (J. A.) English Roots and Ramifications; or, the Derivation and Meaning of Divers Words. Fcap. 8vo. 4*s.*

KUGLER'S (DR. FRANZ) Handbook to the History of Painting (the Italian Schools). Translated from the German. Edited, with Notes, by SIR CHARLES EASTLAKE. *Third Edition.* Woodcuts. 2 Vols. Post 8vo. 30*s.*

——— (the German, Dutch, and Flemish Schools). Translated from the German. *A New Edition.* Edited, with Notes. By DR. WAAGEN. Woodcuts. Post 8vo. *Nearly Ready.*

LABARTE'S (M. JULES) Handbook of the Arts of the Middle Ages and Renaissance. With 200 Woodcuts. 8vo. 18*s.*

LABORDE'S (LEON DE) Journey through Arabia Petræa, to Mount Sinai, and the Excavated City of Petræa,—the Edom of the Prophecies. *Second Edition.* With Plates. 8vo. 18*s.*

LANE'S (E. W.) Arabian Nights. Translated from the Arabic, with Explanatory Notes. *A New Edition.* Edited by E. STANLEY POOLE. With 600 Woodcuts. 3 Vols. 8vo. 42*s.*

LATIN GRAMMAR (KING EDWARD THE VITH's.) For the Use of Schools. *Twelfth Edition.* 12mo. 3*s.* 6*d.*

——— First Book (KING EDWARD VI.); or, the Accidence, Syntax, and Prosody, with English Translation for Junior Classes. *Third Edition.* 12mo. 2*s.*

LAYARD'S (A. H.) Nineveh and its Remains. Being a Narrative of Researches and Discoveries amidst the Ruins of Assyria. With an Account of the Chaldean Christians of Kurdistan; the Yezedis, or Devil-worshippers; and an Enquiry into the Manners and Arts of the Ancient Assyrians. *Sixth Edition.* Plates and Woodcuts. 2 Vols. 8vo. 36*s.*

——— Nineveh and Babylon; being the Result of a Second Expedition to Assyria. *Fourteenth Thousand.* Plates. 8vo. 21*s.* Or Fine Paper, 2 Vols. 8vo. 30*s.*

——— Popular Account of Nineveh. 15*th Edition.* With Woodcuts. Post 8vo. 5*s.*

LESLIE'S (C. R.) Handbook for Young Painters. With Illustrations. Post 8vo. 10*s.* 6*d.*

——— Life of Sir Joshua Reynolds. With an Account of his Works, and a Sketch of his Cotemporaries. Fcap. 4to. *In the Press.*

LEAKE'S (Col. W. Martin) Topography of Athens, with Remarks on its Antiquities; to which is added, the Demi of Attica. *Second Edition*. Plates. 2 Vols. 8vo. 30*s*.

——— Travels in Northern Greece. Maps. 4 Vols. 8vo. 60*s*.

——— Disputed Questions of Ancient Geography. Map. 8vo. 6*s*. 6*d*.

——— Numismata Hellenica. A Catalogue of Greek Coins. With Map and Appendix. 4to 63*s*.

——— Peloponnesiaca: A Supplement to Travels in the Morea. 8vo. 15*s*.

——— Thoughts on the Degradation of Science in England. 8vo. 3*s*. 6*d*.

LETTERS FROM THE SHORES OF THE BALTIC. By a Lady. Post 8vo. 2*s*. 6*d*.

——— Madras; or, First Impressions of Life and Manners in India. By a Lady. Post 8vo. 2*s*. 6*d*.

——— Sierra Leone, written to Friends at Home. By a Lady. Edited by Mrs. Norton. Post 8vo. 6*s*.

——— Head Quarters; or, The Realities of the War in the Crimea. By a Staff Officer. *Popular Edition*. Plans. Post 8vo. 6*s*.

LEXINGTON (The) PAPERS; or, Some Account of the Courts of London and Vienna at the end of the 17th Century. Edited by Hon. H. Manners Sutton. 8vo. 14*s*.

LEWIS' (Sir G. C.) Essay on the Government of Dependencies. 8vo. 12*s*.

——— Glossary of Provincial Words used in Herefordshire and some of the adjoining Counties. 12mo. 4*s*. 6*d*.

——— (Lady Theresa) Friends and Contemporaries of the Lord Chancellor Clarendon, illustrative of Portraits in his Gallery. With a Descriptive Account of the Pictures, and Origin of the Collection. Portraits. 3 Vols. 8vo. 42*s*.

——— (M. G.) Journal of a Residence among the Negroes in the West Indies. Post 8vo. 2*s*. 6*d*.

LIDDELL'S (Dean) History of Rome. From the Earliest Times to the Establishment of the Empire. With the History of Literature and Art. *Library Edition*. 2 Vols. 8vo. 28*s*.

——— SCHOOL HISTORY OF ROME. Abridged from the Larger Work. *Eighth Thousand*. With 100 Woodcuts. Post 8vo. 7*s*. 6*d*. [*Uniform with* Dr. Wm. Smith's History of Greece].

LINDSAY'S (Lord) Lives of the Lindsays; or, a Memoir of the Houses of Crawford and Balcarres. With Extracts from Official Papers and Personal Narratives. *Second Edition*. 3 Vols. 8vo. 24*s*.

———Report of the Claim of James, Earl of Crawfurd and Balcarres, to the Original Dukedom of Montrose, created in 1488. Folio. 15*s*.

LITTLE ARTHUR'S HISTORY OF ENGLAND. By Lady Callcott. *Eighteenth Edition*. With 20 Woodcuts. Fcap. 8vo. 2*s*. 6*d*.

LIVINGSTONE'S (Rev. Dr.) Missionary Travels and Researches in South Africa; including a Sketch of Sixteen Years' Residence in the Interior of Africa, and a Journey from the Cape of Good Hope to Loanda on the West Coast; thence across the Continent, down the River Zambesi, to the Eastern Ocean. *Thirtieth Thousand.* Map, Plates, and Index. 8vo. 21*s.*

LIVONIAN TALES.—The Disponent.—The Wolves.—The Jewess. By the Author of "Letters from the Baltic." Post 8vo. 2*s.* 6*d.*

LOCKHART'S (J. G.) Ancient Spanish Ballads. Historical and Romantic. Translated, with Notes. *Illustrated Edition.* 4to. 21*s.* Or, *Popular Edition.* Post 8vo. 2*s.* 6*d.*

——— Life of Robert Burns. *Fifth Edition.* Fcap. 8vo. 3*s.*

LOUDON'S (Mrs.) Instructions in Gardening for Ladies. With Directions and Calendar of Operations for Every Month. *Eighth Edition.* Woodcuts. Fcap. 8vo. 5*s.*

——— Modern Botany; a Popular Introduction to the Natural System of Plants. *Second Edition.* Woodcuts. Fcap. 8vo. 6*s.*

LOWE'S (Sir Hudson) Letters and Journals, during the Captivity of Napoleon at St. Helena. By William Forsyth. Portrait. 3 Vols. 8vo. 45*s.*

LUCKNOW: A Lady's Diary of the Siege. Written for Friends at Home. *Fourth Thousand.* Fcap. 8vo. 4*s.* 6*d.*

LYELL'S (Sir Charles) Principles of Geology; or, the Modern Changes of the Earth and its Inhabitants considered as illustrative of Geology. *Ninth Edition.* Woodcuts. 8vo. 18*s.*

——— Manual of Elementary Geology; or, the Ancient Changes of the Earth and its Inhabitants illustrated by its Geological Monuments. *Fifth Edition.* Woodcuts. 8vo. 14*s.*

———Visits to the United States, 1841-46. *Second Edition.* Plates. 4 Vols. Post 8vo. 24*s.*

MAHON'S (Lord) History of England, from the Peace of Utrecht to the Peace of Versailles, 1713—83. *Library Edition.* 7 Vols. 8vo. 93*s.*

——— *Popular Edition.* 7 Vols. Post 8vo. 35*s.*

——— "Forty-Five;" a Narrative of the Rebellion in Scotland. Post 8vo. 3*s.*

——— The Rise of our Indian Empire. Being the History of British India from its Origin till the Peace of 1783. Extracted from his "History of England." Post 8vo. 3*s.* 6*d.*

——— History of the War of the Succession in Spain. *Second Edition.* Map. 8vo. 15*s.*

——— Spain under Charles the Second; or, Extracts from the Correspondence of the Hon. Alexander Stanhope, British Minister at Madrid from 1690 to 1700. *Second Edition.* Post 8vo. 6*s.* 6*d.*

——— Life of Louis Prince of Condé, surnamed the Great. Post 8vo. 6*s.*

——— Life of Belisarius. *Second Edition.* Post 8vo. 10*s.* 6*d.*

——— Historical and Critical Essays. Post 8vo. 6*s.*

——— Story of Joan of Arc. Fcap. 8vo. 1*s.*

——— Addresses Delivered at Manchester, Leeds, and Birmingham. Fcap. 8vo. 1*s.*

M'CULLOCH'S (J. R.) Collected Edition of RICARDO'S Political Works. With Notes and Memoir. *Second Edition.* 8vo. 16*s*.

MALCOLM'S (SIR JOHN) Sketches of Persia. *Third Edition.* Post 8vo. 6*s*.

MANSEL'S (REV. H. L.) The Limits of Religious Thought Examined. Being the Bampton Lectures for 1858. *Second Edition.* 8vo. 12*s*.

MANTELL'S (GIDEON A.) Thoughts on Animalcules; or, the Invisible World, as revealed by the Microscope. *Second Edition.* Plates. 16mo. 6*s*.

MANUAL OF SCIENTIFIC ENQUIRY, Prepared for the Use of Officers and Travellers. By various Writers. *Third Edition revised.* Maps. Post 8vo. (*Published by order of the Lords of the Admiralty.*)

MARKHAM'S (MRS.) History of England. From the First Invasion by the Romans, down to the fourteenth year of Queen Victoria's Reign. *98th Edition.* Woodcuts. 12mo. 6*s*.

——— History of France. From the Conquest by the Gauls, to the Death of Louis Philippe. *58th Edition.* Woodcuts. 12mo. 6*s*.

——— History of Germany. From the Invasion by Marius, to the present time. *6th Edition.* Woodcuts. 12mo. 6*s*.

——— School History of Greece. From the Earliest Times of the Roman Conquest. With the History of Literature and Art. By DR. WM. SMITH. *Sixteenth Thousand.* Woodcuts. 12mo. 7*s*. 6*d*. (*Questions.* 12mo. 2*s*.)

——— School History of Rome, from the Earliest Times to the Establishment of the Empire. With the History of Literature and Art. By DEAN LIDDELL. *Eighth Thousand.* Woodcuts. 12mo. 7*s*. 6*d*.

MARKLAND'S (J. H.) Reverence due to Holy Places. *Third Edition.* Fcap. 8vo. 2*s*.

MARRYAT'S (JOSEPH) History of Modern and Mediæval Pottery and Porcelain. With a Description of the Manufacture, a Glossary, and a List of Monograms. *Second Edition.* Plates and Woodcuts. 8vo. 31*s*. 6*d*.

MATTHIÆ'S (AUGUSTUS) Greek Grammar for Schools. Abridged from the Larger Grammar. By Blomfield. *Ninth Edition.* Revised by EDWARDS. 12mo. 3*s*.

MAUREL'S (JULES) Essay on the Character, Actions, and Writings of the Duke of Wellington. *Second Edition.* Fcap. 8vo. 1*s*. 6*d*.

MAWE'S (H. L.) Journal of a Passage from the Pacific to the Atlantic, crossing the Andes in the Northern Provinces of Peru, and descending the great River Maranon. 8vo. 12*s*.

MAXIMS AND HINTS for an Angler, and the Miseries of Fishing. By RICHARD PENN. *New Edition.* Woodcuts. 12mo. 1*s*.

MAYO'S (DR.) Pathology of the Human Mind. Fcap. 8vo. 5*s*. 6*d*.

MELVILLE'S (HERMANN) Typee and Omoo; or, Adventures amongst the Marquesas and South Sea Islands. 2 Vols. Post 8vo.

MENDELSSOHN'S (Felix Bartholdy) Life. By Jules Benedict. 8vo. 2*s*. 6*d*.

MEREDITH'S (Mrs. Charles) Notes and Sketches of New South Wales, during a Residence from 1839 to 1844. Post 8vo. 2*s*. 6*d*.

——— Tasmania, during a Residence of Nine Years. With Illustrations. 2 Vols. Post 8vo. 18*s*.

MERRIFIELD (Mrs.) on the Arts of Painting in Oil, Miniature, Mosaic, and Glass; Gilding, Dyeing, and the Preparation of Colours and Artificial Gems, described in several old Manuscripts. 2 Vols. 8vo. 30*s*.

MILLS (Arthur) India in 1858; A Summary of the Existing Administration—Political, Fiscal, and Judicial; with Laws and Public Documents, from the earliest to the present time. *Second Edition*. With Coloured Revenue Map. 8vo. 10*s*. 6*d*.

MITCHELL'S (Thomas) Plays of Aristophanes. With English Notes. 8vo.—1. CLOUDS, 10*s*.—2. WASPS, 10*s*.—3. FROGS, 15*s*.

MILMAN'S (Dean) History of Christianity, from the Birth of Christ to the Extinction of Paganism in the Roman Empire. 3 Vols. 8vo. 36*s*.

——— History of Latin Christianity; including that of the Popes to the Pontificate of Nicholas V. *Second Edition*. 6 Vols. 8vo. 72*s*.

——— Character and Conduct of the Apostles considered as an Evidence of Christianity. 8vo. 10*s*. 6*d*.

——— Life and Works of Horace. With 300 Woodcuts. *New Edition*. 2 Vols. Crown 8vo. 30*s*.

——— Poetical Works. Plates. 3 Vols. Fcap. 8vo. 18*s*.

——— Fall of Jerusalem. Fcap. 8vo. 1*s*.

——— (Capt. E. A.) Wayside Cross; or, the Raid of Gomez. A Tale of the Carlist War. Post 8vo. 2*s*. 6*d*.

MODERN DOMESTIC COOKERY. Founded on Principles of Economy and Practical Knowledge, and adapted for Private Families. *New Edition*. Woodcuts. Fcap. 8vo. 5*s*.

MOLTKE'S (Baron) Russian Campaigns on the Danube and the Passage of the Balkan, 1828—9. Plans. 8vo. 14*s*.

MONASTERY AND THE MOUNTAIN CHURCH. By Author of "Sunlight through the Mist." Woodcuts. 16mo. 4*s*.

MOORE'S (Thomas) Life and Letters of Lord Byron. *Cabinet Edition*. 6 Vols. Fcap. 8vo. 18*s*.

——— Life and Letters of Lord Byron. *Popular Edition*. With Portrait and Vignette. One Volume. Royal 8vo. 12*s*.

MOZLEY'S (Rev. J. B.) Treatise on the Augustinian Doctrine of Predestination. 8vo. 14*s*.

——— Primitive Doctrine of Baptismal Regeneration. 8vo. 7*s*. 6*d*.

MUCK MANUAL (The) for the Use of Farmers. A Practical Treatise on the Chemical Properties, Management, and Application of Manures. By Frederick Falkner. *Second Edition*. Fcap. 8vo. 5*s*.

MUNDY'S (Gen.) Pen and Pencil Sketches during a Tour in India. *Third Edition.* Plates. Post 8vo. 7*s.* 6*d.*

MUNRO'S (General Sir Thomas) Life and Letters. By the Rev. G. R. Gleig. Post 8vo. 6*s.*

MURCHISON'S (Sir Roderick) Russia in Europe and the Ural Mountains; Geologically Illustrated. With Coloured Maps, Plates, Sections, &c. 2 Vols. Royal 4to.

——— Siluria; or, a History of the Oldest Rocks containing Organic Remains. *Second Edition.* Map and Plates. 8vo.

MURRAY'S (Capt. A.) Naval Life and Services of Admiral Sir Philip Durham. 8vo. 5*s.* 6*d.*

MURRAY'S RAILWAY READING. For all classes of Readers.

[*The following are published:*]

Wellington. By Lord Ellesmere. 6*d.*
Nimrod on the Chase, 1*s.*
Essays from "The Times." 2 Vols. 8*s.*
Music and Dress. 1*s.*
Layard's Account of Nineveh. 5*s.*
Milman's Fall of Jerusalem. 1*s.*
Mahon's "Forty-Five." 3*s.*
Life of Theodore Hook. 1*s.*
Deeds of Naval Daring. 2 Vols. 5*s.*
The Honey Bee. 1*s.*
James' Æsop's Fables. 2*s.* 6*d.*
Nimrod on the Turf. 1*s.* 6*d.*
Oliphant's Nepaul. 2*s.* 6*d.*
Art of Dining. 1*s.* 6*d.*
Hallam's Literary Essays. 2*s.*
Mahon's Joan of Arc. 1*s.*
Head's Emigrant. 2*s.* 6*d.*
Nimrod on the Road. 1*s.*
Wilkinson's Ancient Egyptians. 12*s.*
Croker on the Guillotine. 1*s.*
Hollway's Norway. 2*s.*
Maurel's Wellington. 1*s.* 6*d.*
Campbell's Life of Bacon. 2*s.* 6*d.*
The Flower Garden. 1*s.*
Lockhart's Spanish Ballads. 2*s.* 6*d.*
Lucas on History. 6*d.*
Beauties of Byron. 3*s.*
Taylor's Notes from Life. 2*s.*
Rejected Addresses. 1*s.*
Penn's Hints on Angling. 1*s.*

MUSIC AND DRESS. Two Essays, by a Lady. Reprinted from the "Quarterly Review." Fcap. 8vo. 1*s.*

NAPIER'S (Sir Wm.) English Battles and Sieges of the Peninsular War. *Third Edition.* Portrait. Post 8vo. 10*s.* 6*d.*

——— Life and Opinions of General Sir Charles Napier; chiefly derived from his Journals, Letters, and Familiar Correspondence. *Second Edition.* Portraits. 4 Vols. Post 8vo. 48*s.*

NAUTICAL ALMANACK (The). Royal 8vo. 2*s.* 6*d.* (*Published by Authority.*)

NAVY LIST (The Quarterly). (*Published by Authority.*) Post 8vo. 2*s.* 6*d.*

NEWBOLD'S (Lieut.) Straits of Malacca, Penang, and Singapore. 2 Vols. 8vo. 26*s.*

NEWDEGATE'S (C. N.) Customs' Tariffs of all Nations; collected and arranged up to the year 1855. 4to. 30*s.*

NICHOLLS' (Sir George) History of the British Poor: Being an Historical Account of the English, Scotch, and Irish Poor Law: in connection with the Condition of the People. 4 Vols. 8vo.

The work may be had separately:—

History of the English Poor. 2 Vols. 8vo. 28*s.*
——— the Irish Poor. 8vo. 14*s.*
——— the Scotch Poor. 8vo. 12*s.*

——— (Rev. H. G.) FOREST OF DEAN. An Historical and Descriptive Account, derived from Personal Observation and other Sources, Public, Private, Legendary, and Local. Woodcuts &c. Post 8vo. 10*s.* 6*d.*

NICOLAS' (SIR HARRIS) Historic Peerage of England. Exhibiting, under Alphabetical Arrangement, the Origin, Descent, and Present State of every Title of Peerage which has existed in this Country since the Conquest. Being a New Edition of the "Synopsis of the Peerage." Revised, Corrected, and Continued to the Present Time. By WILLIAM COURTHOPE, Somerset Herald. 8vo. 30*s.*

NIMROD On the Chace—The Turf—and The Road. Reprinted from the "Quarterly Review." Woodcuts. Fcap. 8vo. 3*s.* 6*d.*

O'CONNOR'S (R.) Field Sports of France; or, Hunting, Shooting, and Fishing on the Continent. Woodcuts. 12mo. 7*s.* 6*d.*

OLIPHANT'S (LAURENCE) Journey to Katmandu, with Visit to the Camp of the Nepaulese Ambassador. Fcap. 8vo. 2*s.* 6*d.*

OWEN'S (PROFESSOR) Manual of Fossil Mammals. Including the substance of the course of Lectures on Osteology and Palæontology of the class Mammalia, delivered at the Metropolitan School of Science, Jermyn Street. Illustrations. 8vo. *In the Press.*

OXENHAM'S (REV. W.) English Notes for Latin Elegiacs; designed for early Proficients in the Art of Latin Versification, with Prefatory Rules of Composition in Elegiac Metre. *Third Edition.* 12mo. 4*s.*

PAGET'S (JOHN) Hungary and Transylvania. With Remarks on their Condition, Social, Political, and Economical. *Third Edition.* Woodcuts. 2 Vols. 8vo. 18*s.*

PARIS' (DR.) Philosophy in Sport made Science in Earnest; or, the First Principles of Natural Philosophy inculcated by aid of the Toys and Sports of Youth. *Eighth Edition.* Woodcuts. Post 8vo. 9*s.*

PARISH'S (SIR WOODBINE) Buenos Ayres and the Provinces of the Rio de la Plata. Their First Discovery and Conquest, Present State, Trade, Debt, &c. *Second Edition.* Map and Woodcuts. 8vo. 15*s.*

PARKYNS' (MANSFIELD) Personal Narrative of Three Years' Residence and Adventures in Abyssinia. Woodcuts. 2 Vols. 8vo. 30*s.*

PEEL'S (SIR ROBT.) MEMOIRS. Left in MSS. Edited by EARL STANHOPE and the Right Hon. EDWARD CARDWELL. 2 Vols. Post 8vo. 7*s.* 6*d.* each.

PEILE'S (REV. DR.) Agamemnon and Choephoræ of Æschylus. A New Edition of the Text, with Notes. *Second Edition.* 2 Vols. 8vo. 9*s.* each.

PENN'S (RICHARD) Maxims and Hints for an Angler, and the Miseries of Fishing. To which is added, Maxims and Hints for Chess-player. *New Edition.* Woodcuts. Fcap. 8vo. 1*s.*

PENROSE'S (REV. JOHN) Faith and Practice; an Exposition of the Principles and Duties of Natural and Revealed Religion. Post 8vo. 8*s.* 6*d.*

——————— (F. C.) Principles of Athenian Architecture, and the Optical Refinements exhibited in the Construction of the Ancient Buildings at Athens, from a Survey. With 40 Plates. Folio. 5*l.* 5*s.* (*Published under the direction of the Dilettanti Society.*)

PERRY'S (SIR ERSKINE) Bird's-Eye View of India. With Extracts from a Journal kept in the Provinces, Nepaul, &c. Fcap. 8vo. 5*s.*

PHILLIPS' (JOHN) Memoirs of William Smith, LL.D. (the Geologist). Portrait. 8vo. 7*s*. 6*d*.

——— Geology of Yorkshire, The Yorkshire Coast, and the Mountain-Limestone District. Plates 4to. Part I., 20*s*. –Part II., 30*s*.

——— Rivers, Mountains, and Sea Coast of Yorkshire. With Essays on the Climate, Scenery, and Ancient Inhabitants of the Country. *Second Edition*, with 36 Plates. 8vo. 15*s*.

PHILPOTT'S (BISHOP) Letters to the late Charles Butler, on the Theological parts of his "Book of the Roman Catholic Church;" with Remarks on certain Works of Dr. Milner and Dr. Lingard, and on some parts of the Evidence of Dr. Doyle. *Second Edition*. 8vo. 16*s*.

PHIPPS' (HON. EDMUND) Memoir, Correspondence, Literary and Unpublished Diaries of Robert Plumer Ward. Portrait. 2 Vols. 8vo. 28*s*.

POPE'S (ALEXANDER) WORKS. An entirely New Edition. Edited, with Notes. 8vo *In the Press*.

PORTER'S (REV. J. L.) Five Years in Damascus. With Travels to Palmyra, Lebanon, and other Scripture Sites. Map and Woodcuts. 2 vols. Post 8vo. 21*s*.

——— HANDBOOK FOR SYRIA AND PALESTINE: including an Account of the Geography, History, Antiquities, and Inhabitants of these Countries, the Peninsula of Sinai, Edom, and the Syrian Desert. Maps. 2 Vols. Post 8vo. 24*s*.

——— (MRS. G. R.) Rational Arithmetic for Schools and for Private Instruction. 12mo. 3*s*. 6*d*.

PRAYER-BOOK (The Illustrated), with 1000 Illustrations of Borders, Initials, Vignettes, &c. Medium 8vo. Cloth, 21*s*.; Calf, 31*s*. 6*d*.; Morocco, 42*s*.

PRECEPTS FOR THE CONDUCT OF LIFE. Exhortations to a Virtuous Course and Dissuasions from a Vicious Career. Extracted from the Scriptures. *Second Edition*. Fcap. 8vo. 1*s*.

PRINSEP'S (JAS.) Essays on Indian Antiquities, Historic, Numismatic, and Palæographic, with Tables, illustrative of Indian History, Chronology, Modern Coinages, Weights, Measures, &c. Edited by EDWARD THOMAS. Illustrations. 2 Vols. 8vo. 52*s*. 6*d*.

PROGRESS OF RUSSIA IN THE EAST. An Historical Summary, continued to the Present Time. With Map by ARROWSMITH. *Third Edition*. 8vo. 6*s*. 6*d*.

PUSS IN BOOTS. With 12 Illustrations; for Old and Young. By OTTO SPECKTER. *A New Edition*. 16mo. 1s. 6*d*.

QUARTERLY REVIEW (THE). 8vo. 6*s*.

RANKE'S (LEOPOLD) Political and Ecclesiastical History of the Popes of Rome, during the Sixteenth and Seventeenth Centuries. Translated from the German by MRS. AUSTIN. *Third Edition*. 2 Vols. 8vo. 24*s*.

RAWLINSON'S (REV. GEORGE) Herodotus. A New English Version. Edited with Notes and Essays. Assisted by SIR HENRY RAWLINSON and SIR J. G. WILKINSON. Maps and Woodcuts. 4 Vols. 8vo. 18*s*. each.

REJECTED ADDRESSES (THE). By JAMES AND HORACE SMITH. With Biographies of the Authors, and additional Notes. *New Edition, with the Author's latest Corrections*. Fcap. 8vo. 1*s*., or *Fine Paper*, with Portrait. Fcap. 8vo. 5*s*.

RENNIE'S (JAMES) Insect Architecture. To which are added Chapters on the Ravages, the Preservation, for Purposes of Study, and the Classification of Insects. *New Edition.* Woodcuts. Post 8vo. 5*s.*

RICARDO'S (DAVID) Political Works. With a Notice of his Life and Writings. By J. R. M'CULLOCH. *New Edition.* 8vo. 16*s.*

RIPA'S (FATHER) Memoirs during Thirteen Years' Residence at the Court of Peking, in the Service of the Emperor of China. Translated from the Italian. By FORTUNATO PRANDI. Post 8vo. 2*s.* 6*d.*

ROBERTSON'S (REV. J. C.) History of the Christian Church, From the Apostolic Age to the Pontificate of Gregory the Great, A.D. 590. *Second and Revised Edition.* Vol. 1. 8vo. 16*s.*

——— Second Period, from A.D. 590 to the Concordat of Worms. A.D. 1123. Vol. 2. 8vo. 18*s.*

ROBINSON'S (REV. DR.) Biblical Researches in the Holy Land. Being a Journal of Travels in 1838, and of Later Researches in 1852. With New Maps. 3 Vols. 8vo. 36*s.*

*** *The "Later Researches" may be had separately.* 8vo. 15*s.*

ROMILLY'S (SIR SAMUEL) Memoirs and Political Diary. By his SONS. *Third Edition.* Portrait. 2 Vols. Fcap. 8vo. 12*s.*

ROSS'S (SIR JAMES) Voyage of Discovery and Research in the Southern and Antarctic Regions during the years 1839-43. Plates. 2 Vols. 8vo. 36*s.*

RUNDELL'S (MRS.) Domestic Cookery, founded on Principles of Economy and Practice, and adapted for Private Families. *New and Revised Edition.* Woodcuts. Fcap. 8vo. 5*s.*

RUSSIA; A Memoir of the Remarkable Events which attended the Accession of the Emperor Nicholas. By BARON M. KORFF, Secretary of State. 8vo. 10*s.* 6*d.* (*Published by Imperial Command.*)

RUXTON'S (GEORGE F.) Travels in Mexico; with Adventures among the Wild Tribes and Animals of the Prairies and Rocky Mountains. Post 8vo. 6*s.*

SALE'S (LADY) Journal of the Disasters in Affghanistan. *Eighth Edition.* Post 8vo. 12*s.*

——— (SIR ROBERT) Brigade in Affghanistan. With an Account of the Seizure and Defence of Jellalabad. By REV. G. R. GLEIG. Post 8vo. 2*s.* 6*d.*

SANDWITH'S (HUMPHRY) Narrative of the Siege of Kars and of the Six Months' Resistance by the Turkish Garrison unde General Williams. *Seventh Thousand.* Post 8vo. 3*s.* 6*d.*

SCOTT'S (G. GILBERT) Remarks on Secular and Domestic Architecture, Present and Future. *Second Edition.* 8vo. 9*s.*

SCROPE'S (WILLIAM) Days of Deer-Stalking in the Forest of Atholl; with some Account of the Nature and Habits of the Red Deer. *Third Edition.* Woodcuts. Crown 8vo. 20*s.*

——— Days and Nights of Salmon Fishing in the Tweed; with a short Account of the Natural History and Habits of the Salmon. *Second Edition.* Woodcuts. Royal 8vo. 31*s.* 6*d.*

——— (G. P.) Memoir of Lord Sydenham, and his Administration in Canada. *Second Edition.* Portrait. 8vo. 9*s.* 6*d.*

——— Geology and Extinct Volcanos of Central France. *Second Edition*, revised and enlarged. Illustrations. Medium 8vo. 30*s.*

SHAW'S (THOS. B.) Outlines of English Literature, for the Use of Young Students. Post 8vo. 12*s.*

SIERRA LEONE; Described in a Series of Letters to Friends at Home. By A LADY. Edited by MRS. NORTON. Post 8vo. 6*s.*

SMITH'S (WM., LL.D.) Dictionary of Greek and Roman Antiquities. *Second Edition.* With 500 Woodcuts. 8vo. 42*s.*

——— Smaller Dictionary of Greek and Roman Antiquities. Abridged from the above work. *Fourth Edition.* With 200 Woodcuts. Crown 8vo. 7*s.* 6*d.*

——— Dictionary of Greek and Roman Biography and Mythology. With 500 Woodcuts. 3 Vols. 8vo. 5*l.* 15*s.* 6*d.*

——— Dictionary of Greek and Roman Geography. With Woodcuts. 2 Vols. 8vo. 80*s.*

——— Atlas of Ancient Geography. 4to. [*In preparation.*

——— Classical Dictionary for the Higher Forms in Schools. Compiled from the above two works. *Fourth Edition.* With 750 Woodcuts. 8vo. 18*s.*

——— Smaller Classical Dictionary. Abridged from the above work. *Fifth Edition.* With 200 Woodcuts. Crown 8vo. 7*s.* 6*d.*

——— Latin-English Dictionary. Based upon the Works of Forcellini and Freund. *Fifth Thousand.* 8vo. 21*s.*

——— Smaller Latin-English Dictionary. Abridged from the above work. *Twelfth Thousand.* Square 12mo. 7*s.* 6*d.*

——— English-Latin Dictionary. Assisted by JOHN ROBSON, B.A. 8vo. and 12mo. [*In preparation.*

——— Mediæval Latin-English Dictionary. Selected from the great work of DUCANGE. 8vo. [*Uniform with* DR. SMITH'S "Latin-English Dictionary."]

——— Dictionary of Biblical Antiquities, Biography, Geography, and Natural History. Woodcuts. 8vo. [*In the Press.*

——— Gibbon's History of the Decline and Fall of the Roman Empire. Edited, with Notes. Portrait and Map. 8 Vols. 8vo. 60*s.* (Murray's British Classics.)

——— Student's Gibbon; being the History of the Decline and Fall, Abridged. Incorporating the Researches of Recent Commentators. *Sixth Thousand.* Woodcuts. Post 8vo. 7*s.* 6*d.*

——— Student's Hume. A History of England from the Invasion of Julius Cæsar. Abridged from Hume, and continued to the present time. With woodcuts. Post 8vo. 7*s.* 6*d.*

——— History of Greece; from the Earliest Times to the Roman Conquest. With the History of Literature and Art. *Sixteenth Thousand.* Woodcuts. Crown 8vo. 7*s.* 6*d.* (Questions. 12mo. 2*s.*)

——— History of Rome; from the Earliest Times to the Establishment of the Empire. With the History of Literature and Art. By H. G. LIDDELL, D.D. *Eighth Thousand.* Woodcuts. Crown 8vo. 7*s.* 6*d.* [*Uniform with* SMITH'S "HISTORY OF GREECE."].

——— (WM. JAS.) Grenville Letters and Diaries, including MR. GRENVILLE'S DIARY OF POLITICAL EVENTS, while First Lord of the Treasury. Edited, with Notes. 4 Vols. 8vo. 64*s.*

——— (JAMES & HORACE) Rejected Addresses. *Twenty-third Edition.* Fcap. 8vo. 1*s.*, or *Fine Paper*, with Portrait. Fcap. 8vo. 5*s.*

SOMERVILLE'S (MARY) Physical Geography. *Fourth Edition.* Portrait. Post 8vo. 9*s.*

———— Connexion of the Physical Sciences. *Ninth Edition.* Woodcuts. Post 8vo. 9*s.*

SOUTH'S (JOHN F.) Household Surgery; or, Hints on Emergencies. *Seventeenth Thousand.* Woodcuts. Fcp. 8vo. 4*s.* 6*d.*

SOUTHEY'S (ROBERT) Book of the Church; with Notes containing the Authorities, and an Index. *Seventh Edition.* Post 8vo. 7*s.* 6*d.*

———— Lives of John Bunyan & Oliver Cromwell. Post 8vo. 2*s.* 6*d.*

SPECKTER'S (OTTO) Puss in Boots, suited to the Tastes of Old and Young. *A New Edition.* With 12 Woodcuts. Square 12mo. 1*s.* 6*d.*

———— Charmed Roe; or, the Story of the Little Brother and Sister. Illustrated. 16mo.

STANLEY'S (Rev. A. P.) ADDRESSES AND CHARGES OF THE LATE BISHOP STANLEY. With a Memoir of his Life. *Second Edition.* 8vo. 10*s.* 6*d.*

———— Sermons preached in Canterbury Cathedral, on the Unity of Evangelical and Apostolical Teaching. Post 8vo.

———— Commentary on St. Paul's Epistles to the Corinthians. with Notes and Dissertations. *Second, and revised Edition.* 8vo. 18*s.*

———— Historical Memorials of Canterbury. The Landing of Augustine—The Murder of Becket—The Black Prince—The Shrine of Becket. *Third Edition.* Woodcuts. Post 8vo. 7*s.* 6*d.*

———— Sinai and Palestine, in Connexion with their History. *Fifth Edition.* Map. 8vo. 16*s.*

ST. JOHN'S (CHARLES) Wild Sports and Natural History of the Highlands. Post 8vo. 6*s.*

———— (BAYLE) Adventures in the Libyan Desert and the Oasis of Jupiter Ammon. Woodcuts. Post 8vo. 2*s.* 6*d.*

STEPHENSON'S (GEORGE) Life. The Railway Engineer. By SAMUEL SMILES. *Fifth Edition.* Portrait. 8vo. 16*s.*

STOTHARD'S (THOS., R. A.) Life. With Personal Reminiscences. By Mrs. BRAY. With Portrait and 60 Woodcuts. 4to.

STREET'S (G. E.) Brick and Marble Architecture of Italy, in the Middle Ages. Plates. 8vo. 21*s.*

STRIFE FOR THE MASTERY. Two Allegories. With Illustrations. Crown 8vo. 6*s.*

SWIFT'S (JONATHAN) Life, Letters and Journals. By JOHN FORSTER. 8vo. *In Preparation.*

———— Works. Edited, with Notes. By JOHN FORSTER. 8vo. *In Preparation.*

SYDENHAM'S (LORD) Memoirs. With his Administration in Canada. By G. POULET SCROPE, M.P. *Second Edition.* Portrait. 8vo. 9*s.* 6*d.*

SYME'S (JAS.) Principles of Surgery. *Fourth Edition.* 8vo. 14*s.*

TAYLOR'S (HENRY) Notes from Life. Fcap 8vo. 2*s.*

———— (J. E.) Fairy Ring. A Collection of Stories for Young Persons. From the German. With Illustrations by RICHARD DOYLE *Second Edition.* Woodcuts. Fcap. 8vo.

TENNENT'S (Sir J. E.) Christianity in Ceylon. Its Introduction and Progress under the Portuguese, Dutch, British, and American Missions. With an Historical Sketch of the Brahmanical and Buddhist Superstitions. Woodcuts. 8vo. 14*s.*

THREE-LEAVED MANUAL OF FAMILY PRAYER; arranged so as to save the trouble of turning the Pages backwards and forwards. Royal 8vo. 2*s.*

TICKNOR'S (George) History of Spanish Literature. With Criticisms on particular Works, and Biographical Notices of Prominent Writers. *Second Edition.* 3 Vols. 8vo. 24*s.*

TOCQUEVILLE'S (M. de) State of France before the Revolution, 1789, and on the Causes of that Event. Translated by Henry Reeve, Esq. 8vo. 14*s.*

TREMENHEERE'S (H. S.) Political Experience of the Ancients, in its bearing on Modern Times. Fcap. 8vo. 2*s.* 6*d.*

——— Notes on Public Subjects, made during a Tour in the United States and Canada. Post 8vo. 10*s.* 6*d.*

——— Constitution of the United States compared with our own. Post 8vo. 9*s.* 6*d.*

TWISS' (Horace) Public and Private Life of Lord Chancellor Eldon, with Selections from his Correspondence. Portrait. *Third Edition.* 2 Vols. Post 8vo. 21*s.*

TYTLER (Patrick Fraser), A Memoir of. By his Friend, Rev. J. W. Burgon, M.A. 8vo. *In the Press.*

UBICINI'S (M. A.) Letters on Turkey and its Inhabitants—the Moslems, Greeks, Armenians, &c. Translated by Lady Easthope. 2 Vols. Post 8vo. 21*s.*

VAUGHAN'S (Rev. Dr.) Sermons preached in Harrow School. 8vo. 10*s.* 6*d.*

——— New Sermons. 12mo. 5*s.*

VENABLES' (Rev. R. L.) Domestic Scenes in Russia during a Year's Residence, chiefly in the Interior. *Second Edition.* Post 8vo. 5*s.*

VOYAGE to the Mauritius and back, touching at the Cape of Good Hope, and St. Helena. By Author of "Paddiana." Post 8vo. 9*s.* 6*d.*

WAAGEN'S (Dr.) Treasures of Art in Great Britain. Being an Account of the Chief Collections of Paintings, Sculpture, Manuscripts, Miniatures, &c. &c., in this Country. Obtained from Personal Inspection during Visits to England. 3 Vols. 8vo. 36*s.*

——— Galleries and Cabinets of Art in England. Being an Account of more than Forty Collections, visited in 1854-56 and never before described. With Index. 8vo. 18*s.*

WADDINGTON'S (Dean) Condition and Prospects of the Greek Church. *New Edition.* Fcap. 8vo. 3*s.* 6*d.*

WAKEFIELD'S (E. J.) Adventures in New Zealand. With some Account of the Beginning of the British Colonisation of the Island. Map. 2 Vols. 8vo. 28*s.*

WALKS AND TALKS. A Story-book for Young Children. By Aunt Ida. With Woodcuts. 16mo. 5*s.*

WARD'S (Robert Plumer) Memoir, Correspondence, Literary and Unpublished Diaries and Remains. By the Hon. Edmund Phipps. Portrait. 2 Vols. 8vo. 28*s.*

WATT'S (James) Life. Incorporating the most interesting passages from his Private and Public Correspondence. By James P. Muirhead, M.A. Portraits and Woodcuts. 8vo. 16*s.*

——— Origin and Progress of his Mechanical Inventions. Illustrated by his Correspondence with his Friends. Edited by J. P. Muirhead. Plates. 3 vols. 8vo. 45*s.*, or Large Paper. 3 Vols. 4to.

WELLINGTON'S (The Duke of) Despatches during his various Campaigns. Compiled from Official and other Authentic Documents. By Col. Gurwood, C.B. *New Enlarged Edition.* 8 Vols. 8vo. 21*s.* each.

——— Supplementary Letters, Despatches, and other Papers. Edited by his Son. Vols. 1 and 2. 8vo. 20*s.* each.

——— Selections from his Despatches and General Orders. By Colonel Gurwood. 8vo. 18*s.*

——— Speeches in Parliament. 2 Vols. 8vo. 42*s.*

WILKIE'S (Sir David) Life, Journals, Tours, and Critical Remarks on Works of Art, with a Selection from his Correspondence. By Allan Cunningham. Portrait. 3 Vols. 8vo. 42*s.*

WILKINSON'S (Sir J. G.) Popular Account of the Private Life, Manners, and Customs of the Ancient Egyptians. *New Edition.* Revised and Condensed. With 500 Woodcuts. 2 Vols. Post 8vo. 12*s.*

——— Dalmatia and Montenegro; with a Journey to Mostar in Hertzegovina, and Remarks on the Slavonic Nations. Plates and Woodcuts. 2 Vols. 8vo. 42*s.*

——— Handbook for Egypt.—Thebes, the Nile, Alexandria, Cairo, the Pyramids, Mount Sinai, &c. Map. Post 8vo. 15*s.*

——— On Colour, and on the Necessity for a General Diffusion of Taste among all Classes; with Remarks on laying out Dressed or Geometrical Gardens. With Coloured Illustrations and Woodcuts. 8vo. 18*s.*

——— (G. B.) Working Man's Handbook to South Australia; with Advice to the Farmer, and Detailed Information for the several Classes of Labourers and Artisans. Map. 18mo. 1*s.* 6*d.*

WOOD'S (Lieut.) Voyage up the Indus to the Source of the River Oxus, by Kabul and Badakhshan. Map. 8vo. 14*s.*

WORDSWORTH'S (Rev. Dr.) Athens and Attica. Journal of a Tour. *Third Edition.* Plates. Post 8vo. 8*s.* 6*d.*

——— Greece: Pictorial, Descriptive, and Historical, with a History of Greek Art, by G. Scharf, F.S.A. *New Edition.* With 600 Woodcuts. Royal 8vo. 28*s.*

——— King Edward VIth's Latin Grammar, for the Use of Schools. 12*th Edition*, revised. 12mo. 3*s.* 6*d.*

——— First Latin Book, or the Accidence, Syntax and Prosody, with English Translation for Junior Classes. *Third Edition.* 12mo. 2*s.*

WORNUM (Ralph). A Biographical Dictionary of Italian Painters: with a Table of the Contemporary Schools of Italy. By a Lady. Post 8vo. 6*s.* 6*d.*

YOUNG'S (Dr. Thos.) Life and Miscellaneous Works, edited by Dean Peacock and John Leitch. Portrait and Plates. 4 Vols. 8vo. 15*s.* each.

BRADBURY AND EVANS, PRINTERS, WHITEFRIARS.